The Singular Anomaly

The Singular Anomaly

Women Novelists
of the Nineteenth Century

Vineta Colby

New York • *NEW YORK UNIVERSITY PRESS*
London • *UNIVERSITY OF LONDON PRESS LTD* 1970

© 1970 by New York University Press
Library of Congress Catalog Card Number: 70-92522
SBN: 8147 0096-9 (cloth)
SBN: 8147-0097-7 (paper)
Manufactured in the United States of America

Acknowledgments

In the making of this book I have incurred many obligations which I am happy to acknowledge. For their advice and cooperation I am indebted to E. Marie Becker of the Fales Collection, New York University; Kenneth Freyer and Mimi Penchansky of the Paul Klapper Library. Queens College of the City University of New York; Martin Gilbert of Merton College, Oxford; Kenneth A. Lohf, Librarian for Rare Books and Manuscripts, Columbia University; Patrick Smith of the University of California at Davis; and Lola L. Szladits, Curator of the Berg Collection of the New York Public Library. Queens College of the City University of New York has granted me sabbatical leave and various other forms of assistance, including the typing services of Florence G. Waldheter and her staff.

For permission to publish Max Beerbohm's parody of John Oliver Hobbes I am grateful to William Heinemann, Ltd. and the Estate of the late Max Beerbohm. Libraries that have given me permission to quote from their books and manuscripts are: the Henry W. and Albert A. Berg Collection of the New York Public Library, Astor, Lenox and Tilden Foundations; Columbia University; the Harvard College Library; and the Fales Collection, New York University. Among pubishers I have received permissions from William Blackwood and Sons, Ltd. and the National Library of Scotland to publish passages from the letters of Eliza Lynn Linton; Bobbs-Merrill Company for a passage from Laurence Housman's *The Unexpected Years;* Curtis Brown, Ltd. and the Estate of Roy Campbell for the poem "Buffel's Kop"; Random House, Inc. and William Heinemann Medical Books, Ltd. for an excerpt from Havelock Ellis' *Studies in the Psychology of Sex;* Charles Scribner's Sons for passages from *The Letters of Henry James,* edited by Percy Lubbock.

Chiefly—and beyond hope of any adequate recognition here—I am grateful to Robert A. Colby, my colleague, fellow-scholar, and husband. His knowledge of the nineteenth-century English novel is equalled only by his sound critical judgment and excelled only by his generosity in sharing all this with me.

V. C.

Contents

And that singular anomaly, the lady novelist,
I don't think she'd be missed—I'm *sure* she'd
not be missed!

—from Ko-Ko's "Little List,"
in *The Mikado*

It was not originally the intention of the writer to adopt the form of fiction as the instrument to scatter his suggestions, but, after reflection, he resolved to avail himself of a method which, in the temper of the times, offered the best chance of influencing opinion.
— Benjamin Disraeli, Preface to the Fifth Edition of *Coningsby* (1849)

Introduction

The essays which follow consider a mixed bag of women novelists. The phrase is not felicitous, but it is intended to suggest the variety of types and quality of a certain group of late nineteenth-century English novels and novelists. These have in common three very large and loose characteristics: they are novels with a purpose essentially ethical and didactic; they are novels which for a brief period enjoyed a considerable and sometimes astonishing amount of attention; they were all written by women. The singular anomaly is sex, but the fact that the novelists are women is relatively unimportant. Of far greater significance is the form itself—the late nineteenth-century English novel—so rich, so flexible, and so multi-faceted that it could simultaneously and effectively serve the purposes of art, mass entertainment, public communication, popular education, propaganda, and polemics.

This book is an attempt to study the novel of the period not as a work of art, but as a vehicle for the expression and dissemination of ideas. The concentration upon women novelists reflects merely an attempt to narrow the focus and to turn it more emphatically upon the novel's ethical-didactic functions. Many men were writing the same kinds of novels during this period. To study the novels of Eliza Lynn Linton and Olive Schreiner rather

1

than those of Grant Allen, Walter Besant, or W. H. Mallock—
Mrs. Humphry Ward rather than J. H. Shorthouse, Mark
Rutherford, or George Gissing—John Oliver Hobbes rather than
Stanley J. Weyman or Henry Harland—Vernon Lee rather than
Walter Pater—is only to impose some necessary limits upon the
scope of one's work.

Nevertheless, there is no denying that the sex of these novelists places a particular stamp upon the nature of their work, the
circumstances of its composition, and its reception. Late Victorian England, a largely bourgeois, domestic society ruled by a
queen, was far more woman-conscious than its neighbors in
western Europe. One need only consider the differences in attitudes toward the two Georges, Sand and Eliot. Both were
honored literary figures, enjoying popular acclaim as well as
critical respect. But the French George was not a literary phenomenon in her own land. She was one of many—a woman who
wrote novels, alongside of and equal with men who wrote novels.
Unlike the English, the French designate the sex of their novelists in their language—*romancier; romancière*. But the designa-
tion is merely nominal, while the English, who make no such
distinction in language, are keenly and constantly sensitive to the
sex. In the last quarter of the nineteenth century in particular,
as women became more vocal and more militant in their feminism, women novelists became more and more a distinct literary
breed. Midpoint in the century (1856), an unsigned article in
the *Westminster Review* roundly condemned "Silly Novels by
Lady Novelists." The anonymous author was George Eliot, who
never wrote a silly novel in her life. At the end of the century
(1904), W. L. Courtney titled his long and serious critical book
The Feminine Note in Fiction. In the years between, the lady
novelist had become a critical category.

It was not that there were more women writing novels in
1900 than there had been in 1800. In her study *The Popular
Novel in England, 1770 to 1800*, J. M. S. Tompkins cites an
impressive number of flourishing women novelists and observes
that "women of all ranks are writing, from the Duchess of
Devonshire and Lady Craven down to the Bristol milk woman

and a farmer's daughter of Gloucestershire." But there were at least two major changes within the century. First, women were writing more and different kinds of novels. They were no longer mere spinners of yarns, or—more accurately—they were, in addition to that, many other things—reformers, educators, polemicists. The homely domestic tale, the frivolous love story, the escapist romance continued to be the staple of the writing ladies, but no longer were their only merchandise. As their education and experience expanded, the "fair authoresses" of the eighteenth century became professional writers. Their "proper sphere" widened proportionately from the heart to the head, from the domestic hearth to the world outside, from the sentimental and emotional problems of individual characters to the intellectually challenging social, moral, ethical, and religious problems of society-at-large.[1]

Accordingly they demanded, and received, more sober critical and public attention. A vestige of the past, the male pseudonym, lingered on through the nineteenth century, but it had lost its original purpose. When the Brontës assumed their Acton, Currer, and Ellis Bell disguises, they were concealing their femininity in the hope that their work would be read more seriously, that they might be regarded as professional writers rather than as light-weight literary ladies, parsons' daughters with nothing better to do with their time than to write books.[2] But by the end of the century the pseudonym had become mere affectation. Mrs. Pearl Craigie called herself John Oliver Hobbes because she published her first novel in Unwin's Pseudonym Library and had to supply a pseudonym to qualify. She retained it as a whim. It amused her when a first-night audience, applauding her comedy *The Ambassador*, called for the author and then shouted in amazement, "Where is John?" as she appeared, bowing, in a white satin gown.

The changing attitude toward women novelists reflects a changing attitude toward the novel itself. The seriousness and dignity brought to the form by Sir Walter Scott and carried on by the major works of Dickens, Thackeray, the Brontës, and George Eliot, created a totally new image of the novelist as now not a mere story-teller but a prophet and a sage. As John Hollo-way has observed, the nineteenth-century English novelist was regarded as "every bit as well equipped as the discursive essayist to mediate a way of life." [3] The narrowly didactic function of the eighteenth-century novel had broadened into a vast moral-ethical-philosophical one. George Meredith was not mocking the fiction-writing of his heroine but expressing a widely held con-viction when he said in the first chapter of *Diana of the Cross-ways* that "the fiction which is the summary of actual Life, the within and without of us, is, prose or verse, plodding or soaring, philosophy's elect handmaiden." Only a few years later, in 1890, hailing the "New Spirit" of the coming twentieth century, Have-lock Ellis called the novel "the great art of the century . . . contemporary moral history in a deeper sense than the De Gon-courts meant. Many novels of today will be found to express the distinctive features of our age as truly as the distinctive features of another age, its whole inner and outer life, are expressed in Gothic architecture."

With its new exalted status, the English novel did not change in essence. It remained fundamentally realistic and do-mestic even while it assumed qualities of the epic. And since it was domestic, it invited both the woman reader and the woman writer. "Of all departments of literature," George Henry Lewes wrote in 1852, four years before George Eliot began to write fiction herself, "Fiction is the one to which, by nature and by circumstance, women are best adapted . . . novels are their forte." In spite of the fact that George Eliot was to demonstrate the narrowness of his view, Lewes probably would not have altered his explanation for this attraction of women to the novel: "The domestic experiences which form the bulk of woman's knowledge find an appropriate form in novels: while the very nature of fiction calls for that predominance of Sentiment which we have already attributed to the feminine mind. Love is the very staple of fiction, for it 'forms the story of a woman's life.' " [4] Almost half a century later, in 1899, in her preface to the Haworth edition of Charlotte Brontë's *Villette*, Mrs. Humphry Ward proclaimed the triumph of women in the field of the novel, but offered an explanation little different from Lewes's:

In other fields of art they are still either relatively amateurs, or their performance, however good, awakens a kindly surprise. Their position is hardly assured; they are still on sufferance. Whereas in fiction the great names of the past, within their own sphere, are the equals of all the world, accepted, discussed, analyzed, by the masculine critic, with precisely the same keenness and under the same canons as he applied to Thackeray or Stevenson, to Balzac or Loti.

She accounts for their remarkable achievement by suggesting that women came to novel-writing equipped by their experience in letter-writing, which gave them training in language, and by the very limitations of their experience of life. The one subject that they solidly know is love—which happens to be the principal subject matter of novels. Thus, experts on the emotions, especially love, sheltered from the distractions of worldly life, and trained in what she calls "the arts of society and of letter-writing," women have only to look into their hearts to write novels.

A more realistic explanation of this phenomenon was offered in her *Autobiography* by the enormously prolific novelist Mrs. Oliphant, who said simply: "I have written because it gave me pleasure, because it came natural to me, because it was like talking or breathing, besides the big fact that it was necessary for me to work for my children." A score of other women novelists from Mrs. Gore, Frances Trollope, and Caroline Norton, through Henry James' fictional but typical Greville Fane, might have echoed those words. The hand could wield the pen while the foot rocked the cradle. The nineteenth-century English novel was the "home epic" not only because it concentrated largely upon bourgeois, domestic life, but also because it could be written in the home. In Eliza Lynn Linton's *Sowing the Wind* (1867), a genteel woman, left suddenly helpless with a child to support, earns some money by fancy needlework:

This was all that Isola could do towards filling the gaping void of the family purse. She was not a woman of trained intellect, and could not have taken up literature as a pro-

fession. . . . I doubt if she could have written a novel, given
bigamy, murder and suicide as the triple basis, or even a bit
of goody-goody vapidness fit for village schools. She could
have been a daily governess . . . [but] she preferred work of
a lower range which kept her at home and near her baby.

The practical businesslike outlook of Mrs. Oliphant and the
dilemma of the heroine Isola reflect the far more fundamental
reason why novel-writing appealed to such large numbers of
women—namely, the nature of Victorian society, which denied
them professional outlets for their talents and energies. The
women we are studying in this book were not artistic, creative
novelists in the sense that Jane Austen, the Brontës, and George
Eliot were. They were intelligent, articulate women with much
inclination and some gift for expression in writing. Forbidden
the pulpit, the university lecture platform, the seat in Parliament, they turned to an outlet in which they were welcome and
through which they could express their ideas and wield an influence otherwise denied them. The novel was an expedient, a
means to an end. Their more perceptive contemporaries recognized this, and they acknowledged it themselves—no one more
candidly and eloquently than Olive Schreiner in *Women and
Labour:*

It is sometimes stated, that as several women of genius in
modern times have sought to find expression for their creative powers in the art of fiction, there must be some in-
herent connection in the human brain between the ovarian
sex function and the art of fiction. The fact is that modern
fiction, being merely a description of human life in any of
its phases, and being the only art that can be exercised
without special training or special appliances and produced
in the moments stolen from the multifarious, brain-destroy-
ing occupations which fill the average woman's life, they
have been driven to find this outlet for their powers as the
only one presenting itself. How far otherwise might have
been the directions in which their genius would naturally

have expressed itself can be known only to the women themselves; what the world has lost by that compulsory expression of genius, in a form which may not have been its most natural form of expression, or only one of its forms, no one can ever know. Even in the little third-rate novelist whose works cumber the ground, we see often a pathetic figure when we recognize that beneath that failure in a complex and difficult art, may lie buried a sound legislator, an able architect, an original scientific investigator, or a good judge. Scientifically speaking, it is as unproven that there is any organic relation between the brain of the female and the production of art in the form of fiction as that there is an organic relation between the hand of woman and the typewriter. Both the creative writer and the typist, in their respective spheres, are merely finding outlets for their powers in the direction of least mental resistance. The tendency of women at the present day to undertake certain forms of labour proves only that in the crabbed, walled-in and bound conditions surrounding women at the present day, these are the lines along which action is most possible to her (Ch. IV).

Many a shrewd Victorian critic recognized that popular novelists like Mrs. Humphry Ward were a phenomenon of the social and cultural climate of the times—the vast novel-reading middle class seeking self-improvement, practical instruction, social and ethical guidance. In the year 1886 more novels were published in England than any other single category of new books, significantly outdistancing even books on religion. Two years later, in a review of Mrs. Ward's spectacularly best-selling *Robert Elsmere*, the *Athenaeum* (March 31, 1888) commented:

Having a great deal to say and exceptional ability for saying it, Mrs. Humphry Ward no doubt chose the novel for the form of her work as being that which would best attract the attention of those she wished to reach. It is impossible to find fault with her decision. Few subjects are inadmissable in the novel of today, and through the novel alone can one speak effectively to the masses.

Like so many of her contemporaries, Mrs. Ward became a novelist, and a successful one, without any basic talent for the novel, without even any strong creative impulse. What Edmund Gosse wrote of her in *Silhouettes* in 1925 holds true for all these "singular anomalies":

> She found her easiest path to fortune in writing novels. That she toiled up this road untiringly for forty years is a tribute to her powers of concentration and to her violence of will. She was so immensely clever, so clear-brained, so finely equipped, so resolute, so intelligent, that she wrote novels as, if she had chosen to do so, she could undoubtedly have painted landscapes or conducted a business. But it was done against the grain, until, after experiment upon experiment, she had learned every trick of the trade, and the effort, having become mechanical, appeared to be crowned with success.

The same force of will drove John Oliver Hobbes to write novels when her primary interests were history and religion. She confessed to a manager arranging a lecture tour for her: "The subject I am engrossed in at present is *Spanish history*—Spain under Philip and the Bourbons: the Carlist War, etc., etc. Novels are not, as a matter of fact, my 'real line.' I could certainly not read from them or lecture about them." [5] Olive Schreiner admitted that she rarely read novels, and she wrote them laboriously, far happier in the more overtly didactic forms of allegory and polemical nonfiction. Dedicated almost religiously to aesthetics, Vernon Lee had a faint contempt for the novel even while she acknowledged its practical power to influence and persuade the reader. "The novel," she wrote, "has less value in art, but more importance in life."

For many intelligent, articulate, ambitious young women in the late nineteenth century the novel was a vocation, not in the sense of a real calling so much as an occupation that one might choose as a rational and practical course of life. In the late 1880's young Beatrice Potter, later the famous sociologist Mrs. Sidney Webb, debated the choice of a life's work, giving serious thought

to becoming "not a worker in the field of sociology, but a descriptive psychologist; either in the novel, to which I was from
time to time tempted or (if I had been born thirty years later)
in a scientific analysis of the mental make-up of individual men
and women, and their behaviour under particular conditions."
Happily, Mrs. Webb found her outlet in the newly emerging
field of what she called the "science of social organization." But
had she been born a few years earlier, she might well have chan-
neled those same energies into the writing of fiction. As she and
her contemporaries were fully aware, the novel was a medium
for the expression of ideas about the society in which man lives.
The vital issues of the day, as young Beatrice Potter saw them,
were also the issues of much of the fiction of her age—"the relation of the individual to some particular social organization,
the big enterprise, or to Parliament, to the profession of law, or
of medicine or of the Church," and the "new" motivation—"the
transference of the emotion of self-sacrificing service from God
to man." [6] Such questions obviously offered no easy escape into
daydreaming romance and fantasy but demanded sound, intelligent, informed presentation and analysis. No serious intellectual
or practical issue, from the place of God in the universe to the
effects on society of the development of cotton-weaving machines,
eluded the nineteenth-century novelist. He—and she as well—
had a sense of mission, a categorical imperative to observe, to
write, and to influence readers. The "problem novel," the "issue
novel," the "novel with a purpose," or the "novel of ideas,"—at
least a half-dozen terms describe in the end the same thing: the
use of an art form for public edification and instruction. The
writers who wrote such novels took themselves seriously, and
their readers took them seriously. Amy Cruse recalled the enormous power of the novel in her study of late-Victorian reading:
"Those of us who were young in those days will remember the
high seriousness with which we came to our books, how we
weighed the views they expressed, and discussed them with the
gravity of elder statesmen as well as the eager audacity of
youth." [7]

An enormous debt for the prestige enjoyed by women novelists was owed by them to the single influence of George Eliot.

They acknowledged that indebtedness freely and fully. No critical tribute paid Mrs. Humphry Ward for *Robert Elsmere* was more appreciated by her than the frequent comparisons made of her novel to the works of George Eliot. John Oliver Hobbes wrote an almost reverential article on George Eliot for the tenth edition of the *Encyclopedia Britannica*. Consciously or unconsciously, Olive Schreiner paid her the supreme compliment of imitation in her tender pictures of childhood which remind her readers of *The Mill on the Floss*. Eliza Lynn Linton, while somewhat piqued by the adulation she enjoyed, nevertheless hailed her as the finest woman writer of this or any other age. Even Vernon Lee, who, along with so many turn-of-the-century critics patronizingly referred to her "heavy-handed" moralizing and her "old-fashioned" Victorian narrative technique, considered her "a great writer," ranking with Balzac, Flaubert, and Zola.

What these novelists shared with their great model and inspiration was not her creative genius but, to some degree at least, her commitment, within the form of the novel, to the exploration of the most serious social and ethical questions of her time. Like George Elliot they had first-rate minds which they knew how to use. But, to observe a distinction George Eliot herself made, they had only the talent "which makes the effective use of materials . . . [and] awakens your curiosity"; they lacked the genius "which absorbs material and reproduces it as a living whole." [8] They could never assimilate and integrate their knowledge and their ideas into a work of art. Mrs. Ward, Max Beerbohm observed in a comment equally appropriate to the others, "has a very firm grasp of problems but is not very creational." [9] A professional musician once said of John Oliver Hobbes, a talented amateur pianist, "She plays with her brain." The trouble with these "singular anomalies" is that they wrote with their brains. George Eliot described a truly cultured woman as one "whose mind had absorbed her knowledge instead of being absorbed by it." Unhappily, the women novelists who imitated her were absorbed by their knowledge. They displayed it at times gracefully and attractively but more often heavily and clumsily. They *used* the novel as a medium of instruction; often they exploited it. They were women of intellect, taste, and talent, but they were not artists. That they should have been so widely acclaimed, as most of them were, so honored and influential, is a comment on the power and prestige of the novel itself.

By the late nineteenth century the English novel had reached that level of eminence and security where it could weather the stormy fictional passions of Ouida and Marie Corelli with no loss of dignity. Such novelists have no place in this study, not because their work is mainly vulgar sensationalism, but because they were not primarily intellectuals. The mere spinner of yarns continued to flourish, but rivaling and sometimes even outdistancing her was the serious intelligent novelist of purpose or ideas. Mrs. Ward's *Robert Elsmere,* a work of formidable erudition, was the fiction best-seller of 1888, competing handily with Marie Corelli's *A Romance of Two Worlds,* Hall Caine's *The Deemster,* and Rider Haggard's *She.* Olive Schreiner's *Story of an African Farm,* according to one of Marie Corelli's biographers, "put *Thelma's* nose out of joint." [10] Neither novel was "easy" reading, but the public was buying and apparently reading them avidly. The novelist of purpose felt no need to apologize for writing this form of novel. Mrs. Ward proudly and confidently challenged the "decadents" and the "aesthetes":

> Chateaubriand, George Sand, and Victor Hugo have bent the novel to all the purposes of propaganda in turn. Theology, politics, social problems and reforms, they have laid hands on them all, and have but stirred the more vibrations thereby in the life of their time. And which of them, from "Don Quixote" downwards, will you save from this opprobrious category of "novels with a purpose"?—which of them has not tried in its own way and with its own vehemence to "reform" the world? [11]

In the last years of the Victorian era, the woman novelist of the kind we are studying here was really neither singular nor anomalous. She was, on the contrary, a register and a spokesman for her age, reflecting its earnestness, its restless urge for self-improvement, its conformity and respectability, as well as its iconoclasm and rebellion against past values and the present order. She also registered its dark spiritual confusion and despair. In some way or another, each of the novelists studied here confronted the major problem of nineteenth-century thought—the challenge of science to established faith and dogma. Significantly, while rejecting the Establishment Church of England, each reacted with a "substitute" faith. Only one, John Oliver Hobbes, turned to an older, even more established Church—Rome. The others chose instead some form of secular or social idealism: Eliza Lynn Linton's hearty, vigorous social altruism and meliorism, Mrs. Humphry Ward's philanthropy and social welfare work, Olive Schreiner's vision of a revolutionary rebirth of the human spirit, Vernon Lee's religion of art as the redeeming, reforming agent of mankind.

Nor was there any anomaly in their use of the novel as a medium of expression. The Victorian novel was broad and flexible enough to be adapted exactly to their "purposes." It retained from its eighteenth-century roots a tradition of didacticism and moral instruction. It remained what George Eliot called the "aesthetic teacher" (though too often, in these later years, subordinating aesthetics to polemics), even while it was moving toward those new areas which James proclaimed in "The Art of Fiction" —"of having a theory, a conviction, a consciousness of itself behind it—of being the expression of an artistic faith. . . ."

Since Queen Victoria's time, the function of the "novel with a purpose" has been gradually absorbed by journalism, the documentary film, television, and the tape recorder. Never a major art form, it nevertheless performed a practical and important service to the public. Its death too is in some way connected with the apparent decline and disappearance, in our own time, of the whole genre of the serious novel—the novel which interprets life in broadly philosophical and imaginative terms—the works of the major Victorians, of Tolstoy, Dostoevsky, and, in the twentieth century, Joyce, Lawrence, Mann, and Faulkner. This kind of novel, many critics agree, has been superseded by the nonfiction novel, whose "purpose" may be to report and inform but not, as in the nineteenth century, to illuminate, interpret, and reform. A contemporary novelist, Doris Lessing, describes precisely this development in her novel *The Golden Notebook:*

The point is, that the function of the novel seems to be changing; it has become an outpost of journalism; we read novels for information about areas of life we don't know— Nigeria, South Africa, the American army, a coal-mining village, coteries in Chelsea, etc. We read *to find out what is going on*. One novel in five hundred or a thousand has the quality a novel should have to make it a novel—the quality of philosophy, I find that I read with the *same kind of curiosity* most novels, and a book of reportage. Most novels, if they are successful at all, are original in the sense that they report the existence of an area of society, a type of person, not yet admitted to the general literate consciousness. The novel has become a function of the fragmented society, the fragmented consciousness.

> (Part I: The Notebooks, her italics)

Where the Victorian novel was plastic enough to embrace a variety of forms and purposes and the Victorian reading public hungry enough to devour them all, neither the form nor the readership of the contemporary novel shows promise of similar strength and growth. The modern novelist, Mary McCarthy has observed, has become isolated from his public. He writes for other writers and for students of writing and has "nothing in common" with the businessman, the working man, the public-at-large. The novel itself, she argues, "seems to be dissolving into its component parts: the essay, the travel book, reporting, on the one hand, and the 'pure fiction' of the tale on the other." The essence of the novel is, and has always been, reality, reporting the news of life, *fact*—but fact related to a rational, ordered universe, such as indeed the Victorian world still gave the illusion of being. In our chaotic, irrational, improbable contemporary world of Buchenwald and the Bomb, fact becomes blurred and unreal. "We know that the real world exists," Miss McCarthy writes, "but we can no longer imagine it." [12] The "singular anomaly" of our present literary age is certainly not the lady novelist. It may well be the novel itself.

Notes

1. For a discussion of attitudes toward women novelists in the mid-nineteenth century see Inga-Stina Ewbank's *Their Proper Sphere: A Study of the Brontë Sisters as Early Victorian Female Novelists* (Cambridge, Mass., 1966), Ch. I.
2. According to Mrs. Gaskell, Charlotte Brontë "especially disliked the lowering of the standard by which to judge a work of fiction, if it proceeded from a feminine pen; and praise mingled with pseudo-gallant allusions to her sex mortified her far more than actual blame" (*Life of Charlotte Brontë* [Haworth ed., London, 1929], p. 423).
3. *The Victorian Sage: Studies in Argument* (London, 1953), p. 12.
4. "The Lady Novelists," *Westminister Review*, LVIII (July, 1852), 133.
5. A. L. S. to Major Pond, August 15, 1897, Fales Collection, New York University; her italics.
6. *My Apprenticeship* (London and New York, 1950), p. 95.
7. *After the Victorians* (London, 1938), p. 13.
8. "Three Novels," *Westminister Review*, LXVI (October, 1856), 571–78. See also her "Silly Novels by Lady Novelists," *Ibid.* Both are reprinted in *Essays of George Eliot*, ed. Thomas Pinney (New York, 1963).
9. "A Clergyman," *And Even Now* (New York, 1921), p. 239.
10. Eileen Bigland, *Marie Corelli, The Woman and the Legend* (London and New York, 1953), p. 99.
11. Preface to *David Grieve* (Westmoreland ed., London, 1911), p. xvii.
12. "The Fact in Fiction," *Partisan Review*, XXVII (Summer, 1960), 438–58.

1.

Wild Women, Revolting Daughters, and The Shrieking Sisterhood: Mrs. Eliza Lynn Linton

The nineteenth-century English parsonage was an incubator and a hatchery for lady novelists. From Steventon in Hampshire, where Jane Austen's talents were nurtured, to Haworth in Yorkshire, where the Brontë sisters wove their childhood webs of fancy, the houses of the clergy produced an impressive number of literary young women. Their talents were not always so impressive as their numbers, but something in the serious, bookish atmosphere of country parsonages seems to have stimulated literary composition. For every Jane Austen and Emily and Charlotte Brontë, there were perhaps a half-dozen of the more modestly gifted—Charlotte Yonge, for example, born of a clerical family (though her father had been an army officer) in Otterbourne, near Winchester; Rhoda Broughton, daughter of a clergyman in Denbigh, North Wales; the Devonshire-born "Lucas Malet" (pen name of Mrs. Mary St. Leger Harrison), daughter of the crusading "muscular Christian" Canon Charles Kingsley; Mary Cholmondeley, author of *Red Pottage,* a best-seller of 1900, and daughter of the Rector of Hodnet in Shropshire as well as niece of the celebrated hymn-writing Bishop Heber. And for every half-dozen of these there were probably dozens of respectable, plodding novelists of little or no talent at all.

To judge merely by survival power, the parson's daughter Eliza Lynn Linton belongs in this last category; but she was perhaps the supreme example of the self-made, self-proclaimed Victorian lady novelist-polemicist—the hardiest, the longest lived, the most businesslike and professional. A rebel from the start (a "revolting daughter" to use the Victorian epithet), at twenty-three, in 1845, she set out from her father's parsonage at Crosthwaite, in the Lake Country, to storm literary London. Characteristically, she began her siege from the Reading Room of the British Museum, compiling rather than writing two prodigiously learned historical novels, *Azeth the Egyptian* and *Amymone, a Romance of the Days of Pericles,* to which almost nobody except Walter Savage Landor has ever paid any attention. Nevertheless, Miss Lynn made her mark. By 1851 she was a full-fledged, full-time journalist on the staff of the *Morning Chronicle,* at the not inconsiderable salary of twenty guineas a month. She was also contributing regularly to *Household Words,* with the editor Charles Dickens' solid recommendation: "Good for anything and thoroughly reliable." [1] The "anything" was everything—fiction, book and play reviews, travel reporting, social leaders—all of it competent, much of it lively, and some of it so abrasive and controversial that by the 1860's, now Mrs. Linton, she was a national celebrity.

Not surprisingly, her greatest fame was won in polemical journalism rather than in the novel. Although throughout her long career Mrs. Linton treated the subject of women's rights in her novels, she handled it most effectively in nonfiction, in a series of battling, bristling unsigned articles in the *Saturday Review* under the general title "The Girl of the Period." These appeared over some ten years, 1866–1877, the bulk of them in 1866. They were reprinted in a pamphlet in 1868, of which some forty thousand copies circulated; in two American collections entitled *Modern Women and What Is Said of Them* (1868; Second Series, 1870); and finally in 1883 in two volumes published under Mrs. Linton's own name, *The Girl of the Period and Other Social Essays.* Such was their popularity that, according to Mrs. Linton, two others—a clergyman and "a lady of rank well known in London society"—claimed their authorship.[2] The phrase itself won a place in the language. There was a *Girl of the Period Almanack* and a thirty-two-page monthly, *The Girl of the Period Miscellany,* with articles on the typical Irish GP, the French GP, etc. There were GP parasols and articles of ladies' clothing. And Matthew Morgan caricatured the unknown authoress (though many thought the pieces the work of a man) in a wicked cartoon showing a shriveled, high-nosed, bespectacled shrew painting from a sweetly innocent-looking model a portrait of a diabolical female with Satanic horns and wings. Her paint jars are labeled Venom and Gall, and around her skirt is the banner "Saturday Review." [3]

Something of the imagination of a novelist went into Mrs. Linton's creation. The Girl of the Period is indeed a sister of the high-spirited "anti-heroines" who figure in a good deal of minor Victorian fiction from Mrs. Oliphant to Rhoda Broughton and M. E. Braddon. She is the pert modern miss of the sixties, blossoming out in rebellion against the codes and crinolines of mid-Victorianism and flowering (or degenerating, according to one's feminist views) into the belligerent crusading suffragette of the nineties and later. As Mrs. Linton originally conceived her—both in the *Saturday Review* and in some of her early fiction—she was empty-headed, frivolous, self-indulgent: "a creature who dyes her hair and paints her face . . . whose sole idea of life is plenty of fun and luxury, and whose dress is the object of such thought and intellect as she possesses" (March 14, 1868). As she matures, however, her silliness turns to malevolence. She marries for money and social position, is indifferent to her home and children:

> a frisky matron, a fashionable woman, a thing of paints and pads . . . making pleasure her only good, and the world her highest god, it too often means a woman who is not ashamed to supplement her husband with a lover, but who is unwilling to become the honest mother of that husband's children . . . a hybrid creature perverted out of the natural way altogether, affecting the license but ignorant of the strength of

a man, alike as girl or woman valueless for her highest natural duties, and talking largely of liberty while showing at every turn how much she fails in that co-essential of liberty—knowledge how to use it (August 8, 1868).

Ultimately her fate reflects the poetic justice of a work of fiction. She loses the love of her children (see "Modern Mothers," February 29, 1868: "Society has put maternity out of fashion . . ."); the loyalty of her servants (see "Mistress and Maid on Dress and Undress," February 1, 1868); the devotion of her husband (see "Ideal Women," May 9, 1868: "It is the vague restlessness, the fierce extravagance, the neglect of home, the indolent fine-ladyism, the passionate love of pleasure which characterise the modern woman, that saddens men and destroys in them that respect which their very pride prompts them to feel"). Dwindling into middle age and desperately striving to retain her youth, she becomes the ridiculous and pathetic "Femme Passée" (July 11, 1868):

Dressed in the extreme of youthful fashion, her thinning hair dyed and crimped and fired till it is more like red-brown tow than hair, her flaccid cheeks ruddled, her throat whitened . . . her lustreless eyes blackened around the lids, to give the semblance of limpidity to the tarnished whites . . . she stands, the wretched creature who will not consent to grow old.

The Girl of the Period fares little better in Mrs. Linton's fiction. Here one may trace her evolution from the spoiled and impetuous young girls who appear from time to time in her early novels to the ardent and willfully destructive suffragettes in her novels of the 1890's. At the same time that Mrs. Linton was condemning the GP in the *Saturday Review* (during the 1860's) she was introducing in her novel *Sowing the Wind* (1867) a plain, mannish young woman journalist who, while blunt and even crude at times, is nevertheless sympathetic. By 1878 the Girl of the Period had become one of the "Shrieking Sisterhood," and in *The Rebel of the Family* a plain, bespectacled young heroine named Perdita flirts dangerously with the movement. Unappreciated and even persecuted by her shallow, selfish widowed mother and prettier sisters, "longing for some vital interest, and suffocating in the stifling atmosphere to which she was condemned," she is briefly lured into the West Hill Society for Women's Rights by an aggressive older woman, "the Venus of the Emancipated Olympus." Perdita happily has enough character to resist her blandishments and enough luck to meet an attractive young chemist whom she eventually marries.

A more typical GP appears in a late novel, *The One Too Many* (1894); here she has degenerated into the militant suffragette. The novel is dedicated to "the sweet girls still left among us who have no part in the new revolt but are content to be dutiful, innocent, and sheltered." Such a sweet innocent is the heroine of this novel, driven to mental anguish and finally suicide by a cold, egotistical husband. In contrast, the antiheroine, "the prize-girl of Girton and now a B.A. of London," strides vigorously through life, trampling on any who get in her way:

> Emphatically a child of the generation, she had a profound contempt for all that had gone before. Her world dated from yesterday, and the past was only as a cock-shy for ridicule. Nothing was as it had been. Thought, knowledge, morality, humanity, had all come into a new phase: and the rules which had done well for the times that had gone were now but as decayed sticks, which might have kept the sapling straight but were useless to the sturdy tree.

She reads Ibsen, Maeterlinck, Baudelaire, Zola, and Maupassant. She has studied nursing and medicine, assisted at operations without fainting or flinching, studied painting "from the life" in Paris, lived in the slums, visited prisons and doss houses, and "fraternised with thieves, gutter sparrows, and soiled doves." She smokes, talks slang, and wears her hair short; her clothes are masculine and severe. Nevertheless, this "revolting daughter" or, as Mrs. Linton calls her in a series of articles in *The Nineteenth Century,* the "wild woman," comes off better in the novel than in the periodical articles.[4] After a flurry of activity in an anarchist movement, she falls in love with a policeman whom she finally marries. To Mrs. Linton's readers this was a humiliating social descent, but, even if it is at the price of her femininity, this heroine at least gets what she wants: "Not bold nor bad, she had yet lost that ineffable something which gives womankind its essential charm, endows it with its special power, and throws over it, as it were, a veil of mystic beauty."

The "Wild Woman" is treated with less tolerance in Mrs. Linton's novel of 1895, *The New Woman: In Haste and at Leisure,* where a frivolous heroine becomes enmeshed in the feminist activities of the Excelsior Club (". . . they were united as one woman on the great question of the diabolical nature of husbands, the degrading institution of marriage, the shameful burden of maternity, woman's claims to be a County Councillor, a voter, a lawyer, a judge, an M.P."). She neglects her child, destroys her husband's love for her, and comes perilously close to wrecking her marriage. In contrast there is an "ideal" woman here with whom her husband falls in love, but whom he nobly renounces in order to preserve his marriage. This admirable woman is distinguished for her

> absolute purity—her freedom from the very fringes of feminine "fastness." No prurient curiosity ever led her to premature knowledge; no dangerous study had aroused more dangerous speculations, and what evil she was perforce obliged to know neither clung nor rooted, but passed from her mind as a thing with which she had nought to do.

Mrs. Linton's conservatism on the "Woman Question" is ironic in the light of her own bold personality, her striking success as a journalist in keen competition with men, and her outright radicalism in religion. Independent and aggressive, she idealized the modest, shrinking, feminine woman. Woman's instinct, she argued, was to submerge herself in her family: "A woman's own fame is barren. It begins and ends with herself.

Reflected from her husband or her son, it has in it the glory of immortality—of continuance . . . the raison d'être of a woman is maternity. . . . The cradle lies across the door of the polling-booth and bars the way to the senate." [5] Scholarly and hungry for learning herself, Mrs. Linton opposed formal higher education for women. Even more vigorously she deplored the extremes to which some partially educated women were carried in their zeal for education. In *Paston Carew, Millionaire and Miser,* a novel published in 1886, she ridicules a shallow genteel woman who, like many of her sex, has fallen under "the curse of culture":

> They go in for something they are not and can never be. Fragile, anemic, and barely escaping the sick couch for their own parts, they rush off to become hospital nurses or missionaries' wives. Incapable of looking ahead or of forecasting the events of tomorrow from the facts of today, they dash on to platforms and toss up grave political questions like jugglers' balls in the air. Ignorant of grammar . . . they neglect their families, let the children's stockings go in holes, and spend both time and money in chasing the phantom of literary fame.

Apparently Mrs. Linton shared with many writing women of her time a tendency to go to extremes in condemning the extremes of others. Her positions are often inconsistent and contradictory, largely because, pen in hand, she became intoxicated with her powers. Her success as a polemicist in both fiction and nonfiction fortified an already strong urge to preach, teach, and reform. As a result, she frequently spoke more strongly than she probably felt. Like many another second-rate novelist she made her points by unsubtle characterization, verging often on stereotype and caricature. Incapable of suggesting the shades and complexities of human character, she could only extol or condemn. Almost everyone who knew her personally, especially in her mature years, was impressed with her kindness, gentleness, and warmth. The novelist Beatrice Harraden, who was for some years Mrs. Linton's protegée, observed of her posthumously published

memoirs *My Literary Life,* with its outspoken and sometimes indiscreet comments on Dickens, George Eliot, and George Henry
Lewes: "It is to be regretted also that she is not here herself to
tone down some of her more pungent remarks and criticisms,
hastily thrown off in bitter moments such as come to us all. Mrs.
Linton's pen was ever harsher than her speech, and those who
loved and knew her have the right to emphasize this fact." [6]
Another friend, Algernon Charles Swinburne, spoke of her as
"not only one of the most brilliant and gifted, but one of the
kindest and most generous of women," and wrote a long poem
on her death that begins:

> Kind, wise, and true as truth's own heart,
>   A soul that here
> Chose and held fast the better part
>   And cast out fear. [7]

The stridency and abusiveness of Mrs. Linton's published
work are in marked contrast to these impressions. One can only
conclude that her writing does not represent her fairly. To seek
consistency in her passionate pronouncements, in both her fiction
and her nonfiction, is futile. Her inconsistency, however, is not
mere waywardness, nor the reflection of an irrational, hysterical
nature. It is easy to dismiss Mrs. Linton as a clown-caricature
figure: she invites ridicule. But her contemporaries respected her
—and her writing, shrill and intemperate as it is, suggests that
she was a sound and faithful register of the times in which she
lived. On the Woman Question, politics, religion, and social
problems, she spoke her mind, a mind troubled, groping, confused by the rapid revolutionary changes that everywhere be-
sieged it, yet eager to come to terms with progress and the "new"
world.

No doubt there were personal sources as well for her con-
fusions and inconsistencies. Mrs. Linton was a public figure most
of her life, and her private life was closely bound up with her
public one. She had little of the reticence one expects from Vic-

torians and expressed herself as freely on most personal matters as she did on public ones. Characteristically, in 1885, she published her autobiography as a three-volume novel, so candid (even to using many real names) that her biographer George Somes Layard reprinted long passages of it. But this free-speaking nonfiction novel makes one extraordinary departure from reality. It changes the sex of the protagonist and becomes *The Autobiography of Christopher Kirkland,* promising thereby fascinating insights into transvestitism and unconscious masculinity but offering, in fact, so thin a sexual disguise and so transparent an authorial point of view that the reader promptly forgets the disguise.

As exposé and roman à clef, *Christopher Kirkland* is a dull and disappointing book, but it is an interesting expression of an intelligent Victorian's struggle to find a way of life for herself. The issue of the book—as it was the issue of her life and the problem of many other Victorians—was to find something to compensate for the loss of faith, something to fill the void. It is not a religious book, although religion figures strongly in it, but a book about a search for values. As Christopher Kirkland, Mrs. Linton traces her spiritual evolution from the fervent religious orthodoxy of her childhood through various stages of atheism, agnosticism, Unitarianism, necessitarianism, spiritualism and, finally, to a Comtist philosophy of humanitarianism and social meliorism which she called altruism. Eliza Lynn was born, a country parson's daughter, in 1822: "I was born before the age of railroads, steamboats, electric telegraphs, or the penny post; and when society in the remote country districts of England was very little changed from what it had been a hundred years before." Her childhood home was a parsonage near Keswick, Cumberland, in the beautiful Lake Country that was later to be the scene of many of her stories. Her parents were eminently respectable church people—her mother Charlotte Goodenough, a bishop's daughter; her father James Lynn, B.A. Wadham College, Oxford, the Vicar of Crosthwaite. She was the youngest of twelve children, and never knew her mother, who survived her birth only a few months. Left with the responsibilities of a large family of which the eldest was only sixteen, the Reverend Mr. Lynn turned resignedly to Providence and abandoned the education of his children to chance and their own efforts:

> There was one thing I have never understood; why my father, so well read and even learned in his own person, did not care to give his children the education proper to their birth and his own standing. The elders among us came off best, for the mother had had her hand on them, and the bishop [her grandfather, Samuel Goodenough, Bishop of Carlisle] too had had his say; but the younger ones were lamentably neglected. I do not know why. We were not poor. . . . At the worst, my father might have taught us himself. He was a good classic and a sound historian; and though his mathematics did not go very deep, they were better than our ignorance. But he was both too impatient and too indolent to be able to teach. And I doubt if the experiment would have answered had he tried it.[8]

Most of the boys managed to get to school. Eliza foraged as best she could, hoping, like Maggie Tulliver, that some of her brothers' education might rub off on her, reading omnivorously in a typical Church of England clergyman's library everything from Doddridge's *Family Expositor* and Miss Edgeworth's *Moral Tales* to *Faust* and *Don Quixote*. Resolving to teach herself, she plunged recklessly into Latin, Greek, and Hebrew, where she made no spectacular progress. She managed to pick up a working knowledge of French, and a smattering of Italian, Spanish, and German. Her passion for learning was fed by adolescent surges of religious fanaticism—ardent prayer, mystic communings.

> In a word, I lived in the Christian's sanctified egotism— believing that all the forces of heaven and hell were mainly occupied with the salvation or destruction of my one poor miserable little soul, and that the most important thing between earth and sky was, whether a hot-blooded girl with more sincerity than judgment flew into a rage when she should have curbed her temper, or heroically checked her

impulses of sensuality in the matter of jam-pudding and the fruit garden.[9]

Her religious fervor led her to the study of theology and philosophy, and she emerged understandably dizzy from reading heady mixtures like Ovid's *Metamorphoses* and the Old Testament. The struggle was all the more intense and painful because she had no one to turn to for guidance: "What agony I went through! What an infinite sense of being fated to sin, foredoomed to perdition, possessed me, as I felt that I was left to fight with my wild beasts unhelped—to struggle to get free, that I might take refuge in God, and to be hopelessly in the clutch of the devil." [10]

By the time she reached seventeen Eliza Lynn was an avowed skeptic:

Ever and ever the Mystery of the Incarnation became more and more a subject of perplexity and doubt. . . . Brought into line with these legends of former times—contrasted with the old classic myths and the stories in the very Bible itself—it suddenly seemed to lose its special character and to be merely one like others. It was no longer exceptional and divine—it had become historic and human.[11]

An independent, inquiring mind had been formed. A few years later, fortified with manuscripts and some verses she had published in *Ainsworth's Magazine,* she sought her father's permission to go to London to earn her living as a writer. His answer was unequivocal: "If you go to London, as you propose, you go without my consent, and the curse of God rests on disobedient children to the ends of their lives." [12] Mr. Lynn's firm resolution, however, was no stronger than any of the other powers he failed to exercise over his family. Eliza persuaded the family solicitor to intervene on her behalf and her father agreed to a trial year in London. There she settled in a respectable boarding house in Montague Place, only a few steps from the British Museum. She spent her year of liberation in the Reading Room, under the strict but kindly paternal eye of its famous librarian Antonio

Panizzi. Every day she went faithfully to "that badly-lighted, ill-ventilated, and queerly tenanted old room," stimulated and all but intoxicated by "the consciousness of living in the midst of such boundless stores, and of being the potential possessor of all this wealth." [13] Turned loose in "this rich pasturage," she took a year to gather "material for my magnum opus" and produced a novel of staggering erudition. *Azeth the Egyptian*, which she managed to persuade Newby to publish—at her own expense of £50. The *Times* reviewer was kind to the book. Another reviewer astoundingly called the final pages of the novel "equal to anything in the *Antigone* of Sophocles!" [14] Little wonder then that Mr. Lynn was at last convinced that his daughter belonged in London and, after this trial period, granted her an annual allowance of £30. A literary career had been launched out of the raw materials of intelligence, industry, and superb self-confidence.

In 1848 Eliza Lynn, parson's daughter turned budding novelist and journalist, settled down in London as an independent career woman. Only two years later another young woman writer would follow much the same course—Marian Evans, also self-educated and, after an adolescence of religious fervor, now a free thinker. Their lives met and crossed curiously in London. The emancipated Miss Lynn responded eagerly to the revolutionary activity in Europe in the late 1840's and '50s. She met Mazzini, Louis Blanc, Kossuth, Herbert Spencer, Robert Owen, Charles Bray:

> The French Revolution was the divine birthday of European liberty—I am not far from the same belief now! . . . I undutifully rejoiced in the discomfiture of my country in the American War of Independence. I believed in Greece and abjured Turkey. . . . Joan of Arc, the Maid of Saragosa, and Charlotte Corday were my feminine ideals.

Her London circle included the publisher John Chapman and the young radicals who published the magazine *The Leader*—"like the beginning of a moral and intellectual millennium. How ardent and eager we all were! How bravely Thornton Hunt and

George Henry Lewes and other young lions roared in its columns!" These were the notorious "Free-lovers, whose ultimate transaction was the most notable example of matrimony void of contract of our day." [15]

For some reason consistent only with Eliza Lynn's characteristic inconsistency, she took a violent dislike to Lewes, while defending Hunt. It was probably Lewes whom she portrayed as the villainous theatrical manager Vasty Vaughan in her novel of 1851, *Realities,* and it was certainly Lewes of whom she wrote, in judgment on his union with George Eliot:

> The one whom society set itself to honour, partly because of the transcendent genius of his companion, partly because of his own brilliancy and facility, was less solid than specious. The other, whom all men, not knowing him, reviled, was a moral hero. The former betrayed his own principles when he made capital out of his "desecrated hearth." . . . It must never be forgotten too that he who afterwards posed as the husband betrayed by the trusted friend, was, in the days when I first knew them all, the most pronounced Free-lover of the group, and openly took for himself the liberty he expressly sanctioned in his wife.[16]

Nevertheless she maintained a polite if cool social relationship with George Eliot and Lewes. For years, she confided in Herbert Spencer, she was prejudiced against Miss Evans "as a girl of infinitely bad taste, to say nothing more. How she *could* have liked him was to me a marvel! . . . Mr. Lewes and Miss Evans were perfectly justified in their union—perfectly—but they were not justified in their assumption of special sacredness, nor was the world, in its attitude of special reverence, which was more than condonation." [17] Perhaps there was personal pique in Mrs. Linton's comments. Even her admiration for George Eliot's novels was grudging; there was a lurking resentment of her "laboured style," "pedantry," and "artificial pose." But Mrs. Linton was a good enough judge of fiction to conclude that George Eliot was "the finest woman writer we have had or probably shall have . . . head and shoulders above the rest." [18]

La vie bohème was largely a spectator sport for the young Miss Lynn. She worked hard—both for art and for income. A second novel, *Amymone,* again with a background of ancient history, brought her £100 in 1848, but she could not hope to live on her fiction. Therefore she turned to journalism. On her earnings she was able to manage a reasonably comfortable living in London and, financed by free-lance work, a long stay in Paris, where she met Thackeray, the Brownings, Fanny Kemble, and more of the artists and radicals whom she cultivated—Ary Scheffer, Pierre-Jean Béranger, the Italian leader Daniele Manin.

Her success in a highly competitive, unfeminine, and often antifeminine field like journalism can be attributed only to her persistence and her industry. She was not a remarkable writer, but she was thoroughly competent and, as at least one of her editors, Dickens, had testified, reliable. In *Sowing the Wind* she introduced an aggressive, plain, and masculine young girl who pushes her way into journalism in order to support an indigent widowed mother. In *Christopher Kirkland* she expands the episode with much autobiographical detail, describing her first interview with the gruff, forbidding editor of the *Morning Chronicle,* John Douglas Cook. He managed to awe and frighten even the imperturbable Miss Lynn: "So! you are the little girl who has written that queer book [*Amymone*] and want to be one of the press-gang, are you?" To her meek reply, "Yes, I am the woman," he answered, "Woman, you call yourself? I call you a whipper-snapper. But you seem to have something in you. We'll soon find out if you have." He thereupon assigned her a leader, to be composed on the spot, based on a technical Blue Book report relating to the economy of mining. She passed the test and for the next two years, until 1851, when she had a violent quarrel with her editor and quit, she worked steadily, turning out some eighty miscellaneous articles and thirty-six reviews.[19]

More even than on her industry, Eliza Lynn's success was based on unshakable self-confidence. Rebuffs never discouraged her. She had resolved on a career in literature and she pursued her goal relentlessly, besieging publishers with no trace of reticence or false modesty. Even as a comparatively established novelist in the 1860's she was constantly on the alert for opportunities. In the files of the publisher William Blackwood and Sons in Edinburgh there are several letters from her, offering manuscripts. Concerning one novel, "Dearly Beloved" (probably *Sowing the Wind*, published in 1867 by Tinsley), she wrote to Major William Blackwood in 1863:

> It would be stupid to praise my own work, but I do think that if *Adam Bede, Jane Eyre, East Lynne* made their mark so quickly and deeply, this of mine will also; for it is not a weaker book than any of these, and certainly it is as faithful and therefore as original a transcript of society and human character as these. So much I think I may say without being conceited or presumptuous.[20]

After the publisher rejected the novel, she wrote John Blackwood an impassioned, almost hysterical plea, offering to make any changes he might suggest and imploring his personal guidance and assistance:

> I am so very sorry you did not like it! Could I not alter it to suit you? Indeed, indeed I am teachable and grateful for criticism, kindly (not if illnaturedly) bestowed, and have very little literary selfwill in the way of holding to my own against the advice of wiser and more experienced people. My object is to get out of periodical literature and succeed as a writer of good novels; but to really succeed I must have a first-class publisher. If you think that I could change the tone of that book—add story—take out certain characters —insert new, perhaps healthier and pleasanter characters— I would set to work at once on it. . . . I have never been befriended once in my whole literary life. I have never been advised, never guided, never helped. It has been a hard, solitary, fierce struggle for what I have gained. . . . I have faculties that might be utilized to the making of beautiful books and to my own good fortune, if I were befriended. If I could but interest such a man as yourself I could fear nothing and would gladly farm out my talent to his guidance and to his advantage as well as my own. This is not the letter of an author to a publisher—from any but my point

of view it is utterly mad—and outrageous—but it is the appeal of one human being to another; the one wanting such support as the other might possibly be able to give.[21]

Her plea fell on deaf ears. Blackwood did not publish this or any of her novels[22]—but other publishers were more obliging. Ultimately there is no mystery about Mrs. Linton's success as a woman of letters. She was an irresistible force before whom there were no immovable objects.

Although her success was self-engendered, Mrs. Linton never hesitated to use others where necessary to advance her career. Indeed, her pathetic complaint to John Blackwood that she had never been befriended or guided in her literary career is a downright untruth. But her motives do not appear to have been ruthless or entirely self-serving. Rather, she seems to have been so single-minded in her pursuit of a career that she was blind to how her actions might be interpreted by others. Certainly the friends from whose assistance and prestige she benefited did not feel themselves exploited. Walter Savage Landor, whose patronage she sought, was rewarded by the kind of hero-worshiping devotion that brought joy to his otherwise unhappy old age. He was seventy-three and she twenty-five when they first met in Bath. Long an admirer of his *Imaginary Conversations,* she dashed up to him, she recalled, "as if he had been a god suddenly revealed." Landor responded with touching, if naive, pleasure, writing of this first meeting: "A few days ago I was presented to a lady of extraordinary genius. . . . [Her noble Romances] filled me with delight and wonder. She is truly admirable for the strength and simplicity of her character. [Though the granddaughter of a bishop and a daughter of a vicar] her spirit, I suspect, is no haunter of churches." [23]

Eliza Lynn reaped immediate benefit from the friendship. Landor reviewed *Amymone* in *Fraser's Magazine* (October, 1848), giving high praise to this work of an unknown young novelist, and persuaded John Forster to publish a favorable notice of it in the *Examiner.* Further, he wrote a poem which the *Examiner* published (July 22, 1848)—"To Eliza Lynn on her 'Amymone'"

—where he named her in the distinguished company of Erinna, Corinna, Sappho, and Mme de Staël, concluding:

> In our days, so sweet,
> So potent, so diversified, is none
> As thine, Protectress of Aspasia's fame
> Thine, golden shield of matchless Pericles,
> Pure heart and lofty soul, Eliza Lynn! [24]

Calling her his "dear daughter," he campaigned vigorously for her career. When her third novel, *Realities,* which she dedicated to him, was published in 1851, Landor wrote to Forster urging him to be kind in his review:

> It appears to me, from a letter of yours, that you fancy there is something bold and unfeminine in her Novel. Bold indeed there is much, unfeminine there is nothing at all. Her boldness is the boldness of innocence and truth. . . . I have red [sic] only this first volume; and I find it a mirror which diminishes me. I defy the whole world to exhibit such *animated truth.*

A few years later he described her as a writer "high in the ranks of literature . . . there are sentences in her work not surpassed in eloquence by De Staël or by Rousseau. If a sculptor is about to produce a statue of Truth, let him choose for the purpose a pure and spotless marble, and let him study the features of Eliza Lynn." [25]

Granted that Landor was in his dotage, and hardly objective in his literary and personal judgments, he was nevertheless an influential friend. And Eliza Lynn apparently gave as much as she received—attention, admiration, companionship, and loyalty. Many years later another admirer of Landor, Algernon Charles Swinburne, acknowledged her friendship in a graceful dedicatory poem, part of a longer memorial poem he was writing on Landor:

A.C.S. to E.L.L.

Daughter in spirit elect and consecrate
     By love and reverence of the Olympian sire
Whom I too love and worshipped, seeing so great,
     And found so gracious toward my long desire
To bid that love in song before his gate
     Sound, and my lute be loyal to his lyre,
To none save one it now may dedicate
     Song's new burnt-offering on a century's pyre.

     And though the gift be light
     As ashes in men's sight
Left by the flame of no ethereal fire,
     Yet, for love's worthier sake
     Than words are worthless, take
This wreath of words ere yet their hour expire:
So, haply, from some heaven above,
He, seeing, may set next yours my sacrifice of love.[26]

After Landor's death, Mrs. Linton became involved in a controversy over him. She attacked both Forster and Sidney Colvin for their biographies of him, with special bitterness toward Forster for "his want of loyalty to the man, dead, whose feet he had kissed while living." The cause for her indignation was Forster's failure to mention her in his book.

He never forgave me my intimacy with the Samson who had already generously endowed him with the copyright of his books, and whose kindness, he was afraid, would be diverted to me. Probably he thought I was as self-seeking as himself. In the days to come he made me feel his enmity; and of all the queer things in my strange life, one of the queerest is the determination with which he, first, and then subsequent biographers of Mr. Landor, have agreed to ignore my friendship with him.[27]

Whatever practical benefits the relationship with Landor offered Eliza Lynn, there seems no doubt that genuine affection existed between them. She was his "dear daughter" and he her "spiritual father." One can readily understand her need for such a relationship. Her own father, who had made no claim upon her affection, died in 1855. Her older sisters and brothers were married, with lives of their own. A bluestocking and never a beauty, Eliza Lynn appears to have had no brilliant marriage prospects. She was not unattractive to men, however, and had many free and casual friendships with the opposite sex. Though rather short and heavy and handicapped with poor eyesight, which she attempted to correct with thick spectacles, she nevertheless had qualities much admired by the Victorians—rich profuse brown-gold hair, an excellent complexion, a stately manner, and good taste in clothes. Her biographer Layard reports that she had only one love in her life, a devout Catholic identified only as "Brother Edward." Because she was intractable in her agnosticism there was no possibility of marriage for them.

Her marriage, when it did at last take place, was a curious, indeed in some ways an absurd one. Quite possibly it could only have occurred in Victorian England, where those odd mixtures of idealism and practicality, personal candor and sexual naïveté, seem to have been so frequent. Not the oddest aspect of this marriage is that Mrs. Linton wrote of it so frankly in *Christopher Kirkland,* simply transposing the sexes of herself and her husband. In 1854, already in her thirties and launched on an independent career, Eliza Lynn became acquainted with the Lintons, who lived at Coniston, in the Lake Country, in Brantwood, the house that Ruskin purchased in 1871.[28] They were a large, lively family—William James Linton, ten years Eliza Lynn's senior, was an artist-engraver, writer, radical, and idealist: "an artist, shiftless, dreamy, unpractical, morally self-indulgent, personally pure and ascetic; a man who could live on bread and spring-water but who would not work in his studio when he wanted to be out in the sunshine, and who exhaled in thought all the strength that should have gone into action." [29] Linton's first wife had died, leaving him two children. His second wife, sister of his first wife whom he married in defiance of the Deceased Wife's Sister marriage ban, bore him five children. A cheerful, easygoing woman, "indifferent to material comforts," she reared their brood in a noisy, hearty, permissive Bohemian atmosphere. Eliza Lynn became attached to the mother and the children, one of whom was named for her. In 1857 the second Mrs. Linton died, with a deathbed request to her friend to look after the younger children. Having witnessed in her own family the results of parental neglect and indifference to the education of children, Eliza Lynn took her responsibilities to heart. In March 1858 she married Linton—not without some misgivings, but resolved to put into successful practice her theories of domestic life.[30]

"Christopher Kirkland" marries Esther, the idealistic widow of his artist-friend Joshua Lambert, in order to provide for her large family. "I was in that frame of mind which made benevolence my greatest solace and my only happiness. I had the desire to sacrifice myself for the well-being of others. . . . I wanted to give myself as an offering to God, through man." The real-life Linton was not unattractive, nor was the marriage altogether self-immolation on Eliza's part. "I do not mean to say," Kirkland writes, "that I married with any personal reluctance, but I do say that I married with more sense of duty than of attraction." The marriage lasted almost seven years. Mrs. Linton assumed the whole financial burden, moved the family to London, and sent the children to school. At first they lived comfortably, entertained generously, and seemed happy. The children responded well to the new discipline. But Linton could not accommodate himself to household routines, regularly scheduled meals, and living on a strict budget. There were quarrels which made it difficult for Mrs. Linton to keep up with her writing assignments and thereby meet the household expenses. In 1864 Linton returned with the children to Brantwood. His wife remained in London, though she continued to spend her summers with the family. In 1867 Linton went to America to seek his fortune. There was no legal separation; the Lintons simply drifted apart. Christopher Kirkland's wife, an ardent champion of women's rights, also emigrates to America. Christopher—and we may assume Mrs. Linton—reflects:

Had things been different between us, I would have thrown up everything in England, and I would have gone with her. I could have written in America as well as here, and perhaps with even better results. Had my wife still loved and respected me—had she not begun to treat me with systematic neglect and intolerable contempt . . . I would have kept with her to the end.

Linton made no mention of his marriage in his memoirs, *Threescore and Ten Years, 1820–1890: Recollections,* which he published in 1894. When he returned to England on a visit in 1889 he did not see his wife, although he wrote to her warmly:

Dear old Love—We must not lose sight of each other again. Now that I am leaving, and satisfied that we have done wisely by not meeting, I may say that it has been hard for me too. I would have been glad to hold you to my heart again, my lips on yours—but the parting would have been too painful. Dearest, believe me, I would knit our lives together again if I thought it might be; but in some things we have been unsuited, and if in the first fervour of our love this difference could part us, might it not occur again? I could dare to face it, but it would be rank unwisdom. God bless you, darling! . . . And now farewell, still dearly loved! You love me too.—Your old lover, W. J. Linton.

He died in Hamden, Connecticut, in December, 1897. Mrs. Linton, herself then close to death, received the news with resignation: "He was eighty-five, and quite worn out. Life had no more to give him now but pain and sorrow, and existence had become a burden. It is best so." [31]

The failure of her marriage did not dampen Mrs. Linton's enthusiasm for life and work. Restored to single blessedness in the mid-60's, she plunged even more energetically into writing and produced a steady stream of novels and journalism. She wrote her sensational Girl of the Period pieces and her most popular novels: *Lizzie Lorton of Greyrigg* (1866), *Sowing the*

Wind (1867), *Joshua Davidson* (1872), *Patricia Kemball* (1875), *The Atonement of Leam Dundas* (1876), and *Under Which Lord?* (1879). Layard estimates that from 1870 to 1871 she published at least 225 essays and stories in such respected periodicals as *Saturday Review, All the Year Around,* and *Queen.*[32] Her income now permitted her to indulge her taste for travel, and she spent several years abroad, visiting in France and living in Italy, a country of which she was especially fond. There she became part of the English colony and knew the W. W. Storys, the T. A. Trollopes, Ouida, and Vernon Lee. She wrote as industriously abroad as she did at home, adding travel reporting to the many varieties of articles she produced.

At best, Mrs. Linton's novels can be read today only with clinical curiosity to see *how* she managed to capture a public in spite of a conspicuous lack of creative ability. The answer lies in the extraordinary tolerance of the Victorian reading public for anything that smacked of serious ideas and partly in Mrs. Linton's shrewd recognition that that public also wanted thrills and vicarious stimulation. In a review of a now forgotten three-decker, *Hester's Sacrifice* ("by the Author of 'St. Olav's,' 'Janita's Cross,' etc. etc."), which Mrs. Linton wrote for the *Saturday Review* (April 21, 1866), she ridiculed the unnamed authoress for failing to rise to the passions of her own plot. Her manly hero, for example, has "the heart of a hare and the conscience of an hysterical woman," and is ultimately reduced to "a mass of invertebrate pulp." These "rose-water" novels were not to Mrs. Linton's hearty taste:

> As there are people who buy raspberry-rock and cocoanut paste, and who find the diet exhilarating, so there are people who read such books as *Hester's Sacrifice,* and who rest and are thankful after the process. Meat for men and milk for babes truly. Milk and water rather, and more of the latter than of the former, is such literary food as is here offered.

Meat, tough and fibrous though not necessarily raw, was what Mrs. Linton offered her readers. Her novels tend toward the sensational, although her serious moral and social preoccupations kept her from producing the outright sensational novel. She persists in cluttering her plots of intrigue, suspense, and even murder with her hobby-horses—religious skepticism, the Woman Question, regionalism (mainly the local color and folklore of the Lake Country). With characteristic bluntness she never hesitated to introduce elements of the gruesome and the grotesque. Murder, madness, and melancholia were basic ingredients of many of her stories. In *Lizzie Lorton of Greyrigg* a tempestuous heroine stirs up a peaceful Cumberland village by jealously accusing the man she loves of murder and finally killing herself. In *Sowing the Wind* a psychopathic husband persecutes his loving wife and attempts to murder his sister's child. In *Patricia Kemball* a young man murders his rival and allows an innocent man to hang for the crime. In *The World Well Lost* a genteel family conceals from society the fact that the father is a convict.

But Mrs. Linton was too intelligent to be satisfied with grinding out mere formula fiction. Her interests were serious and controversial. Her feelings on every issue were intense; her conviction and self-confidence were boundless. The polemical novel, therefore, was a natural outlet and, while it never brought her the critical acclaim and popular success enjoyed by Mrs. Humphry Ward, it did bring a fair measure of financial reward and passing attention from critics and public alike.[33] That a clergyman's daughter should turn, in her serious fiction, to the subject of religion is not surprising. But with characteristic independence of spirit, Mrs. Linton used her religious novels as platforms for denouncing religious orthodoxy. She was certainly not alone among her contemporaries in criticizing the Church of England, but her rebellion was more personal and extreme than most. Even in her childhood reading, as we have already observed, she confronted problems of faith with curiosity and skepticism. Throughout her life she remained "spiritually inclined." That is, she speculated on religious questions and scrutinized every variety of spiritualism, mesmerism, and psychic investigation. Ultimately she settled for agnosticism, heavily tinged with social idealism in the form of a secular philosophy of altruism: "It is the Agnostic who . . . preaches afresh the democracy of souls—

who, in his belief that the religious idea is one to be improved and finally perfected by evolution and knowledge, sees the true salvation of men and their final redemption from error." [34] When they treat of religious subjects, her novels show a straight and unflinching course out of the sheltered family parsonage into the maelstrom of modern nineteenth-century intellectual life—a head-on confrontation with science, socialism, free thought, every major challenge of her day.

As early as 1851, in a novel of her contemporary society, *Realities*, Mrs. Linton ridiculed a High Churchman for emphasizing ritual, portraying him as arrogant and hypocritical. In *Lizzie Lorton of Greyrigg* she treated more sympathetically an idealistic clergyman who hopes "to establish a kind of Christian socialism on a High Church basis." [35] Her most sensational and scandalous attack on orthodoxy is in *The True History of Joshua Davidson, Christian and Communist*. A none too subtle allegory of the life of Christ, her story introduces young Joshua Davidson (Jesus—David's son), son of a carpenter in Cornwall, who sets out in nineteenth-century England to relive the life of Christ. Not surprisingly, he is scorned, abused, and finally murdered by a mob incited by an old clergyman from his native village. The writing is feverish and shrill: "Let us then strip our Christianity," Joshua preaches, "of all the mythology, the fetichism that has grown about it. Let us abandon the idolatry with which we have obscured the meaning of Life; let us go back to the MAN, and carry on His work in its essential spirit in the direction suited to our times and social conditions"; the premise is unoriginal, and, as she develops it, unimaginative. Yet the book stirred considerable excitement. The first edition, published anonymously, sold out immediately. Within three months there was a second and then a third edition, with the author's name now on the title page, and by 1890 it had reached a tenth edition in England and had sold widely in America as well.[35] The atheist Charles Bradlaugh bought a thousand copies for distribution; John Bright endorsed it enthusiastically—but the 1870's and '80's were crowded with religious controversy, and *Joshua Davidson* was forgotten.[37] Nevertheless, the book made her as famous a novelist as the Girl of the Period had made her a journalist.

Mrs. Linton treated religious questions again in the more conventional novel *Under Which Lord?*—the story of a marriage wrecked by the interference of a fanatically high clergyman. This is a characteristic Linton novel—outspoken, bristling with issues and arguments, implausible in plot yet so vigorous that it holds a reader's interest even while it jars his aesthetic sensibilities and common sense. The central characters are a middle-aged couple who had married romantically and impulsively but who now find themselves alienated—she vaguely restless, yearning for deep emotional experience, he absorbed in scientific reading and in lecturing on agnosticism to working men's clubs ("What has the Church ever taught that has been of the smallest permanent or real good to man?" he asks). They have one daughter, a sensitive, idealistic girl who "wanted religion, not philosophy; faith, not scepticism; adoration of God and the angels, not critical examination of verbal forms and isolated facts in natural history."

Into the lives of this family comes the new vicar, the Reverend Launcelot Lascelles. He is very high, "a Roman Catholic in all save name and obedience," who reads from Wiseman's *Fabiola* and Newman's *Apologia* to the ladies' sewing circle and exploits the starved emotions of his women parishioners. In the guise of a spiritual confessor he makes love to one repressed spinster: "He questioned her of her waking thoughts and nightly dreams; he probed now the yearning and now the suffering, to which she gave fancy names that disguised the truth from herself but not from him." He persuades the heroine to rebel against her husband and sign over her money to him: "You had to choose your master. Which was it to be—God or man?—the Church or your home?—your Saviour or your husband?—me as your guide in the way of salvation or him as your leader into inevitable destruction?" By the end of the novel he has lured the daughter into joining a Roman Catholic nunnery and destroyed the marriage of her parents. The agnostic husband dies nobly with the sentiments of altruism on his lips:

> He kept his dying eyes still fixed on the sun—his face irradiated with a kind of divine glory, as before his mind, marshalled in grand and long procession, passed thoughts of

the noble victories over superstition and the glorious truths made manifest, the peace of nations, the spread of knowledge, the abolition of vice and misery and ignorance, the sublime light of universal freedom and the unfettered progress of humanity which should inform and govern the future through the supreme triumphs of True Knowledge.

"Man the God incarnate!" he said; "Yes, the myth was true."

His more gullible wife is left without child, husband, money, or reputation. "But," Mrs. Linton concludes bitterly, "she had gained the blessing of the Church which denies science, asserts impossibilities, and refuses to admit the evidence of facts."

Early in her life Mrs. Linton had taken the plunge into the void and broken with established religion. "The presence of God recedes as science advances," she proclaimed. Her hearty, untroubled acceptance of the scientific revolution appealed to many readers. Such an attitude was enlightened and intellectual, to the extent that it was based on reading and reason, but uncomplicated, easy to grasp. Writing as Christopher Kirkland of her own emergence from doubt and despair to positive faith in mankind's future, she voiced the Victorian yearning for certainty and affirmation: "What a glorious time it was! . . . Everywhere was a shaking of the dry bones, and the clothing of flesh and sinew on what had been dead and useless fragments buried in the earth. . . . It was the birth-hour of a new Truth. . . ." [38]

Such a joyous, vigorous affirmation not only pleased Mrs. Linton's readers but, for most of her long life, sustained her happily. She spent her last years in London, in an attractive flat in Queen Anne's Mansions, just off St. James' Park. She entertained and was entertained by many literary notables—Kipling, Rider Haggard, Marie Corelli, Andrew Lang, Swinburne, Thomas Hardy. She corresponded with Henry James who, with typical gallantry and diplomacy, complimented her without praising her work.[39] Now a kind of grey eminence among women writers, she gave interviews to the press and advised and patronized many aspiring young writers.[40] Usually she had living with her some young woman friend or relative whom she educated and assisted financially. The most successful of her protegés was Beatrice Harraden, author of the best-seller of 1893, *Ships that Pass in the Night*. "She had the tenderest heart imaginable," Miss Harraden wrote in an affectionate memoir:

> Even at the risk of appearing to be sentimental, I dwell with lingering emphasis on the gentler side of her character, because it is as true of her as the pugilistic side. She took me into her heart from the onset, and though she distinctly gave me to understand that she did not approve of me—for I had committed the terrible sin of receiving a modern young woman's education—yet she was prepared to overlook a great deal because she loved me.[41]

In spite of the many gratifications of her old age, however, Mrs. Linton had the disquieting experience of realizing that she had outlived her time. During most of her life she had been a rebel and a radical. Even her passionate antifeminism was iconoclastic. She advocated divorce, when by mutual consent, and a woman's rights to own property and have full guardianship of her children. She prided herself on her humanitarianism and her adaptability to the course of man's progress. Morality, she boldly asserted, was relative and flexible: "Morality is as much a matter of climate, age, sex, education, as is the growth of an oak from an acorn in England, of a palm from a date-stone in Syria. It is as shifting as the thermometer—as local as vegetation. The morality of one age is not that of another." [42] But no amount of affirmation could deny the realities of old age and the alienation of one generation from another. In 1890 she wrote, querulously perhaps, that current literature was frivolous and superficial: "The democratic wave which has spread over all society—and washed down something which had better been left standing—has swept through the whole province of literature." [43]

Mrs. Linton died in London at seventy-six, on July 14, 1898. She left unpublished a novel about an old woman who, after a serious illness, finds that she has miraculously regained her youth. The consequences are unhappy: people distrust her and suspect her of witchcraft; she is lonely, cut off from her own generation in a new and radically altered world. The novel, published in 1900 as *The Second Youth of Theodora Desanges,* is ludicrous, but it contains several passages that are moving for their personal expression: "Born in the backward ages, when society was constructed on such different lines, I am at cross corners with modern thoughts and ways. The easy familiarity of the young men and the ungraceful masculinity of the young women revolt me. The loss of dignity, of respect, of beauty of sex-differences, destroys the charm of social intercourse." Finding life increasingly burdensome, Theodora Desanges finally welcomes death, "that sweet-faced genius who is our release from pain and perplexity."

Eliza Lynn Linton was a self-made writer and a totally synthetic novelist. She demonstrates the power and prestige that, in nineteenth-century England, a career in literature could bring to a woman of no particular creative talent but of intelligence, industry, and determination. Her achievement was admirably summed up in her obituary in the *Athenaeum* (July 23, 1898):

> Naturally she was an essayist rather than a novelist. She wrote novels simply because the novel was the accredited form of literature in her day; had she lived in the opening of the seventeenth century she would have written plays. She had no innate talent for fiction, for she was no judge nor observer of character, and she had no ability for creating living personages. She had an excellent faculty of writing, and her knowledge of literature enabled her to devise a plot and to construct personages to act respectably in the scenes of her planning; but they had no real life in them.

Whatever her limitations as a novelist, she understood the needs of her public—at least of that large, restless segment of Victorian England whose religious faith had crumbled, but who clung stubbornly and fiercely to the institutions and traditions of the early nineteenth century. A radical conservative, a militantly feminine antifeminist, a skeptical idealist and a believing atheist, Mrs. Linton consistently mirrored the inconsistencies of her times.

Notes

1. George Somes Layard, *Mrs. Lynn Linton, Her Life, Letters, and Opinions* (London, 1901), pp. 60, 81. See also M. M. Bevington, *The Saturday Review, 1855–1868* (New York, 1941), pp. 33–34.
2. See her preface to *The Girl of the Period,* I (London, 1883), vii–viii. By the time this collection was published, the furor over the Girl of the Period had died down. Although the publisher, Bentley, advertised the book widely, sales were disappointing. See Royal A. Gettmann, *A Victorian Publisher: A Study of the Bentley Papers* (Cambridge, 1960), p. 128.
3. Layard, p. 143. In 1869 Samuel Bracebridge Hemyng cribbed the title *The Girl of the Period* for a novel and followed through the next year with *The Man of the Period.*
4. "The Wild Women. No. I. as Politician," XXX (July, 1891), 79–88; "The Wild Women as Social Insurgents," XXX (October, 1891), 596–605; "The Partisans of the Wild Women," XXXI (March, 1892), 455–64.
5. "The Wild Women No. I. as Politician" p. 80.
6. Prefatory note to Mrs. Linton's *My Literary Life* (London, 1899), pp. 5–6.
7. See his letter to Alice Swinburne, July 26, 1898, in *The Swinburne Letters,* ed. C. Y. Lang, VI (New Haven, 1959), 130. The poem is printed in full in *The Complete Works of Algernon Charles Swinburne,* Bonchurch Edition, VI (London, 1925–27), 287–88. It was originally published in his *A Channel Passage and Other Poems* (1904).
8. Layard, p. 5. Parallel passages to this and others quoted here appear in *The Autobiography of Christopher Kirkland.*
9. Layard, p. 31.
10. *Kirkland,* I, 90.
11. Layard, p. 37.
12. *Ibid.,* p. 47.
13. *Kirkland,* I, 239–40.
14. Layard, p. 54.
15. *Kirkland,* I, 99; II, 13–14.
16. *Ibid.,* I, 278–79. See also Gordon S. Haight, *George Eliot* (New York, 1968), p. 132.
17. Layard, p. 251.
18. For her personal impressions of Lewes and George Eliot see also *My Literary Life,* pp. 86–87. Her evaluation of George Eliot as a novelist appears in *Women Novelists of Queen Victoria's Reign* (London, 1897), pp. 63–115. George Eliot seems to have been amused and somewhat overwhelmed by Eliza Lynn. She referred to her as "altogether an L. L. [Literary Lady] looking person" (*The George Eliot Letters,* ed. Gordon S. Haight, I [New Haven, 1954], 337) but admired her idealism (see below, n. 30). In 1866 George Eliot wrote twice to apologize for not

being at home at the Priory when Mrs. Linton called and to postpone another announced visit (IV, 319, 326).

19. Layard, pp. 57–58, 60. Layard of course changes the text to restore the feminine gender.

2c. Blackwood MSS. 4183, January 17, 1863. The Blackwood Letters are in the National Library in Edinburgh.

21. Blackwood MSS. 4183, April 22, 1863.

22. See her letter to Blackwood of October 7, 1894 (MSS. 4618), thanking him for his kindness to Beatrice Harraden: "I am unfortunate in all I have attempted with you but not in my friends."

23. R. H. Super, *Walter Savage Landor, A Biography* (New York, 1954), p. 585, n. 27.

24. The poem is reprinted by Layard, p. 376.

25. R. H. Super, "Landor's 'Dear Daughter,' Eliza Lynn Linton," *PMLA*, LIX (December, 1944), 1061, 1063.

26. *Swinburne Letters*, IV, 149.

27. *Kirkland*, II, 297.

28. By coincidence, another house in which Eliza Lynn Linton lived had important literary associations—Gad's Hill, which her father had bought early in the century and which was later purchased by Charles Dickens.

29. *Kirkland*, III, 14.

30. See Landor's letter to her: "You are now bound by honor, the holiest of sacraments, to complete an engagement which was formed inconsiderately. . . . I look forward with anxiety to your future . . . I could have wished that Mr. L. had overcome his passion for you" (*PMLA*, LIX, 1063). George Eliot commented on the marriage in a letter to Mrs. Charles Bray (June 5, 1857): "Your description of her devotion to those seven children is very pretty. Her large-hearted energy is something to admire and love her for" (*Letters*, II, 339–40).

31. Layard, pp. 270, 339.

32. *Ibid.*, p. 163.

33. In the 1880's she was receiving from £600 to £800 for the book rights to her novels. Most of them appeared serially in magazines as well, from which she realized about £500 additionally (Layard, pp. 220, 253). Bentley lost considerable money on *Christopher Kirkland* because she asked £250 for it instead of a royalty. The book sold very poorly (Gettman, *A Victorian Publisher*, p. 128).

34. *The Order of Creation: The Conflict between Genesis and Geology*. A Controversy between W. E. Gladstone, T. H. Huxley, Max-Müller, M. Reville, E. Lynn Linton. (New York: The Truth Seeker [1886]), p. 171. Mrs. Linton's "A Protest and a Plea" is the last essay in this little book (pp. 161–78), an answer to Gladstone's article, "The Dawn of Creation and of Worship," which had originally appeared in *The Nineteenth Century*. Without naming Mrs. Linton, Gladstone had included her in his attack on a number of writers who, "unimpeached in character and abounding in talent," deny the idea of a ruling deity with "a joy and exultation that might almost recall the frantic orgies of the Commune." In her defense, Mrs. Linton outlined her philosophy of altruism and

emphasized her faith in humanity to guide itself to a higher, more glorious future.

35. Joseph Baker. *The Novel and the Oxford Movement*. No. 8 (Princeton Studies in English, 1932), pp. 80, 158–59.

36. Layard, pp. 179–80.

37. It had a brief moment of revival in 1960 when Professor E. E. Evans-Prichard, scheduled to give the Aquinas Lecture at Blackfriars, Oxford, found a copy of the novel on a six-penny bookstall and was inspired by one sentence in it: "If sociology is a scientific truth, then Jesus of Nazareth preached and practised not only in vain, but against unchangeable law." His lecture, "Religion and the Anthropologists," pointing out that all anthropologists regard religion as superstition, was the subject of an editorial in the *Times Literary Supplement*, May 20, 1960.

38. *Kirkland*, III, 84–85.

39. Layard, p. 233, prints a letter from James in reply to a letter of hers praising but also asking questions about the interpretation of *Daisy Miller*. (The letter also appears in *The Selected Letters of Henry James*, ed. Leon Edel [New York, 1955], pp. 138–40.) In another letter, James acknowledges with thanks her praise of *Portrait of a Lady*: "One writes *for* the public, perhaps—but one writes *to* those few. I shall always write to you in future—most intelligent and liberal of readers, most positive of friends" (*A Letter from Henry James to Mrs. Linton* [Privately printed at the Sign of the George, Dover, Mass., 1932]; the MS of this letter is at Harvard).

40. See "Mrs. Lynn Linton," interview by Helen C. Black in *Notable Women Authors* (Glasgow, 1893), pp. 1–10 (originally published in *Lady's Pictorial*); "A Chat with Mrs. Lynn Linton," by Mrs. Alec Tweedie, *Temple Bar*, CII (July, 1894), pp. 355–64; F. J. Gould, *Chats with Pioneers of Modern Thought* (London, 1898), pp. 17–21.

41. Layard, pp. 295–96. See also her memorial article, "Mrs. Lynn Linton," *The* (London) *Bookman*, XIV (August, 1898), 124–25.

42. *Kirkland*, III, 170.

43. "Literature: Then and Now," *Fortnightly*, LIII (April, 1890), 527. In the same year, along with Hardy and Walter Besant, she participated in a discussion on "Candour in English Fiction" in *The New Review*. Here again she condemned contemporary fiction as "the weakest . . . the most insincere, the most jejune, the least impressive and the least tragic." She attributed this decline of the novel to the blandness and hypocrisy of English morality (II [January–June, 1890], 10–14).

. . . letter-writing was a form of her imperative impulse to express her-self to others, and constituted also a mild form of physical exercise. She once said to me of herself that, just as walking or other muscular exertion was essential to the bodily health of some people, so talking was to others, that talking was not merely a mental relief and stimulus, but was, in its other effect, a physical and renovating exercise. . . .
—Samuel Cronwright-Schreiner, Preface to
The Letters of Olive Schreiner

In after times when strength or courage fail,
May I recall this lonely hour; the gloom
Moving one way: all heaven in the gale
Roaring: and high above the insulated tomb
An eagle anchored on full spread of sail
That from its wings lets fall a silver plume.
—Roy Campbell, "Buffel's Kop: Olive Scrreiner's Grave" 1

2.

The Imperative Impulse:
Olive Schreiner

I

Every generation or so a handful of readers—usually young, ardent, and idealistic—rediscovers Olive Schreiner and her *Story of an African Farm*. The experience tends to be intense but ephemeral. In 1955, the centenary of her birth, the BBC offered a series of programs on her, and in South Africa there was a flurry of ceremonial activity in her honor. A writer in *The New York Times Book Review* (May 22, 1955) observed patronizingly that an entire generation had grown up without having heard of her:

And if that generation inquired . . . "Why should we have?"
—we confess we'd be pretty mute. Somehow the whole thing
is a little sad. Miss Schreiner wrote a fine book when she
was just a kid of about 25, "The Story of an African Farm,"
but she was no genius—and the rest of her writing . . .
though some of it had distinction, is almost entirely
forgotten.

Yet in 1961 Izaak Dinesen, writing in a preface to the Limited
Editions Club issue of that novel, referred to it as "one of my
favorite books long before I knew that I myself would ever come
to make Africa my home." And in 1968 Doris Lessing, a novelist
not unlike Olive Schreiner in both background and ideology,
wrote a warm tribute to *The Story of an African Farm* and to its
author. She had discovered the novel at fourteen and responded
to it immediately, "realising that this was one of the few rare
books. For it is in that small number of novels, with *Moby Dick,
Jude the Obscure, Wuthering Heights,* perhaps one or two
others, which is on a frontier of the human mind." Ten years
later, Mrs. Lessing confessed, while still remembering the effect
of the novel, she had forgotten all its details. But on rereading it
in the late 1960's she found it powerful and timely: "There is
an atmosphere that is sympathetic to it, particularly among
young people." [2]
 For all then but that handful of readers, Olive Schreiner
remains simply another victim of the literary amnesia that
sweeps away most popular novelists. Her failure to survive is in
large measure a failure of her art. *The Story of an African Farm,*
her only "finished" novel, is a clumsy, uneven book. What interests those of us who read it today is why in its time it was such
a spectacular success and, further, what it was in the character
of the author herself that once so captivated the reading publics
of England and America. For this fat, dumpy, asthmatic little
woman attracted in her time a wide and diverse circle of admirers. These were not crackpots but serious, intelligent people
—Bernard Shaw, Havelock Ellis, Beatrice Webb, Arthur Symons,
Sir Charles Dilke, Cecil Rhodes, Mahatma Gandhi. Granted she
also had her apostles in the lunatic fringe. Herself an emotional,

impulsive, eccentric, and occasionally hysterical woman, she invited hyperbole and downright silliness from some of her admirers.[3] Yet this ungainly bundle of flesh and ardent mysticism
went about her work with a dedication so passionate that no one
who reads her today can deny her profound respect. She was
intelligent and imaginative, a sensitive and sympathetic recorder
of the remote life of the South African farmer, and a propa-
gandist with a zeal for losing causes—the Boers in 1898, pacifism
from 1914 to 1918—as well as for winning ones like feminine
suffrage and sexual emancipation.

Zealots and unabashed idealists are rarely fashionable; in
many quarters they are suspect. If it is not their sincerity that
we impugn, it is their sanity or, at least, their psychological
stability. We question motives and probe at the hidden roots of
human behavior, confident of nothing but the paradoxes and
ambiguities of character. Not so the late Victorians. This is not
to suggest that they were naive or unrealistic. On the contrary,
a dark streak of Calvinism lingered everywhere in Victorian religious thinking, and it was rendered even darker by the scientific
materialism that flourished in the second half of the century.
Nevertheless, it was an age that had come into being during the
flowering of literary romanticism. Mature readers and writers
alike of the 1880's had grown up in the melancholy but affirmative spiritual climate of Goethe, Wordsworth, Emerson, and
Carlyle. Faith in the man, in the deed, in the doing, was perhaps
a little shakier in 1880 than, say, in 1850, but it persisted. It was
an assumption, a premise, a foundation without which all the
social reform movements of the period would have been patently
absurd. To this kind of fundamental idealism or altruism Olive
Schreiner spoke:

I am only a broken and untried possibility—but this I have,
that I can sympathise with all the lives, with all the en-
deavours, with all the accomplished work, even with all the
work attempted and not accomplished, of other men. I love
Nature and I love men; I love music and I love science. I
love poetry and I love practical labour; I like to make a
good pudding and see people eating it; and I like to write a

book that makes their lives fuller. I can do very little, and
have never been so situated that I could do my best—but I
can live all lives in my love and sympathy.[4]

She defines the spirit, the mood, of the young liberals of the
1880's—the coterie that called themselves "The Fellowship of
the New Life," out of which emerged the Fabian Society—the
Webbs, Havelock Ellis, Edward Carpenter, the Hubert Blands
(she the famous children's writer E. Nesbit); the crusading journalism of W. T. Stead; the women's rights movement. *The New
Spirit* was the apt title of Havelock Ellis' first book, published in
1890. In his introduction to these essays on Tolstoy, Whitman,
Heine, and others, Ellis hailed the "lightbearers" who bring
moral enlightenment to "the darkness that surrounds our path":
"this devotion to truth, this instinctive search after the causes of
things, has become what may be called a new faith. The fruits
of this scientific spirit are sincerity, patience, humility, the love
of nature and the love of man."

The London to which Olive Schreiner, an unknown, sickly
governess from South Africa, came in 1883 was teeming with
fresh new ideas, bright and alive with the promise of change. The
South Africa from which she came, the arid plains known as the
Great Karroo, was a vast, primitive emptiness. Life was harsh,
rugged, not unlike that on the American plains a century ago,
except that the settlers, Boers and British alike, had a stronger,
more deeply evangelical religious faith than that of most of the
American pioneers. If one could imagine the New England Puri-
tans trekking west, Cotton Mather driving an ox cart, he might
comprehend the rigid spirit of these African settlers. Olive
Schreiner's parents were English nationals. In later years, when
she was forced to take sides in the Boer War, she made a painful
choice against her own background. "My training was exclusively
and strongly English. I did not begin learning any other language
till I was eight and have never gained the complete mastery of
any other. It is my mother speech and England is my mother
land." [5] The German name came from her father—Gottlob
Schreiner—a native of a tiny Swabian village near Stuttgart. He
was born in 1814, son of a shoemaker, and at eighteen entered

the Moravian Brethren Mission House at Basel, Switzerland, to train for service among the "pagans." From Basel he went on to training in the Missionary Society in London, where he met Rebecca Lyndall, four years his junior, daughter of a Dissenting clergyman and descendant of a long line of strict evangelical clergy. The Lyndall family came from the north of England and traced somewhere in its distant past one Jewish ancestor. With her tendency to romanticize and to identify with the persecuted, Olive liked to speculate on her Jewishness, but the fact is that her ancestry and her upbringing were Christian. Her English mother was fired with the same missionary zeal as possessed her German-born father. When these two young people met, they were of one mind. They married in November, 1837, and almost immediately sailed for South Africa to preach the gospel for the London Missionary Society.

The Africa in which they settled in 1838 was the Dark Continent of the old geography books. Not even Dr. Livingstone (also sent out by the London Missionary Society) had yet penetrated the wilderness. The Schreiners were perhaps more blind than brave in the face of the hardships that confronted them. By the account of all who knew him, Gottlob was a powerfully built but dreamy man—"with his Bible in his pocket and his head in the clouds and his heart with Christ," as his daughter recalled him. He labored mightily, saving heathens' souls, farming, building a succession of primitive houses for his family which grew rapidly until there were twelve children, seven of whom survived childhood. Rebecca was a more complex figure; she shared her husband's religious faith but was more sensitive, witty, shrewd, and mercurial. Late in life she converted to Roman Catholicism, and she lived to a ripe old age, quarreling with her children, as ardent in her enthusiasm for Cecil Rhodes as, decades earlier, she had been for Christ. Olive's relationship with her was never close. "My mother has never been a mother to me," she once wrote to her husband. "I have had no mother. She is a brilliant, wonderful little woman, all intellect and genius. The relation between us is a very curious one; it is *I* who have always had to think for, guide and nurse her since I was a tiny child. *She* seems to me like a very favourite brilliant child of mine!" [5]

In the early years of their marriage the Schreiners moved from one isolated primitive mission station to another. They lived in mud houses with mud floors and thatched roofs, ate the food they could scratch out of the unfriendly soil, occasionally fought off natives and wild animals, then piled their belongings into an ox wagon and moved on. Olive, their ninth child, was born in Wittebergen Mission Station on March 24, 1855. Wittebergen was a mountain outpost in Basutoland, a region then swarming with wild game, one hundred miles from the nearest post office. She lived there until she was six, when the family once again packed the ox wagons and moved to Healdtown, another remote mission station. Although it was a large family, Olive was a lonely child. The older children were already grown up. Her nearest sister, Ettie, was five years older than she. A younger brother, Will, was born in 1857, but Olive formed no deep attachments until a baby sister, Ellie, was born in 1862. Then old enough to be conscious of the need for love and for loving, Olive developed her "first great passion," as she called it, for this child:

> It lasted all the time she lived, and her death, when I was ten years old, altered my life. I had no self, she was myself while she lived. I had no interest in my own life, everything was for her, and I cared very little for anyone else. The love came to me the moment I saw her lying new-born on the nurse's knees. Afterwards I loved Theo and Ettie and Will and Fred, all in an absorbing way, but never with the absolute annihilation of self with which I loved her.[7]

The circumstances of their lives deprived the Schreiner children of formal education, but, thanks to their father's religious connections, the boys at least made out surprisingly well. Frederick, born in 1840, was sent to England, attended the Wesleyan College in Taunton, and took a B.A. at the University of London. He opened a school, the New College, in Eastbourne and had considerable success as an educator. Theophilus (Theo) also attended Wesleyan and the University of London, then returned to South Africa as headmaster of a public school. He later became involved in diamond digging and in politics, serving in the Legislative Assembly and, after the Union, in the South African Parliament. The most distinguished career belonged to Will, the youngest son, who won a scholarship to Cambridge and took a law degree at the Inner Temple. Returning to South Africa, he entered Parliament, became attorney-general during Cecil Rhodes' second ministry, and prime minister from 1898 to 1900. At the time of his death in 1914 he was high commissioner for the Union.[8]

The girls had no such opportunities. Olive's education was scrappy and largely self-administered. Her mother taught her to read. Thereafter she read with the same fervor and lack of discipline evident in all her intellectual activities later in life. A wildly precocious child, she read the Bible, memorized long passages of poetry, and made up her own stories. She never learned to spell, and her manuscripts, from childish scribbling to adult writing, are challenges to the transcriber's ingenuity. She attempted to teach herself Latin, French, and German but acquired only the most rudimentary knowledge of languages. But her love for books—especially for the profound writings of philosophers, theologians, and social thinkers—was an absorbing passion from her earliest years. Some of the most moving scenes in *The Story of an African Farm* describe the young shepherd Waldo's thirst for knowledge. The boy finds a long-neglected box of books in a farmhouse loft:

He stuck his hand in among the books and pulled out two. He felt them, thrust his fingers in among the leaves, and crumpled them a little, as a lover feels the hair of his mistress. The fellow gloated over his treasure. He had had a dozen books in the course of his life; now here was a mine of them opened at his feet. After a while he began to read the titles, and now and again opened a book and read a sentence; but he was too excited to catch the meanings distinctly. At last he came to a dull, brown volume. He read the name, opened it in the centre, and where he opened began to read. 'Twas a chapter on property that he fell upon, —Communism, Fourierism, St. Simonism,—in a work on

Political Economy. He read down one page, and turned over to the next; he read down that without changing his posture by an inch; he read the next, and the next, kneeling all the while with the book in his hand, and his lips parted (Pt. I, Ch. XI).

She read indiscriminately and often without direction, hungrily seeking ideas, often assimilating them without thoroughly digesting them. These habits did not change with maturity: "I personally prize the stimulators most; I like a book you can only read a few pages of then you have to throw it down you have so many thoughts of your own," she wrote to Ellis in 1888. Imaginative literature had little appeal to her. Among the poets, Shelley, Heine, and later Browning were her favorites. Wordsworth, of all the poets the one to whom she was closest in spirit, did not appeal to her in her youth, but the year before she died she wrote, "I read him with more pleasure than even my beloved Browning." [9] She read very few novels in her youth; *Dombey and Son* and some Ouida are the only fiction she mentions. Her prose style was developed largely from the Bible and from one of her lifetime favorite books, Gibbon's *Decline and Fall of the Roman Empire*—noble masters but hardly practical training for a fledgling novelist.

The pattern of Olive Schreiner's intellectual development, while unusual, is not altogether unfamiliar. Clearly she was growing up and out of the narrowly evangelical world of her home and family. Her three novels, *Undine, African Farm,* and *From Man to Man,* describe heroines whose minds flower and expand as they break away from the narrow religious confines of their homes. Like her fictional heroines, her own emergence was dramatic, filled with emotional crises. As a little girl, she told her husband, she was once so inspired by reading the Sermon on the Mount that she rushed to her mother shouting: "Look what I've found! It's what I've known all along. Now we can live like this!" Her mother's cold reproof amazed the child: "But she never forgot it, and knew then for the first time that people did not *want* to live like that, although it was God's command which they professed to accept. She said she never got over the shock." [10] From that time forward, Olive Schreiner was alienated from orthodox Christianity. She became a free-thinker; the books that she read supported her intransigence—Herbert Spencer's *First Principles*, Mill's *Principles of Political Economy*, Ruskin's *Crown of Wild Olive*, Emerson, Carlyle, Buckle, Huxley.

Such was the extraordinary training of this girl who at the age of nineteen went out as a governess. She was obliged to seek work because her father, after years of loyal service as a missionary, had been dismissed from his post in 1865 for engaging in private trade, an infringement of the rules of the Missionary Society. He then went into business for himself, trading with the natives, but was never again able to provide adequately for his large family. The older children scattered. In 1867 Ettie joined Theo, who was teaching in Cradock, to keep house for him. Olive, then twelve, went to live with them, evidently studying informally under her brother's direction. But Theo and Ettie were hard-bitten religious fanatics. As their younger sister moved further toward independence, conflict became inevitable. Olive told Ellis that once when she had been ill her brother wrote that "with her ideas on religion he could not desire her recovery." [11] Gentler, but even more fervent, Ettie nagged her almost beyond endurance. When Theo joined the diamond rush at Kimberley in 1870, Olive went to stay with friends and distant relatives, drifting from one place to another, restless and rootless. Often she made herself useful by assisting in the care of younger children. About 1872 she met and became engaged to a handsome, dandified young man named Julius Gau, whose sister she had nursed through an illness. Apparently he seduced her, promised marriage, then jilted her. Though never reticent about her later love life, Olive seems to have wanted to put this affair out of her mind, for she refers to it only most obscurely in her first novel, *Undine*. Just one letter on the subject exists, addressed to her sister, in which she speaks of planning to marry and go to Europe.[12] A few months later, obviously deeply hurt, Olive traveled to Kimberley and stayed with Theo and Ettie in the rough mining camp. Here she began to write *Undine*, an appallingly juvenile novel that her husband published in 1921, a year after her death. *Undine's* sole interest is as a kind of trial run for *The Story of an African Farm*. Olive herself never considered it for publication: "I ought to have burnt it long ago," she wrote Ellis, "but the biographical element in it made me soft to it." [13]

To the extent that Undine is intelligent and free-thinking she is surely the young Olive Schreiner. Her childhood, a lonely little girl's growing up in a farmhouse in the karroo, is the author's. Undine rebels against the strict religious teachings of her family, announcing, "I would much sooner be wicked and go to hell than be good only because I was afraid of going there." She reads books of theology with a critical, inquiring mind, and she refuses to attend church. After the first chapter, however, the novel moves from autobiography to sheer fantasy. Undine goes to England, watches her beloved aunt go mad, then spurns a fine young man because she has fallen in love with his selfish brother. When the latter jilts her, she marries his wealthy father in order to provide money for this worthless young man. Later she renounces her fortune and returns to Africa, where she works as a humble drudge in the Kimberly mining fields, suffers terrible hardships, sees her selfish lover again on his deathbed, and then dies herself.

The elements of dream fulfillment in *Undine* are obvious. With the exception of the fine passages of nature description in the first chapter, the writing is painfully amateurish. The book is the work of an unhappy girl, lonely and suffering from the first attacks of the asthma that was to torment her throughout her life. Nevertheless there is remarkable spirit and energy here. Writing had already become the emotional release which would sustain her for the rest of her life. In her journal for April 8, 1874, there is an entry referring to an unidentified piece of writing (probably a fragment of *Undine*): "I have not yet finished the first chapter of 'A Queer Little Child' [this is the subtitle of the published *Undine*]. I don't hate myself quite so much as I used to, there's something good in old Olive after all. I am reading Emerson and it is giving me more strength than anything has ever done." [14]

Olive's first job as a governess was in the little town of Colesburg, where she worked for the family of George Weakly, an auctioneer, shopkeeper, and editor-publisher of the local newspaper. In addition to her teaching duties, she was expected to help with the housework, spend several hours every day tending shop, and correct proof for the paper. She devoted her "spare" time to her own writing and reading. After some nine months, she moved on to a new job at Ganna Hoek, with the family of a Boer farmer, the Fouches. Her living conditions—a room with a mud floor where she had to open an umbrella when it rained and where she dug a furrow in the mud for the rain to drain off—were scarcely an improvement. But two factors made this a more endurable situation. One was the Fouches themselves, a thriving, hearty farm family. Mrs. Fouche (who served in some ways as a model for the gross Tant' Sannie in *The Story of an African Farm*), fat and ignorant, was shocked at Olive's habit of washing herself. "Take a piece of meat, now," she once counseled the girl. "If you keep on washing it, won't you wash all the strength out of it? . . . Well, it's just the same with your body; you wash all the strength out of it and you get ill." [15] The Fouches were the first Boers Olive had known intimately, and she developed a deep respect for these simple, hard-working people. "Watching them in all the vicissitudes of life, from birth to marriage and death, I learnt to love the Boer, but more, I learnt to admire him . . . a people who beneath a calm and almost stolid surface hide the intensest passions and the most indomitable resolution." [16]

The other compensation for the hard life at Ganna Hoek was the nearby presence of a large English family Olive had met some time earlier, the Cawoods. To supplement her meager wages from the Fouches she tutored the Cawood children, walking the mile and a half between the two farms to spend her weekends with them. For Mrs. Cawood Olive developed the first really deep emotional attachment of her adult life. Probably it was the first time that she had ever had a sympathetic listener, and she poured out her soul to the older woman, read to her from her manuscripts, and wrote impassioned letters expressing all her loneliness and need for love:

> I wish I could see you. Perhaps it would give you a little happiness and it would do *me* so much good . . . I am so

selfish. I'm not content to love. I want to be loved back again. We talk so much of intellect and of knowledge, but what are they! After all, the heart can't live on them. One would barter all one's knowledge for one kiss and all one's intellect for one tender touch—just one.

* * *

She [Olive's mother] doesn't know how much I would lose if I lost you, and I'm sure you wouldn't keep on loving me as much if you saw what a poor weak miserable creature I am really. . . . But you *are* one of the things that are left to me and I am so afraid of anything that would take you from me.[17]

At both farms Olive was relatively content—many children around her, a family and a social life, a reasonable amount of leisure for reading and writing. Except for occasional attacks of asthma her health was good. Her journal records that she finished *Undine* here and began the novel that was to become *The Story of an African Farm*. Nevertheless, in April, 1876, she left her position to take another, at a larger salary, with the family of a Dutch Reform minister, Mr. Martin, at Ratel Hoek. She continued her writing, revising *Undine* and working on the new book (which she refers to under various titles—"Saints and Sinners," "Thorn Kloopf") and some shorter pieces.

Writing remained a comfort during periods of ill health and despair. Although otherwise sturdy, she was frequently prostrated and terrified by asthma. There seems no question of the psychosomatic origin of these attacks: she acknowledged herself that there was a connection between her physical health and her emotional life.[18] She and the many doctors she consulted over the years were powerless, however, and her "chest" continued to plague her, forcing her to move restlessly about South Africa and Europe in search of a better climate, and ultimately even stunting and disfiguring her. Her emotional life was equally unstable. She seemed to form no attachments except to older women like Mrs. Cawood and Mrs. John Brown. Even these relationships were stormy and uncertain. Her freethinking eventually offended the beloved Mrs. Cawood, and when Olive wrote to inquire about her long silence, she received a shocking answer:

I no longer love you, and cannot act hypocritically. . . . And I have *loved* you, at times with an almost idolatrous love. I have sometimes felt in my heart to say, Olive Schreiner I love you so, that for your sake I could become anything. That is why God in His goodness and wisdom used you as a means to show me what an awful soul-destroying thing free-thinking is.

I must tell you I am not alone in what I now feel. Richard [her husband] and I have both, while pointing out to the children that they owe you gratitude, told them that you are God's enemy and that they cannot love God and you at the same time. . . .

Olive answered with resignation and humility:

I do not at all blame you for not loving me any more. We cannot help love's going, any more than we can help its coming; and when it is gone, it's better to say so.

For myself, I have always liked you not for anything you were to me, but what you were in yourself, and I feel to you as I have felt from the beginning. Therefore, believe me to remain, if not your friend, one who loves you.[19]

The rift was later healed and the correspondence resumed, but the old intimacy was gone.

Her other close friend, Mrs. Brown, the wife of a doctor, was deeply sympathetic to Olive both personally and ideologically. They first met in Fraserburg in 1873 when Olive was only seventeen. Both Browns were ardent liberals. Mrs. Brown later, on her return to England, became active in social work and in women's rights movements. Dr. Brown encouraged Olive's interest in science and her desire to study medicine. Early in 1880, when the Browns were living in Lancashire, they received from Olive the bulky manuscript of *The Story of an African Farm*. They read it enthusiastically and turned it over to an Edinburgh publisher, David Douglass, who found it promising but in need of cutting and revision. The report was encouraging. In her journal for September 30, 1880, Olive wrote: "I think I shall go to England in February . . . I am going to write hard. I have books, Lecky, Carlyle, etc. I'll work harder than ever, not wasting one moment, that is the secret. I seem much like one in a dream the last few days." [20]

Olive sailed for England in March, 1881. Oddly enough, her main purpose in going was not to push the publication of her book but to study medicine. She compared herself at this time to a man with two loves who doesn't know which one to choose. Her interest in the physical world, in nature and in animal life, had been profound ever since her childhood. "The dream of my life was to be a doctor," she wrote Ellis in 1884. "I can't remember a time when I was so small that it was not in my heart." As a child she had dissected ostriches and sheep, puzzling and marveling over the intricacies of physiology. Moreover, medicine was a career that suited her idealistic urge to serve mankind. "It seems to me that a doctor's is the most perfect of all lives; it satisfies the craving to know and also the craving to serve." [21]

At first she planned to study nursing at the Edinburgh Royal Infirmary, but her brother Fred, now head of his own school in Eastbourne, offered to pay for her medical education. In spite of the fact that she met almost none of the academic prerequisites for medical school and that, furthermore, she was totally unfit both constitutionally and psychologically for the grind of systematic study, Olive made a sincere effort to qualify. She spent a few days at the Royal Infirmary but became ill and returned to her brother's home. There she made fitful attempts to study Latin and algebra. In the autumn she nursed for five days at a London hospital. Once again she developed chest trouble, this time so severe that she had to spend the winter on the Isle of Wight. The several months of convalescence were probably fortunate, for during this period she revised the *African Farm,* wrote parts of another novel ("Saints and Sinners," the working title of the book that was to be *From Man to Man*) and a number of short stories or "allegories." Up to this time all that she had in print were two short pieces in the *New College Magazine,* which her brother's school published. In March, 1882, the firm of Bentley and Sons rejected the manuscript of *African Farm;* in April she took it to Chapman and Hall, where a reader, whose name was so unfamiliar to her that she entered it in her journal as "Merithett," recommended its acceptance. The reader was George Meredith.[22]

It is difficult to share the enthusiasm of Meredith and, after its publication in 1883, of so many discriminating readers for this strange book. The title was not inviting; several reviewers observed that they had expected it to be a book about South African agriculture and ostrich breeding. The pseudonym under which it appeared, "Ralph Iron," was no more recognizable or intriguing to the public than the author's real name would have been. But for the very reason of its "strangeness," its evocation of a faraway, exotic scene, it appealed to a public numbed by overexposure to what one of this novel's contemporary reviewers called "the domains of the ordinary novelist . . . Homburg and the Highlands . . . yachts, clubs, hansoms, and Piccadilly." [23]

Once attracted to the subject of the book, the reader of 1883 evidently found much that was arresting beyond the realistic details of South African life. First there was the free-wheeling religious speculation of the novel that coincided with the widespread contemporary interest in religious controversy, especially on questions of orthodoxy, agnosticism, and atheism. Following only a few years after Eliza Lynn Linton's iconoclastic *Joshua Davidson*, the *African Farm* was read and discussed in much the same context. And while it never enjoyed the enormous success of Mrs. Humphry Ward's *Robert Elsmere* (1888), it anticipated the *Elsmere* boom. In addition, through the words of its "emancipated" heroine Lyndall, the novel spoke to seething controversialists on both sides of the Woman Question. This was no mere Girl of the Period but a prophetic symbolic figure who stirred emotions deeply and could certainly not be ignored. Therefore, although it had been almost unnoticed on its first publication in January, 1883, *The Story of an African Farm* sold well enough to warrant a second edition by July of the same year. By 1887, when a third edition was published (the name Olive Shreiner now appearing on the title page in brackets after "Ralph Iron"), it was an international best-seller, doing especially well in the United States where, unfortunately, the author did not possess the copyright. On August 13 of that year the book was the subject of a widely read article in the *Spectator,* "An Agnostic Novel," in which the unsigned writer (it was Canon MacColl), while deploring her religious skepticism, acknowledged with sympathy the very real personal dilemma of the author:

> The truth is, this gifted woman has been driven from her religious and moral moorings—first by the ghastly theology of Calvinism, and then by the difficulty which she finds in reconciling the facts of the world around her, and especially the injustice done to her own sex, with the doctrine of a God who is omnipotent, compassionate, and just.

Apart from the ideological issues that account for its popularity in the 1880's, what is the enduring power of *The Story of an African Farm?* What has kept it alive in the face of its many glaring flaws? It is a loose, formless, rambling narrative, told by an omniscient, frequently intrusive and didactic, author. Doris Lessing accurately describes it as a "hybrid"—"a mixture of journalism and the *Zeitgeist* and autobiography." It is also, however, a work of the most intense passion and conviction. Rarely, even in autobiographical fiction, does one meet an author so committed and engaged as Olive Schreiner. The very failure of art and technique—the illusion that she is speaking directly from the heart, not writing a novel at all—is its success. Furthermore, there are elements in the book, fragmentary and chaotic though they may be, that reflect the spirit if not the letter of a literary artist. Most remarkable of these are the evocation of a sense of place and the re-creation of the mind of childhood. Mrs. Lessing and others have compared the novel to *Wuthering Heights.* There are obvious similarities of plot and character and, more striking, a similar mood of romantic passion feeding itself on the loneliness and isolation of a remote country setting. But an equally telling comparison may be made with *The Mill on the Floss.* As George Eliot traced the growing consciousness of a sensitive child, the influences of physical surroundings, the gradual opening and expansion of intelligence and sensibility in

Maggie Tulliver, so did Olive Schreiner in her hero Waldo and her heroine Lyndall. Environment, nature, the world within and outside the minds of the young—these are the elements of both novels, different as they are in actual scene and in artistic quality. Both are autobiographical in the best nonliteral sense. But where George Eliot maintains her focus steadily on Maggie, Olive Schreiner characteristically diffuses hers and divides it between Waldo and Lyndall. Through Waldo she traces her expanding consciousness of the world of nature, through Lyndall her introduction to the world of ideas. As a result, neither child develops into a full character, and both lose the humanity that Maggie so richly possesses. Waldo grows up into a shadowy, Christlike abstraction, Lyndall into a shrill mouthpiece for the author's views on women's rights.

The most striking passages in the novel are descriptive. Their power lies not only in their poetic evocation of a scene but in their careful integration of scene and character. Olive Schreiner had absorbed her Emerson and, probably without realizing it, her Wordsworth, well and deeply: "The year of infancy, where from the shadowy background of forgetfulness start out pictures of startling clearness, disconnected, but brightly coloured, and indelibly printed in the mind. Much that follows fades, but the colours of those baby-pictures are permanent" (Pt. II, Ch. I). There is nothing sentimentally beautiful in her recreation of the scenes of her childhood. The karroo is lonely and windswept, the vegetation sparse and stunted:

> The full African moon poured down its light from the blue sky into a wide, lonely plain. The dry, sandy earth with its coating of stunted "Karroo" bushes a few inches high, the low hills that skirted the plain, the milk-bushes with their long finger-like leaves, all were touched by a weird and an almost oppressive beauty as they lay in the white light. In one spot only was the solemn monotony of the plain broken. Near the centre a small solitary "kopje" [hillock] rose. Alone it lay there, a heap of round ironstones piled one upon another, as over some giant's grave. Here and there a few tufts of grass or small succulent plants had sprung up among its stones, and on the very summit a clump of prickly pears

lifted their thorny arms, and reflected, as from mirrors, the moonlight on their broad fleshy leaves (Pt. I, Ch. I).

Her hero Waldo and her heroine Lyndall are introduced into this landscape not as idyllic children but as tormented creatures already marked for tragedy. Childhood is as much a part of her tragic vision as any time of later life: "The barb in the arrow of childhood's suffering is this: its intense loneliness, its intense ignorance." For Waldo this suffering is mainly religious. We meet him first as a little boy awakening in the night in the barren hut he shares with his father Otto, a dreamy, kindly old German farm overseer (modeled, certainly, on Gottlob Schreiner). The child listens to the ticking of his father's hunting-watch—a sound which to his impressionable mind, fevered by the Old Testament passages his father has read to him, says endlessly, "Dying, dying, dying." Young as he is, Waldo is already in the throes of a religious crisis, obsessed with the discovery of time passing, of men dying. "And all the while the watch kept ticking on; just like God's will, that never changes or alters, you may do what you please." He prays then to God to save those who are dying every minute, and he weeps.

The first half of the novel is largely Waldo's and describes the growing conflict in his religious faith—his inability to reconcile the teachings of Christ with the suffering of humanity that he sees all around him. As a child he has absolute and literal faith. Out alone in the fields tending his sheep, he builds an altar of stones and offers up as a sacrifice the cold mutton chop that was to have been his dinner. Instead of a vision of the Lord, as he expected, all he sees is a fatty piece of meat melting in the hot sun. Bitterly disillusioned, he laments: "I am like Cain—I am not His. He will not hear my prayer. God hates me." Over the years Waldo's doubts are intensified: "I love Jesus Christ, but I hate God," he proclaims in despair. He sees at first hand the cruelty of his fellow man. His noble, self-sacrificing father is cheated and betrayed by a sadistic newcomer, Bonaparte Blenkins. Blenkins wins the confidence of the mistress of the farm—a fat, ignorant Boer, Tant' Sannie—and prevails on her to dismiss her loyal overseer. The old man, meek and uncomplaining, dies in his sleep, leaving his son Waldo a helpless victim to Blenkins' savage, unmotivated cruelty. He beats the boy, takes away his precious books, wantonly destroys a sheep-shearing machine that he has invented. Little wonder that Waldo loses his faith.

In a long section at the opening of the second book, the author breaks into the narrative and addresses the reader directly, using the universal "we." She describes her own growing up and her emergence from trusting childhood faith into doubt and despair. First she observes the discovery of self:

> One day we sit there and look up at the blue sky, and down at our fat little knees, and suddenly it strikes us, Who are we? This *I*, what is it? We try to look in upon ourself, and ourself beats back upon ourself. Then we get up in great fear and run home as hard as we can. We can't tell anyone what frightened us. We never quite lose that feeling of *self* again.

She traces the child's first enthusiastic reaction to the teachings of the Bible, then his gradually developing doubts as grownups are unable to answer his questions: "Is it good of God to make hell? Was it kind of Him to let no one be forgiven unless Jesus Christ died?" Then she loses her faith and becomes cynical:

> We do not cry and weep; we sit down with cold eyes and look at the world. . . . And, we say it slowly, but without sighing, "Yes, we see it now; there is no God. . . . There is no justice. The ox dies in the yoke, beneath its master's whip. . . . The black man is shot like a dog, and it goes well with the shooter. The innocent are accused, and the accuser triumphs."

Now fully identified with Waldo, the author continues to trace his—and her—developing consciousness of the world of nature: "Every day the karroo shows us a new wonder sleeping in its teeming bosom." She studies flowers and animal life; she

dissects dead animals: "Above are the organs divided by a delicate network of blood-vessels standing out red against the faint
blue background. Each branch of the blood-vessels is comprised
of a trunk, bifurcating and re-bifurcating into the most delicate
hairlike threads, symmetrically arranged. We are struck with its
singular beauty." Out of these observations is born a new faith
and hope, a kind of Wordsworthian pantheism:

> And so it comes to pass in time that the earth ceases for us
> to be a weltering chaos. We walk in the great hall of life,
> looking up and round reverentially. Nothing is despicable,
> —all is part of a whole, whose beginning and end we know
> not. The life that throbs in us is a pulsation from it,—too
> mighty for our comprehension, not too small (Pt. II, Ch. I).

This long digressive passage is followed by another chapter
equally remote from the action—what little there is—of the
story, but foreshadowing the ultimately resigned and tranquil
spirit in which the novel ends. Called "Waldo's Stranger," it introduces a well-dressed young man, never identified, who rides
past Waldo in the fields and stops to talk to him. He suggests,
by his cryptic remarks, some mysterious, supernatural origin: "I
am a man who believes nothing, hopes nothing, fears nothing,
feels nothing. I am beyond the pale of humanity." He tells
Waldo a long allegorical tale confirming such suspicions [24]—the
story of a hunter who sees a beautiful white bird and who spends
the rest of his life on a quest for it. He learns from Wisdom that
the bird is Truth—"He who has once seen her never rests again.
Till death he desires her." In spite of great difficulties he pushes
on through the Valley of Superstition, the Land of Absolute Nega-
tion and Denial, the Mountains of Stern Reality. He grows old
and finally dies, unsuccessful but consoled that he has helped
make a path for others to follow. As he dies, a white feather
flutters down into his hands. The stranger listens to Waldo's life
story and observes that the boy is happier than he thinks. Although he has lost his faith, the stranger tells him, he will learn
through experience "that the laws for a wise and noble life have

a foundation infinitely deeper than the fiat of any being, God or man." He then rides off and never returns. Years later, in the course of his wanderings, Waldo thinks that he has caught a glimpse of him, but he is too shy to approach him.

Parallel with Waldo's growing up is the development of the character of Lyndall, a beautiful little orphan English girl. There is still a third child, her cousin Em, the stepdaughter of Tant' Sannie and actually the owner of the farm. She is a sad, stolid figure who represents normalcy, one who patiently loves, suffers, and waits on the sidelines as the others throw themselves into life's battles. Lyndall is a fighter from the beginning—rebellious, defiant, mercurial. It is easy to see why readers have been reminded of *Wuthering Heights*—Waldo, the neglected, persecuted farm boy, falls in love with his childhood playmate but social superior Lyndall.[25] She is a memorable child figure—especially in one episode where, locked in her bedroom with Em as punishment for her rebelliousness, she attempts to set fire to the room and then resolves, "When that day comes, and I am strong, I will hate everything that has power, and help everything that is weak." But as she grows up she becomes, like Waldo, more symbol than character. Like Catherine Earnshaw of *Wuthering Heights* she disappears from the scene for a while (and, as in that novel, seems to have no particular existence away from it). When she returns, a young lady, she is remote and aloof, though still drawn to her childhood sweetheart. During her absence at school Lyndall has acquired strong views on the independence of women, which she expresses to Waldo in a lengthy monologue. (Later Olive Schreiner expanded these ideas in an influential work of nonfiction, *Woman and Labour*, but as early as this novel she held the same general position—that women are cursed from birth by the nature of our society: "We all enter the world little plastic beings, with so much natural force, perhaps, but for the rest—blank; and the world tells us what we are to be, and shapes us by the ends it sets before us." In modern civilization women no longer have any function other than the merely reproductive one. They are denied careers, petted, spoiled, humiliated, reduced to household drudges or mere playthings.) But Lyndall is a visionary. She looks ahead to a future ideal—"when love is no more bought or sold, when it is not a means of making bread, when each woman's life is filled with earnest, independent labour" (Pt. II, Ch. IV).

Behind Lyndall's lofty pronouncements, there is a personal bitterness. To Waldo she is aloof but always kind. To other men, however, she is coldly contemptuous. A newcomer has settled on the farm—an epicene, half-hysterical young man named Gregory Rose who at first is attracted to the phlegmatic Em. When Lyndall returns, he promptly falls in love with her and breaks his engagement to Em. Lyndall has no interest whatever in him until suddenly she asks him to marry her: "I want nothing more than your name." Before they can marry, still another stranger appears, a mysterious Englishman with whom Lyndall has already had an affair and whose child she is now carrying. She goes away with him but refuses his offer of marriage: "Because if you have me, you would hold me fast. I shall never be free again."

From the moment she leaves the farm this second time Lyndall's doom is inevitable: "Why am I alone, so hard so cold? I am so weary of myself! It is eating my soul to its core—self, self, self! I cannot bear this life! . . . Will nothing free me from myself? . . . I want to love! I want something great and pure to lift me to itself!" She disappears from the novel, and we learn of her fate only later, in the narrative of Gregory Rose, who has followed her. After a long search, he finds her at an inn. She has given birth to a baby who died and she is now near death herself. The faithful and extraordinary Gregory shaves off his beard, puts on woman's clothes, and offers himself to her as a nurse. There follows a long, morbid account of Lyndall's suffering and death.

Waldo, meanwhile, has also left the farm. For more than a year he wanders about, drifting from one menial job to another, seeing everywhere the exploitation of men and of animals, the suffering of all living creatures. When he returns to the farm Em tells him that Lyndall is dead. The book concludes with Waldo's musings on Lyndall's death. He rejects the consolations of "the nineteenth-century Christian, deep into whose soul modern unbelief and thought have crept, though he knows it not. He it is who uses his Bible as the pearl-fishers use their shells, sorting out game from refuse; he sets his pearls after his own fashion, and

he sets them well . . . God is love. You shall see her again."
Waldo can only remember Lyndall living—her vitality, her reality—"Who dares to say the body never dies, because it turns to
grass and flowers? . . . For the soul's fierce cry for immortality is
this, only this: Return to me after death the thing as it was
before . . . your immortality is annihilation, your hereafter is a
lie."

Ultimately, however, Waldo finds peace in his own non-
Christian transcendentalism: "his soul passed down the steps of
contemplation into that vast land where there is always peace—
that land where the soul, gazing long, loses all consciousness of
its little self, and almost feels its hand on the old mystery of
Universal Unity that surrounds it." Once again Olive Schreiner's
vocabulary is romantic, the doctrine of Emerson, the language
of Wordsworth and Shelley:

> It is but the man that dies, the Universal Whole of which
> he is part reworks him into the inmost self. . . . The bars of
> the real are set close about us; we cannot open our wings
> but they strike against them and drop bleeding. But when
> we guide between the bars into the great unknown beyond,
> we may sail forever in the glorious blue, seeing nothing but
> our own shadows.

Happily, from the point of view of art, the book ends not
on this lofty and pretentious note, but in a final chapter of great
simplicity and beauty. As in *Wuthering Heights,* tranquility and
calm descend after the storms of passion. The domestic life of the
farm goes on: black native children play in the sunshine; Tant'
Sannie, who has remarried, comes back on a friendly visit; Em is
going to marry Gregory. After finishing a carpentering job,
Waldo goes out to rest in the sunshine: "An evil world, a deceit-
ful, treacherous, mirage-like world, it might be; but a lovely
world for all that, and to sit there, gloating in the sunlight, was
perfect. It was worth having been a little child, and having cried
and prayed, so one might sit there. He moved his hands as
though he were washing them in the sunshine." He falls asleep,
and when Em brings him some milk, she finds the little chickens

perching on him: "Em did not drive them away; but she covered the grass softly at his side. 'He will wake soon,' she said, 'and be glad of it.' But the chickens were wiser."

II

The modern-day reader can only look with wonder and a little amusement at the furor that *The Story of an African Farm* stirred in its time. He must be reminded of the wave of anti-Zolaism, the prosecution and imprisonment of Zola's English publisher Vizetelly, the public expression of outrage against Hardy's novels, the Wilde trial, the Dilke and Parnell scandals, the first rumblings of the militant suffragette movement—all part of what seemed an alarming revolution in morals during the last two decades of the nineteenth century. Anticipating trouble, Olive Schreiner's publisher, Chapman, asked her to make an alteration in her manuscript:

> . . . just to put in a few sentences saying that Lyndall was secretly married to that man, as if she wasn't married to him the British public would think it wicked, and Smiths, the railway booksellers, would not put it on their stalls! Of course I got in a rage and told him he could leave the book alone and I would take it elsewhere. He climbed down at once, and said it was only out of consideration for me; I was young and people would think I was not respectable if I wrote such a book, but of course if I insisted on saying she was not married to him it must be so. He certainly never mentioned his reader in this matter; and I can't believe Meredith, who *was* an artist, would ever have made the suggestion to Chapman.[26]

Chapman was no doubt canny enough to recognize that such trouble could have its compensations. For every suburban matron who indignantly "took it up in the tongs and put it in the fire," as at least one reported doing, and for every village library that yielded to the pressure of a local vicar or schoolmaster and took it off the shelves, there were hundreds of eager readers.[27]

More painful to Olive Schreiner was the reaction of her own brother, Fred, the Eastbourne schoolmaster, who wrote to say that he wanted nothing more to do with her because her novel "brings him into trouble." But Fred forgave his sister, quite likely ending up proud of this young girl whose first published novel caused so much controversy. All but the most narrow-minded readers gave the book respectful attention and were profoundly impressed by it. Tributes came from very eminent sources. Gladstone admired the book and invited its young author to lunch. Sir Charles Dilke, before being almost ruined by scandal himself, hailed it as "the ablest book ever written by a woman," and told Frank Harris that he thought it greater than *The Pilgrim's Progress*. The historian Lecky considered it "among the best novels in the English language." [28] Most reviewers were less given to hyperbole, but they uniformly acknowledged its timeliness and relevance to the most urgent intellectual and moral issues of the day. To women launching their struggle for legal and civil rights, *The Story of an African Farm* was "a voice from the depths," arousing even the most apathetic of their sex. Havelock Ellis's wife, Edith Lees, an ardent feminist, recalled years later that there were two factors which "drove thinking women further together towards their emancipation. One was . . . *The Story of an African Farm* and the other was the banging of the door in Ibsen's *Doll's House*." [29] Henry Norman, reviewing the novel in the *Fortnightly* for December, 1883, summed up the enthusiasm of its readers.

On the solitary "Kopje" [hillock], in the growth of the mind of the little Dutch Waldo, there comes up for solution one after another the simple questions of human nature and human action that the world has labelled with many big names; and this young lady historian of Boer life . . . faces them as they rise with refreshing temerity, and what is still more surprising and refreshing, she has the right word to say about almost all. Orthodox Christianity, Unitarian Christianity, woman suffrage, marriage, Malthusianism, immortality—they all arise, though not with these names, over the horizon of this African farm.

Norman suggested that the book might be called the "Romance of the New Ethics"—an epitome of that "new spirit" that was revolutionizing European thought and life.

On the basis then of one novel, this obscure South African girl, not yet thirty, found herself a celebrity. The mantle of the sibyl had descended upon her. No one regarded her book as mere entertainment, and many hailed it as a work of inspiration and prophecy. It was a role for which Olive Schreiner's dedication and idealism suited her admirably. To her credit, she resisted the heady intoxication of such acclaim. She remained simple, modest, indeed personally insecure and full of self-doubt. But for better or for worse she had become a professional cause-pleader. Everyone who met her recognized almost immediately an uncommon person. Despite her undistinguished appearance, as soon as she began to speak "she was transfigured." Some no doubt were more susceptible to her power than others. The crusading journalist and mystic W. T. Stead called her "the categorical imperative in petticoats." Adèle Chapin gushed in her memoirs:

> Olive Schreiner was like a pure flame. It did not matter whether you agreed with her or not; it was the way she held her convictions that made her akin to the great souls of history. I can see her now, on one of those Sunday afternoons, where there would be perhaps twenty or thirty men in the drawing-room, dart into the room like a bird—so swift and direct were her movements; coming straight to me, she would sit down, silent and intense, until some subject which touched her was mentioned; then she would burst forth into such eloquence and fervour of language as I have never heard from anyone else.[30]

The reigning queen of popular fiction, Marie Corelli, suddenly found her place usurped by this unknown girl and became furiously jealous.[31] Another literary lady, Katherine Bradley (who with her niece Edith Cooper wrote poetry under the pen name "Michael Field"), reported enviously: "The ambassador pays his respects to her, Watts asks to paint her (he is refused), she goes the round of the great."[32] Even Arthur Symons, whose literary sophistication few would question, was captivated. When someone asked him if she was interesting, he replied, "I stood all one night listening to her talk." [33] She was in fact her own best creation. "The tempestuous force of her personality," one of her biographers remarked, "was wider than the range of her art, and she never invented any character so magnetic and fiery, so perverse and inconsistent as her own." [34]

After an isolated and provincial childhood and youth, she was thrust suddenly into the intellectually seething atmosphere of literary London. Her journals and letters after 1883 are filled with names of celebrities, and this was not mere decorative name dropping. Most of these meetings were easy and casual. She was introduced to Herbert Spencer, whose writings had inspired her in her youth. He proved a signal disappointment—distant, lofty, and worst of all, boring. Instead of expounding on his philosophy, he insisted on talking about bowling. But Spencer did not forget her during the painful days of the Boer War some years later and subscribed to a testimonial gift for her in 1901. H. Rider Haggard called on the young novelist and advised her, somewhat gratuitously, to write more cheerful books. Wilde, Shaw, George Moore, and Frank Harris were impressed by her. Shaw, who was introduced to her by Henry Salt, Edward Carpenter's friend, characterized her succinctly as being "like what she wrote. She astonished me by writing that I was the only man she was ever afraid of. Why, God knows!" [35] At the time of their first meeting Frank Harris found her "distinctly pretty." When, however, she asked him to introduce her to George Moore, for whom she indicated some enthusiasm, Harris was annoyed: "Curiously enough, her admiration for Moore brought my interest in her to an untimely end. No one could be really important to me who admired Moore so intensely." [36] Moore was of course delighted by her admiration, although Olive was hardly the kind of social or sexual conquest he sought. Nevertheless he cultivated her until her candor cooled his ardor. "I enjoyed my walk with Moore pretty well," she wrote Ellis in June, 1885. "As his character grows clearer to me I see that his virtues are all intellectual, not moral. He is very selfish, I think. I told him so." [37] She knew Wilde only slightly. He published some of her short allegories in *Woman's World* and produced at least one characteristic remark in a conversation with her which Ernest Rhys reported in his memoirs. Wilde had asked her why she chose, at one point in her life, to live in the slums of London's East End: "I live in the East End," she said, "because the people don't wear masks." To which Wilde replied, "And I live in the West End because they do." [38]

Olive delighted in this busy, stimulating, free and easy society. Her landladies, however, were shocked and annoyed by the coming and going of her visitors, the lively but no doubt noisy talk, and principally by the fact that an unmarried woman entertained men so casually. Her journals and letters are full of accounts of quarrels with the landladies, enforced sudden moves, frantic searches for new quarters. Although her book was selling well, she never had much money and never established a permanent home during her five years' stay in London. Indifferent to material possessions, she drifted from cheap hotels to lodging houses. Her natural milieu was not the glittering society of wits like Moore and Wilde, but the company of earnest, dedicated social philosophers like the members of the Fellowship of the New Life—the Webbs, the Blands, the Avelings, Edward Carpenter, Havelock Ellis. The two latter were the closest and most stimulating of all her associates.

Carpenter (1844–1929), whose life spanned the Victorian age and extended well into the twentieth century, is part of the ephemera of modern social history—a lively, colorful, controversial, "unforgettable" figure who is swept away in the whirlwind of time. What seemed so audacious to his contemporaries —his book *Towards Democracy* (1883), with its message of a mystic, idealistic socialism, his support of utopian colonies, radical political movements, labor unions, his writings in defense of homosexuality, his friendship with Walt Whitman, his belief in dress reform (he made sandals that his Fabian friends daringly wore in public)—is to us tame and trivial. In the London of the 1880's, however, he was a dashing and influential personality. With the more thoughtful and scholarly Havelock Ellis (1859-1939), he crusaded for sexual emancipation and the recognition of the body and its urges as healthy phenomena of nature, not as a necessary evil for the procreation of the race. Carpenter was a poet, not a scientist like Ellis. In a fellow poet, Whitman, he found the expression of his own deepest ideals: "that character and the statement of Self . . . were all-important; that the body in Man . . . and the quality corresponding to the body in all art and behaviour, was radiant in meaning and beautiful beyond words; and that the production of splendid men and women was the aim and only true aim of State policy."

Such lofty ideals made him immediately compatible with Olive Schreiner, and their friendship was a lasting one. In his autobiography *My Days and Dreams* he recalled his first enthusiastic reaction to *The Story of an African Farm:* "The African sun was in its veins—fire and sweetness, intense love of beauty, fierce rebellion against the things that be, of passion and piety and the pride of Lucifer combined." When he met the young author he saw in her face the same qualities he had found in her book: "a wonderful beauty and vivacity, a lightning-quick mind, fine eyes, a resolute yet mobile mouth, a determined little square-set body." Here was the emancipated woman who shocked her landladies, "who did not wear a veil and seldom wore gloves, and who talked and laughed even in the streets quite naturally and unaffectedly." [39]

With Carpenter, Olive Schreiner could easily maintain the kind of casual free intellectual association that she most enjoyed. There were no complications of love and sex. With Havelock Ellis her relationship was more intense, more intimate and delicate. They were not lovers physically. We may rely on their candor; both spoke and wrote freely about their relationship. "We were not what can be technically, or even ordinarily, called lovers," Ellis wrote flatly. But they were lovers in other senses than the physical. For more than thirty-six years, until Olive's death, they were in communication—although they were often separated by thousands of miles. Both married partners who not only tolerated but were actually sympathetic to the relationship. Olive's husband, S. C. Cronwright, became Ellis' friend. They worked together on Cronwright's biography of Olive and his editions of her writings. Ellis' wife, Edith Lees, became an admirer of Olive's work and lectured on her both in England and America. Nevertheless, the Schreiner-Ellis friendship cooled somewhat in later years. In his autobiography, *My Life*, Ellis claimed that she changed, becoming "less tolerant, less receptive," as she grew older. In 1917, for example, she demanded that Ellis destroy the several thousand letters she had written him, fearing that he would some day publish them. He refused, and they were not reconciled until he agreed to burn some of them.[40]

Ellis' *My Life* was written when he was in his late seventies, long after Olive Schreiner's death, and many years after their friendship had begun. Even so he retained a warm and tender memory of the early years. They had met in 1884 as a result of a sympathetic review that he had written of *The Story of an African Farm*.[41] He called on her at her lodgings in South Kensington and "found a short, active, robust woman, simple and unaffected in manner, and plainly dressed in loosely fitted garments, who sat on the couch with her hands resting on her thighs, her face expressive of latent radiant energy and eager receptivity to new impressions." After that they met frequently at the house of Eleanor Marx Aveling and with other friends of the New Life group; they attended lectures and concerts together. Ellis served as a mentor, recommending books, taking her to art galleries, instructing her in science. "There were all sorts of things which I could introduce to her or help to explain," he wrote. Yet it was truly a reciprocal association, Ellis gaining as much as he gave: "She meant even more to me. She was in some respects the most wonderful woman of her time . . . and that such a woman should be the first woman in the world I was to know by intimate revelation was an overwhelming fact. It might well have disturbed my mental balance, and for a while I was almost intoxicated by the experience." [42]

Their relationship was asexual rather than nonsexual. Olive had several love affairs—the one early unhappy experience in South Africa and at least two affairs during this first stay in London. While her passions seem to have been released more freely in her writing and conversations than in sexual relations,[43] she was at first physically attracted to the handsome young Ellis:

She possessed a powerfully and physically passionate temperament which craved an answering impulse. . . . For a brief period at this early stage of our relationship there passed before her the possibility of a relationship with me such as her own temperament demanded. But she swiftly realised that I was not fitted to play in such a relationship which her elementary primitive nature craved.[44]

Evidently Olive was satisfied with the free and intimate relationship, sublimating whatever sexual urges she had in her vast capacity for intellectual absorption. Years later Ellis recalled their extraordinary "affair"—trips to the country and to Paris, where they frequently shared a room and a bed, Olive walking suddenly into a room naked from her bath "to expound to me at once some idea which had just occurred to her, apparently unconscious of all else." For her too Ellis fulfilled a fundamental need. Other men could give her sex, but they would always be separate persons. Ellis was "the person who is like part of me." Her published letters to him, fragmentary as they are, express a rare and sometimes beautiful intensity of feeling. In November, 1884, she wrote:

When I first knew you I thought here is one person into whose relationship with me no pain will ever enter because we are so near each other and understand each other so. . . . If you could see deep into my soul you would see that the feeling that is yours [i.e., my feeling towards you], is the most pure and perfect feeling I have ever had for anyone— I mean the kind of feeling that can't go away. If I had passion for you perhaps I couldn't have this feeling. . . . It is no figure of speech when I say you are my other self. You have taken a place in my life which no marriage or passionate love of mine could ever take from you. My boy, my own, for so many years I have longed to meet a mind that should understand me, that should take away from the loneliness of my life. Now I have found it. Sweet one, you will feel how you are coming to help and rejoice another human being, and that will make you glad.[45]

These are the words of a very strange and complex woman. Although she had achieved a measure of fame and literary prestige in London, she remained lonely and unhappy. Her health was erratic. Her asthma was aggravated by the English climate. To relieve frightening attacks she often took drugs, suffering agonizing aftereffects. Many of her published letters which strike the casual reader as the work of a deranged mind because of their wild shifts in mood and their extravagance of expression actually reflect the effects of medicine:

> I have taken no chloral today; and have tried to write without leaving off since I got up. I have written a few lines. The pain in the left side is getting steadily worse. . . . I have been crying this afternoon and I cried much of last night.

> That nux vomica is good for me. I feel so strong in the head today. I can remember everything! My legs are still the same, but it's only the "lymphatic system." I was up much last night but took chloral.

> I have had terrible asthma all night; even chloral didn't give me any ease; but I'm afraid work I do in this state won't be good but I can but try.

> I have now taken a dose of chloral, the first narcotic I have allowed myself to take for six weeks, and can write.

In one especially graphic letter to Ellis in February, 1885, she describes her desperate craving for relief:

> All night I thought I was going mad and lay on the floor and walked up and down; at dawn, about half past four, I went to the chemist's just near the corner, in that street that runs down at the bottom of Palace Road. I stood there knocking for half an hour, but no one heard. I wanted bromide or something to make me sleep. I can see that scene just as it looked to me, printed like one of Hogarth's pictures. While I stood there waiting a milkman came with his

pails and he stopped at the house opposite, and a dirty, wicked-looking woman and a girl in curl papers came to the door and talked low talk with him and laughed low laughs. The chemist came down at last in his nightshirt and trousers and gave me the medicine. It had been raining in the night and the street was damp, but it was a fine morning.[46]

These letters offer a clue to what was perhaps the most deeply disturbing of all her problems—her inability to write a worthy successor to *The Story of an African Farm*. They speak of constant work, but except for short articles and a few allegories, she published nothing during these London years. She refers in the letters to many stories that she evidently destroyed or never finished. She also refers to an ambitious work on sex which may or may not have become *Woman and Labour,* published many years later, and to a novel in progress which was the never-completed *From Man to Man*. But after launching so brilliant a career she found herself unable to sustain it. Chapman and Hall wanted a new book. Ernest Rhys, commissioned her to write an introduction to the Everyman edition of Mary Wollstonecraft's *Vindication of the Rights of Women*. She was working furiously, but nothing was finished. London life was full of distractions—practical and emotional. For one who threw herself so deeply into everything she undertook and who gave such total dedication and concentration to her work, a quiet environment was imperative. In 1886 she sought one on the Continent, traveling in Switzerland, France, and Italy. In the small Italian Riviera town of Alassio she found temporary refuge. After visiting the little chapel of Santa Croce there, she was inspired to write one of her most celebrated allegories, "In a Ruined Chapel." "I love this place more and more," she recorded in her journal. "I am going to work now like six devils. If only anything could wake up in me a spark of ambition, if only I could care one straw of what people said of me. The one thing I long for is that they should say nothing. It is such agony to be touched." [47]

Alassio offered only temporary relief. Back in England she again suffered attacks of asthma and depression. Meanwhile some of her family had come to visit from South Africa, and old ties and memories were stirring within her. In October, 1889, sick and discouraged about her inability to publish her allegories, she sailed for home: "I will be better when I get to Africa," she wrote Ellis, more to reassure herself, probably, than him.[48]

III

The South Africa that Olive Schreiner had left in 1881 was a vast, undeveloped, divided frontier country in which the British and Dutch lived more or less at peace simply because there was enough space to prevent their treading on each other's toes. The great Kimberley diamond rush of the early 1870's and the discovery of gold in the Witwatersrand in 1886 rapidly changed the economy and the political climate. During the 1880's two powerful leaders had arisen: for the Uitlanders, the British colonists who had settled in the Cape Colony but were now being drawn north into Dutch territory by the temptations of the Witwatersrand, the "Colossus," Cecil Rhodes, a financial genius with dreams of empire; for the Boers, a sturdy, fanatically religious descendant of the Dutch "trekkers," Stephanus Paulus Kruger, Oom or Uncle Paul.

The South Africa to which Olive Schreiner returned in 1889 was already in the throes of rising nationalism and capitalism. The Dutch were no longer simple pioneer farmers but a people conscious of new wealth, power, and pride. The British were zealous in the protection of their rights and vested colonial interests, and Rhodes thought in grand terms of national union under Britain. The Schreiner family was English. Olive had grown up in an English-speaking household; her mother once punished her severely for using Dutch words. As a child she had played at being Queen Victoria. Until she grew up and actually lived with a Boer family, she had regarded the Boers with all the prejudices of her background, thinking them stupid, dirty, and uncouth. Before she left South Africa, however, she had altered her opinions. Her experiences in liberal freethinking circles in England further opened her eyes and her mind. Nevertheless, she came home to Africa still loyally English, and her

family, her aged mother as well as her brothers, were ardent in
their support of Rhodes.

Olive was happy now in South Africa. In spite of occasional
attacks of asthma, she found the climate congenial. She was at
home—the scene of her novels, the base of her childhood memories. But she continued to move about restlessly. Although Cape
Town was beautiful and lively, she longed for the karroo, where
she could find quiet and get down to serious work. In March,
1890, she settled in Matjesfontein, a lonely village five hundred
miles from Cape Town but on a railway line that linked it with
the outside world. From here, in April, she wrote Ellis that she
had heard of Cecil Rhodes, "whom I think I should like if I could
meet him; he's very fond of *An African Farm*." [49] A few months
later she met the man himself, now prime minister, and immediately pronounced him "a man of genius." "He is even higher
and nobler than I expected; . . . he spoke to me more lovingly
and sympathetically of *An African Farm* than anyone has ever
done." [50] Obviously Olive was flattered by the admiration of so
famous a man. But it was not mere egotism that attracted her to
him. The man was dynamic, fired with zeal for a cause that
seemed noble—the unification of her country. Back in England
her friend W. T. Stead was championing his cause. Her brother
Will was his disciple and became attorney general in his first
ministry. Rhodes preached a new awakened Africa, and he was
strong enough to translate his ideals into action. Even before she
had returned to South Africa, Olive had heard of his gift of
£10,000 to the cause of Irish independence. "He was represented
to me as a millionaire who was going to devote his life to the
freeing of the Irish peasant from the landlord, to the education
of the Native races of South Africa, and to the benefit of all poor
and downtrodden people generally! As painted to me, he seemed
the ideal of human greatness."

In the flesh, however, Rhodes proved to be less inspiring.
"As long as he and I talked of books and scenery, we were very
happy, but when he began on politics and social questions, I
found out to my astonishment that he had been misrepresented
to me." Once at a dinner party he announced, "I prefer land to

niggers," and Olive was outraged. In spite of her shifting feelings, however, she continued her association with him for several years, apparently fascinated and hoping dimly that she might reform him:

> I think Rhodes liked me for the same reason that I liked him, because of his *life* and energy, but we *never once* met without a royal fight. I have copies of *all* the letters I ever wrote him, *and they are one long passionate endeavour to save him from what seemed to me the downward course....* I have gone out of the House of Parliament when he was speaking, and written a note and hired a boy to take it over, imploring him to abstain from damning his own soul as it seemed to me he was doing. With all his genius, with all his beautiful, wonderful gifts, to see it going so! [51]

Olive's bitter disillusion with Rhodes was intensified by events of the next few years—his increasing militancy, his contempt for the natives, his part in the abortive Jameson Raid of 1895.[52] Following that disaster even her brother Will regretfully severed his ties and resigned from Rhodes' cabinet: "Blood has been shed and the position I fill I can no longer hold under you. . . . I have no more bitter sorrow in my life than my loss of you." [53] But perhaps the most influential force in her quarrel with Rhodes and in her ultimate dedication to the Boer cause was a handsome young English South African farmer, Samuel Cron Cronwright, whom she met in December, 1892, and married on February 24, 1894.

At the time of their marriage Olive was thirty-eight, Cronwright thirty. She was, by his own account, middle aged, heavy, her shoulders hunched from the wheezing effects of asthma. But she was also, by his account, enchanting, with bright eyes and a brilliant smile, "the divine child," and when she began to talk, he was captivated. He had already read *An African Farm,* which he found "extraordinary," its language so beautiful as "to put it on an equality with much of what is noblest and holiest in the English tongue." [54] Cronwright was thus infatuated even before he met her; in the more than twenty years of their marriage he never ceased to stand in awe of her genius. An intelligent man, reasonably well educated, public spirited and deeply committed to the cause of African independence, he worshiped in Olive the qualities he most lacked in himself—quick wit, intuitive brilliance, imagination, and passionate emotion. His limitations are obvious in the biography he wrote of her and in his edition of her letters. Although sympathetic and understanding, he never really fathomed her complex, turbulent character. He was so convinced of her genius that he portrayed her as a romantic stereotype, pacing the floor, talking to herself, forgetful, childish, defenseless, pitifully impractical, in need of constant love and attention. These qualities truly were part of her nature, but Cronwright magnified them and ignored the qualities of a reasonable, thoughtful woman who wrote rationally and lucidly, who managed alone most of her life (for she was often separated from her husband) to support herself and conduct her own affairs, who was, beyond a doubt, eccentric and capricious, given to exaggeration in word and deed, but never a mad genius.

Different as these two were in temperament, they shared from their first meeting an opposition to Rhodes and a love for South Africa. Their mutual interests never formed a spiritual bond, as had developed between her and Ellis, but there was, in this case, a strong and mutual physical attraction. For the first time, apparently, Olive had met a man who was both intellectually worthy of her and physically appealing. He was an outdoor man, a farmer and animal breeder, an athlete. "I've always thought I should like to marry a stone-mason or a bricklayer," she wrote him. "My children would be so nice and clean-born if their father always worked hard in the open; and I would like his hard rough hands to touch me. The difficulty has always been that I didn't see how you could get a man with hard hands and a cultured intellect." [55] In the firm masculine good looks of Cronwright she found exactly what she was seeking. But she hesitated to make the final commitment of marriage. In June, 1893, she went to England again, still undecided. Absence seemed to work its predictable magic. Her letters to him were warm and loving. They stressed her need for his love and his strength, her growing confidence and trust in him. Four months after her return to South Africa, they married in a simple ceremony at a magistrate's house and went to live on Cronwright's homestead at Krantz Plaats. She had given up her independence as a single woman, but not without first requiring from her husband that in return he adopt her name. Henceforth, while she remained Olive Schreiner, he was Cronwright-Screiner.

The sacrifice of her independence was a mere gesture. A free spirit like Oliver Schreiner's was not to be confined or subordinated to the interests of anyone else. Fortunately, her enlightened husband shared most of her ideas. "When there is such complete unity," she wrote W. T. Stead about a year after her marriage, "there never arises the least difficulty with regard to friendships with third persons of opposite sex. In my own case marriage has not yet touched one of my friendships. . . . Marriage, perfect marriage of mind and body, is such a lovely and holy thing, that rather than an imperfect travesty of it, I should say none was better." [56] With Cronwright-Schreiner she seems to have achieved that perfect union—for some years at least. Probably it was less than perfect for him. Her poor health made terrible demands upon them both—not only the physical burden of long sleepless nights when Olive paced the house heavily, banging doors and slamming on the walls as she struggled for breath, but also the wearying moves from place to place as she sought a better climate. Only a few months after their marriage it became apparent that Cronwright's beautiful and prospering farm, which they both loved, was deadly for her asthma. He gave it up, and they settled in Kimberley where she could breathe and write. Cronwright said that he made the sacrifice willingly, in the interests of her work, although he knew that there would be little money from that source: "I have always felt, as a kind of religion, that I had her as a trust, and that, at whatever cost, it was my duty to give her, as far as lay in my power, the opportunity to complete her work as a great artist and one of spiritual insight." [57]

On April 30, 1895, Olive gave birth to a baby girl and for several brief hours knew a happiness that even her overwrought prose could not convey. The child died the next morning. "There is something so terrible in the manner of its going," she wrote to a friend, Alice Corthorn. "Neither Cron nor I dare ever say even to each other what was in our hearts. There are some thoughts we shall carry with us to our dying day. Oh, Alice, it was so beautiful to have it." [58] As soon as she regained her strength, Olive plunged into political activity. Her husband was even more strongly convinced than she that Rhodes was a threat to the unified democratic South Africa of which they dreamed. The Jameson Raid confirmed their fears. In spite of denunciation from Olive's family, she joined her husband in a public repudiation of Rhodes and of British policy in general. They collaborated on a treatise, *The Political Situation,* which was widely read both in Africa and in England. Their criticism of Rhodes was outspoken but fair. Even the conservative London *Spectator* (November 7, 1896) praised its "unfailing moderation of tone," its avoidance of "mere emotional appeals."

Events moved swiftly and terribly. Having committed herself to an anti-British policy, Olive Schreiner found herself more and more deeply engaged emotionally. Until now her attitude toward the African native, the Negro and the mixed colored, had been sympathetic but distant. The further she moved away from English colonialism and from Rhodes, the more committed she became not only to the Boer but to the black and colored races. Personally she remained aloof from the native:

> If it be asked whether we are negrophiles, we reply: No— we are trying to be but we are not yet. It would be a lie to say that we love the black man, if by that is meant that we love him as we love the white. But we are resolved to deal with justice and mercy towards him. *We will treat him* as if we loved him; and in time the love may come.[59]

But as a South African looking to the future, she recognized with rare perception that the rapidly approaching twentieth century would break down old social barriers:

> Everywhere European, Asiatic and African will interlard. . . . And the problem which this century will have to solve

is the accomplishment of this interaction of distinct human varieties on the largest and most beneficent lines, making for the development of humanity as a whole, and carried out in a manner consonant with modern ideals and modern social wants. It will not always be the European who forms the upper layer; but in its essentials the problem will be everywhere the same.[60]

Her nonfiction writings on South Africa are remarkable not only for their fervor but for their lucidity and—in the light of events more than half a century later—their prescience. They are certainly superior to the few works of fiction she wrote on these sam questions: a highminded but sentimental story, "Eighteen Ninety-Nine," treating of the sufferings of a Boer farm woman who sees her sons and grandson sacrificed to the cause of freedom against the British, and a shrill propagandistic short novel, *Trooper Peter Halket of Mashonaland* (1897). The book, provoked by an atrocity incident in which the British hanged three natives, was a declaration of open war against Rhodes. The early editions of the novel carried a gruesome photograph of three hanging bodies that was later suppressed, but the flaming rage of the author could not be so easily controlled. Olive and her husband took the manuscript to England in January, 1897. Ironically, Rhodes was a passenger in the very next cabin, but they did not speak to him during the long voyage. *Trooper Peter Halket* provoked considerable controversy in England. Not only was the public divided in their attitude toward events in the distant colony, but critics were sharply divided on its literary merits.

Strictly speaking, *Trooper Peter Halket* is not a novel but a polemical allegory. Olive Schreiner uses the familiar device of introducing Christ as a character and as her spokesman. Since her most recent precedents in fiction for this device had been Eliza Lynn Linton and Marie Corelli, she exposed herself immediately to charges of sacrilege and tastelessness. ("Are these ladies God," one indignant reviewer complained, "that they can divine and express what would be the words of our Lord on any subject, or His opinion?")[61] More serious was the general absence of art and imagination in the novel. A work of pure polemics, it preaches a fervent but essentially shallow message. A young English soldier, perfectly contented in the colonial army in South Africa, contemptuous of the natives, and interested only in emulating Cecil Rhodes by making his fortune in business speculation, meets a mysterious traveler who hails him as "Peter Simon" Halket and speaks movingly of the dignity and mobility of the natives and the rights of all men to equal treatment. When Halket returns to his regiment he is a changed man. No longer a brutal soldier, he treats the natives kindly, sharing his rations with them, and ultimately suffers death helping one to escape imprisonment. The lesson of his life is not lost, for one officer reflects at the end, "I hardly know whether it is not better for him now than for us." Potentially, one reviewer of the novel suggested, *Trooper Peter Halket* might have been another *Uncle Tom's Cabin*.[62] But the inflated sentiments and flowery rhetoric that were acceptable to readers in the 1850's were no longer tolerable to readers and reviewers of 1897. *Trooper Peter Halket* had a brief life during the height of the Anglo-Boer crisis, but it died quickly and bears no revival today in spite of the timelessness and sincerity of the author's convictions.

Trooper Peter Halket was the second and last novel Olive Schreiner published in her lifetime. The only other fiction she produced were some short stories and allegories, and the only major non-fiction between 1897 and her death in 1920 was *Woman and Labour*. For one who had worked unremittingly throughout her life this is indeed a skimpy record. It can be explained only by her undisciplined working habits and her peculiar indifference to fame and material success. She wrote by inspiration. In a letter to Ellis in 1885 she described the erratic and compulsive manner of her work:

> I told you this afternoon I had not been working for some days. I'd sit at my table but nothing would come, only a strange blank feeling in my mind; couldn't think, couldn't feel. Suddenly, this evening, the feeling came to sit down and write. I have been writing hour after hour, page after page. I could write till tomorrow morning. I don't know

where all the ideas come from if they've not been forming slowly these last few days while my mind has felt so blank. I have had the same experience over and over again before. I work very hard for some days, or think very intensely on some subject day and night. Then suddenly my mind strikes work. For a day or two days or three days I seem quite passive. Then suddenly, as in a moment, it all bursts open again, and I find all the thoughts that were half-formed and in confusion when I left work, completed and ready.

Just as compulsively and impetuously she destroyed much of what she wrote, affirming that since her only purpose in writing was self-expression, she had no real desire to give her work to the world. She sometimes regarded her writing as so sacred and private that it pained her to think of others reading it:

The thought that hundreds of thousands will read my work does affect and kindle me, not because I wish to teach them but because, terrible as it is to show them my work at all, the thought of throwing it to them to be trodden under foot is double desecration of it. . . . The best stories and dreams I have had nothing would induce me to write at all because I couldn't bear any person to read them.

When Ellis questioned her once as to why she spent so much time on her introduction to Mary Wollstonecraft's *Vindication of the Rights of Women* (which she never completed), she replied: "How can I do otherwise? Whatever I write must be the best I can write. . . . If I was writing for ten thousand pounds or for three and sixpence, my work would be just the same. Perhaps when it's done you'll wonder that it took so long and see nothing in it, but I see. I expect when it's done I'll throw it in the fire." [63]

At times, however, circumstances beyond her control prevented productive work. Her health was one of these. Another was the Anglo-Boer War, during which she and her husband led a stormy existence in British territory. For some time before the war they had lived in Johannesburg, in the Dutch Transvaal, where Cronwright worked for an attorney in hopes of becoming a lawyer himself. Olive had a small income of her own, based mainly on the sale of the copyrights of her books and the occasional articles and reviews she published in magazines, Believing strongly that women should remain financially independent even when married, she refused to allow her husband to support her. They lived modestly and happily, united in their opposition to jingo war-mongering, sympathetic to the Boers yet sensitive to their own English roots and loyalties. Just before the war Olive became ill, and they moved south to British Cape Town for relief. There, war having broken out, they were obliged to stay. Martial law was declared and British jingo feeling ran high. Nevertheless they persisted in their opposition to the war and Cronwright went to England in 1900 to promote the antiwar cause while Olive spoke at protest meetings in Cape Town. She was a powerful speaker. The journalist H. W. Nevinson described one appearance: "I have heard much indignant eloquence, but never such a molten torrent of white-hot rage. It was overwhelming. When it suddenly ceased, the large audience . . . could hardly gasp. If Olive Schreiner . . . had called on them to storm Government House, they would have thrown themselves upon the bayonets." [64]

To one who lived so intensely as Olive Schreiner, who spent herself so passionately on her ideals, the war was especially tragic. A pacifist and believer in nonviolence in all cases, she suffered physical and mental anguish every moment of the conflict. Furthermore she was bitterly divided from most of her family—her mother and brother Theo rabidly pro-British, her brother Will more restrained but committed to support of Britain. Her house in Johannesburg was hit by a bomb, with a loss of many of her books and papers. She was personally insulted on several occasions, at least once questioned by British authorities, confined to restricted patrolled areas; her letters were opened. In general, however, Olive flourished under persecution. When the war ended, she plunged enthusiastically into plans for establishing a new South African union. Cronwright built a house for them in De Aar, a high dry atmosphere where, in spite of the bouts of illness, she lived in some comfort. He was elected to Parliament where he supported (unsuccessfully) a movement for the enfranchisement of women.

Olive lived at De Aar for six years, wrote a great deal but produced only one new book, *Woman and Labour,* published in 1911. Even this book is the result not simply of these six years of work but, if we are to believe her testimony, of a lifetime. As early as the 1880's she had referred in many of her letters to a great "sex book." She planned it as a history of women from prehistoric times to the present, with detailed studies of the physiology of sex in plant and animal as well as in human life, and of social institutions as they are related to the sexes. She claimed that she had written a large part, all of which was destroyed in the bombing of the Johannesburg house. Cronwright doubted that she ever actually wrote the book: "Her capacity for stating hard, objective facts was often conditioned by her powerful imagination." [65] Certainly she had read and collected material for such a book over many years and discussed it with Ellis and other friends in London. The writing of it was a natural extension of the idealistic views of Lyndall in *The Story of an African Farm* and of her own sweeping transcendentalism. Strangely enough, although the book became "the Bible of the woman's movement" and inspired many ardent young women of the period (Vera Brittain, for one, reading it as a schoolgirl, said it "sounded to the world of 1911 as insistent and inspiring as a trumpet-call summoning the faithful to a vital crusade" [66]), Olive was never herself a militant suffragette. Her pacifism ruled out violent action of any kind. Besides, her feminism was more idealistic than practical. It was reflected not so much in social-political action for the vote as in a spiritual, Christlike love that transcended the differences between the sexes.

In practice as well as in theory Olive herself transcended these barriers. There was some question of her lesbianism, but this was no doubt more a matter of extravagant language than fact. In his psychosexual study of her, Ellis concluded that she had never actually loved a woman and was not inverted. Her excited responses to female attractions were, by her own self-analysis, the result of a vivid imagination which enabled her instinctively to put herself "in the place of a man and [feel] as it seems to her a man would feel." [67] Her letters give evidence of her deep attachment to women—Mrs. Cawood and Mrs. Brown in South Africa, Edith Bland ("E. Nesbit" [68]), Havelock Ellis' sister Louie,[69] and others in London. Olive was fully aware of her bisexual drives and discussed them freely with Ellis. She traced her great sympathy for women back to her childhood love for the baby sister who had died.[70] The loss of her own baby daughter intensified these feelings.

Her response to the suffrage movement was characteristically a defense of the weak and the persecuted:

My heart feels so tender over a baby girl because of all the anguish which may be before it. I always think of it when I touch and hold in my arms the dear little female bodies; which no love can shield from the anguish which may be waiting for them. I have done all I can to help free women, but oh it is so little. Long ages must pass before we really stand free and look out on a world that is ours as well as man's. The poor little political franchise is just a tiny, little, wee step towards it. I don't think you can understand a little how I love those suffragettes in London, those that I do know, and those that I don't. They are women who have freed themselves spiritually fighting for freedom; we, here, have in our little movement only slaves clanking their little chains along as they go, asking for their little franchise.

Inspired by sentiments like these, she lived for a while and worked with the prostitutes of London's East End. She was not alone in her reforming zeal. Her friend W. T. Stead went proudly to jail for his attempts to expose white slavery in the London slums. Olive herself was once stopped by a policeman as she walked with a man friend after midnight in the London streets: "If you had seen the look of the wretch," she wrote ex- ultantly to Ellis "as he came up and said: 'I don't want you, sir, I want her!'" She made a few attempts to "save" some of the prostitutes: "I went to see an old woman in Bolsover St., she is a procuress, I can see, and she has such a pretty girl with her whom I want to get away . . . I love that girl." Later she wrote to Ellis, apparently of another girl: "That prostitute is so darling. You would love her. Would you like to meet her? She wants to read and be intellectual, it's quite pathetic." [71]

Emerging out of idealism as fervent as this, *Woman and Labour* is full of impassioned rhetoric, but the reasoning behind it is logical and the arguments are developed calmly. Obviously its readers of 1911 were more impressed by its sentiments than by its documentation. Olive Schreiner could churn up rhetorical waters vigorously. She reminds her readers, for example, that the "New Woman" is not new but the descendant of hardy, indomitable, ancient Teutonic women who farmed and even fought beside their men:

> We have in us the blood of a womanhood that was never bought and never sold; that wore no veil and had no foot bound; whose realized ideal of marriage was sexual companionship and an equality in duty and labour; who stood side by side with the males they loved in peace or war, and whose children, when they had borne them, sucked manhood from their breasts, and even through their fetal existence heard a brave heart beat above them (Ch. III, "Parasitism").

Her aguments for female emancipation are based on such rational grounds as the changing nature of the modern economy, labor-saving devices, and industrialization, which have reduced woman's work in the home and left her idle, ignorant, useless, and parasitically dependent upon the male. In this new economy a place must be specially made for women. Their demand is useful, constructive work. "We claim, today, all labour for our province!" was the rallying cry of Olive Schreiner's feminism:

> From the judge's seat to the legislator's chair; from the statesman's closet to the merchant's office; from the chemist's laboratory to the astronomer's tower, there is no post or form of toil for which it is not our intention to attempt to fit ourselves; and there is no closed door we do not intend to force open; and there is no fruit in the garden of knowl-

edge it is not our determination to eat (Ch. IV, "Woman and War").

The most eloquent expression of Olive's feminism—in fact, of all her ideals—is in her allegories, most of them published during her lifetime in magazines, and collected in a small volume called *Dreams* (1890) and after her death in *Stories, Dreams and Allegories* (1923). These short, intense lyrical pieces came to her swiftly and were written down usually in a frenzy of emotion. They were ideally suited to her undisciplined working habits— short enough to accommodate the emotional outburst without demanding plot, structure, characterization. Not that they were easy to write. She said that she often spent monhs "agonizing" over one of them, polishing and perfecting. But they gave her the richest satisfaction. They were, she told Arthur Symons, "the only artistic expression of the passion of abstract ideas, which to her are the keenest, the deepest in her nature; and in these allegories one can express humanity, not merely this man or that." [72] Their thinly disguised polemics were very evident to her contemporaries. The ardent suffragette Lady Constance Lytton described in her memoirs, *Prisons and Prisoners*, how one of these allegories, "Three Dreams in a Desert," was read to a group of women in prison. In this story the narrator, wandering through a desert, finds a woman paralyzed by the Burden of Inevitable Necessity. Beside her is a man also paralyzed. But as the Age of Muscular Force yields to the Knife of Mechanical Invention, the woman begins to move. She is held back, how- ever, by the man and remains a prisoner: "He does not under- stand. When she moves she draws the bond that binds them, and hurts him, and he moves farther from her. The day will come when he will understand and will know what she is doing." To Lady Lytton and her sister suffragettes, the message was power- ful: "It fell on our ears more like an ABC railway guide to our journey than a figurative parable, though its poetic strength was all the greater for that." [73]

IV

The power to persuade and stir her readers was strong in Olive Schreiner. Unfortunately, it was not a staying power. Conviction, vitality, sincerity—qualities of her writing that her contemporary admirers often singled out for special remark—are not enduring unless they are supported by the firmer structure of art. She completed only one significant novel, her *African Farm,* a fine but flawed book. The major work of her life was a novel that she never completed, *From Man to Man.* It was published in 1926 by her husband, who added a summary of the conclusion she had planned and a long, detailed account of its composition. Forty-five years in the making and never finished nor polished by its maker, it is understandably an odd and imperfect book. Her involvement with it was too intimate and emotional to permit any sense of artistic detachment and objectivity. Her confused conception of the novel as a whole is exposed in many ways—her inability to complete it, the many working titles (the earliest, 1875, "Other Men's Sins," also "Saints and Sinners," "The Camel Thorn," "Thorn Kloopf," "Perhaps Only"; the final title comes from John Morley: "From man to man nothing matters but . . . charity"); her conflicting moods of confidence and despair over the writing of it; her endless revisions; the inevitable inconsistencies caused by her growth and development over these many years.

Lacking in art though it is, *From Man to Man* is a striking and, in some ways, beautiful book, superior even to the better-known *Story of an African Farm* because its scope is larger; its characters operate not only in their private worlds but also within society, interacting and acted upon. Its failure to impress readers as *African Farm* had done is more a matter of unlucky timing than of quality. The latter had appeared in the Victorian era, when it seemed daring and spoke directly to the rebellious new generation. In 1926 *From Man to Man* found a less receptive public. Largely a passionate plea for woman's right to self-fulfillment, it came too late. Even the South African setting of most of the action was less exotic and remote than it had been in 1883. And the central moral issues of the novel—the wages of adultery and prostitution—were somewhat quaint by the mid 1920's.[74]

Like *African Farm,* this novel is intensely personal and autobiographical. The author identifies herself with her two main female characters—sisters, children of devoutly religious English parents who live on a lonely South African farm. The identification with Rebekah, the older sister, is the more complete and literal, but the pretty, doomed younger sister, Bertie, is Olive's romanticized vision of herself, just as Waldo and Lyndall represent two facets of her personality. Rebekah is the more articulate, intelligent, and better adjusted sister. Trapped in an unhappy marriage she finds fulfillment in motherhood and self-expression in writing a private journal. Bertie is more merciful and vulnerable; she becomes the victim of the narrow bigoted society in which she lives. An early indiscretion (she is seduced by her tutor) causes a scandal, and she is hounded until her fine spirit is broken and she becomes first the apathetic mistress of a wealthy Jew, then, after further melodramatic incident, a prostitute.

Loose as it is in structure, the novel has a unifying theme— the redeeming powers of love and idealism—strengthened by Olive's characteristic fervor. After years of work on it, she wrote to her husband in 1907:

> If only the powers that shape existence give me the strength to finish this book, I shall not have that agonized feeling over my life that I have over the last ten years, that I have done nothing of good for any human creature. I am not sure of the book's artistic worth: to judge of that from the purely intellectual standpoint one must stand at a distance from one's own or anyone else's work. But I know it gives a voice to that which exists in the hearts of many women and some men, I know I have only tried to give expression to what was absolutely forced on me, that I have not made up one line for the sake of making it up.[75]

Cronwright-Schreiner said that she "loved this book more than anything else she ever wrote." Certainly it was closest to her own life, especially in the opening section with its Wordsworthian title, "The Prelude" (subtitled "The Child's Day"), and its Wordsworthian spirit of recollection and re-creation of the experiences of childhood. There are striking parallels here to the opening chapter of the early and far inferior *Undine* and to numerous passages in *African Farm*. The lonely child Rebekah, aged five, plays while her mother is in labor with twins. She is building a house of little stones for the mice:

> She had built it in two stories, so that the family could live on the lower floor and keep their grain on the top. She had put a great flat stone to roof the lower story, and another flat stone for the roof at the very top, and she had put a moss carpet on the lower floor for them to sleep on, and corn, ready for them to use, above. She stepped very softly up to the house and peeped in at the little door; there was nothing there but the brown moss. She sat down flat on the stone before it and peered in. Half, she expected the mice to come; and half, she knew they never would.

Then she wanders into the spare room where the body of a dead baby, one of the twins, has been laid out. Thinking the baby asleep, she kisses its hair and offers to it as a gift her odd little treasure collection—stones, candy, "a head of Queen Victoria cut out of the tinsel label of a sardine tin." She considers this her baby since she has found it. Later she dreams that she has her own baby and makes up stories to amuse it: "I write books!" she says proudly to her make-believe child. "When I was little I used to scribble them in a copybook with a stick, when I didn't know how to write. But when I grew up I learned to write;—and I wrote real books, a whole roomful! I've written a book about birds, and about animals, and about the world; and one day I'm going to write a book something like the Bible."

This opening section continues with further description of a child's day—her dreams, her imaginary playmate Charles, her attempts to learn her spelling and arithmetic lessons, her encounter with a cobra which frightens but does not harm her. At the end of the day she sees her father and the servants taking the dead baby out for burial, and she dimly grasps "something of what birth and death mean, which she had not known before." That night she visits her mother, who is nursing the surviving twin, and she falls asleep with the baby. The nurse finds them, "the hands of the sisters so interlocked, and the arm of the elder sister so closely round the younger, that she could not remove it without awakening both."

Nothing in the remainder of the novel matches the sensitivity of insight nor the richness of language that she achieves in this opening. Later she incorporates long passages of allegory and philosophical reflection that Rebekah writes in her journal. Her portrayal of the artistic, creative woman who is hungry for intellectual stimulation is sympathetic and at times moving. Rebekah is a devoted mother, but she is physically exhausted by childbearing and emotionally troubled by her husband's lack of understanding. She has set aside one tiny room of her house as a place of refuge, going there every night after the children are asleep, to think and to write: "Often at night, as she sat alone in that room, she had pictured to herself what great works of art must be like, or great orchestral music. She had seen or heard neither, but she dreamed of them, as she dreamed of what it must be to be one of a company of men and women in a room together, all sharing somewhat the same outlook on life" (Ch. VII). But Rebekah's musings dwindle into the vague, sweeping abstractions to which Olive Schreiner was unfortunately prone. Author and character are one. Rebekah is Olive Schreiner, pacing the floor of the little room as she works out her lofty ideas, scribbling these down hurriedly "in a large sprawling hand." She boldly embraces all fields of knowledge—science, anthropology, evolution, history, the march of human civilizations, social reform—interrupting her meditations from time to time to nurse her baby. She returns to write an allegory in which the Spirit of the Ages finds a woman, beautiful from the waist up but fettered by chains on her feet. The Spirit tells her that she makes herself a prisoner and will be free only when she strikes off the chains herself. Before he leaves he asks her name, and she tells him it is Humanity (Ch. VIII).

Olive delighted in free-rambling expression of this kind. She wrote with feverish inspiration, pouring herself into the book.

Later in the novel Rebekah writes a letter of prodigious length to her husband, who had been unfaithful to her, and it too becomes a passionate polemic in the cause of women's rights:

> I had loved so to bear for you and to work for you. Now nothing mattered; I couldn't read, I couldn't think! Oh, it isn't only the body of a woman that a man touches when he takes her in his hands; it's her brain, it's her intellect, it's her whole life! He puts his hand in among the finest cords of her being and rends and tears them if he will, so that they never produce anything more but discord and disharmony, or he puts his hand on them gently, and draws out all the music and makes them strong (Ch. VIII).

Still later, she makes an agreement whereby she will remain with her husband to raise their children (including a half-Negro child he has had by a servant) but will have no further intimacy with him; she tells her children stories and allegories preaching equality of the races and the brotherhood of man.

These passages, not surprisingly, are tedious. Their intention —to represent the development of Rebekah's mind—is interesting, but they are insufficiently dramatized, repetitious, and inflated.[76] Far more damaging to the novel, however, are the author's clumsy attempts at melodrama and lurid realism. These involve the younger sister Bertie who, after her seduction and her indiscreet confession of it to the straitlaced young man she loves and hopes to marry, suffers misery at the hands of two vicious, self-righteous, monstrous women. Olive was never successful in the portrayal of wicked characters. They emerge either as crude comic caricatures (notably the grotesque Bonaparte Blenkins in *African Farm,* who, she admitted to Ellis in 1884, was drawn in "hard straight lines without shading and is not artistic nor idealised enough" [77]) or snaky hypocrites so unsubtle that we expect them at any moment to crawl and hiss. The villainesses of *From Man to Man* are respectable women, secure in a society which rejects a sweet innocent like Bertie. "The great criminal," Rebekah reflects, "was not necessarily the murderer, the ruffian, the drunkard, the prostitute, or even the frank, direct, and open liar; but maybe a spirit encased in a fair and gentle body . . . openly breaking no social law . . . a rotten apple with dead seeds and a worm at its core."

Bertie's martyrdom follows pretty well the cheap fictional formula of the fallen woman. It is redeemed only by Olive's intense compassion for the character and her moving account of the girl's gradual withdrawal from reality. The Jew who takes her to London treats her with kindness and generosity, but isolates her from other people. Having been wounded by society, Bertie submits passively to him, living in an almost catatonic state shut up in rooms in London. Only once does she express a positive desire—to visit the country. She goes, accompanied by a servant, Isaac:

> "This—this," said Isaac slowly, "is country."
> She looked about her.
> On the slope about everywhere there were the marks of cows' feet, which had sunk deep into the soft soaked turf. Some of the footprints were full of clear water, in some blue flowers had been growing which raised themselves stooping and half crushed. She looked round at the gray sky, at the damp bushes, at the barn a few hundred feet off with its red roof, damp with yellow lichens, and at the mud and grass at their feet. The high heels of her little shoes were sinking deep into the grass as the cows' hoofs had done. She drew her skirt tight about her and stood looking.
> "Let us go back," she said, and turned, Isaac following her (Ch. XI).

On the basis of passages like these, many of Olive Schreiner's readers have felt that she might have been more successful as a poet than as a novelist. She had a sharp eye for nature and a sensitive ear for the rhythms of language. Steeped from childhood in the prose of the King James Bible, she echoed its rhythms:

> At last came the year of the great drought, the year of 1862. From end to end of the land the earth cried for water. Man and beast turned their eyes to the pitiless sky, that like

the roof of some brazen oven arched overhead. On the farm, day after day, month after month, the water in the dams fell lower and lower; the sheep died in the fields; the cattle, scarcely able to crawl, tottered as they moved from spot to spot in search of food. Week after week, month after month, the sun looked down from the cloudless sky, till the karroo bushes were leafless sticks, broken into the earth, and the earth itself was naked and bare; and only the milk-bushes, like old hags, pointed their shrivelled fingers heavenwards, praying for the rain that never came (*Story of an African Farm*, Pt. I, Ch. II).

Much as she advocated simplicity and forthrightness of expression, she admitted to occasional decorating of her prose, borrowing a term from knitting—the "ribbed" style:

I never know *why* I write things in a certain way when I write them, but I can generally find out if I think afterwards. . . . I am changing a whole chapter of *From Man to Man* from what I call the plain into the "ribbed" style. Sometimes the plain is right, sometimes the ribbed. I *think* I generally write descriptions in the plain and philosophise or paint thought in the ribbed.[78]

From Man to Man is Olive Schreiner's final and total expression as a novelist. In spite of its flaws, it is her best and richest work. The mind behind it is strong and interesting; the heart is warm and sympathetic. Her inability to complete it was one of the great disappointments of her life. In March, 1913, she wrote poignantly to Emily Hobhouse: "It isn't the pain and weakness one minds, it's the not being able to work. My one novel especially I would have liked to finish. I feel that if only one lonely and struggling woman read it and found strength and comfort from it one would not feel one had lived quite in vain. I seem to have done so little with my life." [79]

A sense of failure and frustration dominated, although it did not embitter, Olive's last years. Old age and ill health were destructive to the image of flaming, ardent crusader which she had cultivated. Her ardor had not cooled, but her energy and vitality were now severely limited. Many honored her as a writer and as a leader in social reform, but the facts of politics, both in Africa and in Europe, testified to the failure of her ideals. The outbreak of the First World War almost crushed her spirit. She had returned to Europe late in 1913 in another desperate search for health; a doctor in Florence had been recommended for treatment of heart disease and a general change of atmosphere was advised. Cronwright, who was then in business in De Aar, stayed behind. Whether their marriage was foundering or whether, as he explained, it was simply a matter of the war and other circumstances, they did not see each other again for nearly seven years, although they kept up an affectionate correspondence. During this time Olive suffered keenly. She was in London through most of the aerial bombings. Her German-sounding name and odd "foreign" appearance caused her trouble with landladies, and she was forever moving from one lodging to another. Her anti-war views were unpopular. She published little except a few short articles and one or two pacifist allegories—"Who Knocks at the Door?" (*Fortnightly Review,* November, 1917, reprinted in *Stories, Dreams and Allegories*), a nightmare vision of a world in which men kill each other until all humanity is destroyed, and "The Dawn of Civilisation." This, her last writing, was planned as part of a longer, never completed book and printed after her death in *The Nation and The Athenaeum,* March 26, 1921. It is an attempt to explain the pacifist position, not as a rational argument—althogh she was perfectly capable of that—but as a "psychic compulsion." A short, fragmentary essay, it is interesting mainly for her reminiscences of a childhood experience. At about the age of nine, she recalls, she suffered from a terrible mood of despair: "All the world seemed wrong to me. It was not only that sense of the small misunderstandings and tiny injustices of daily life, which perhaps all sensitive children feel at some time pressing down on them; but the whole Universe seemed to be weighing on me."

At daybreak she wanders off into the mountains where she watches the sun rise; suddenly, in a moment of mystic-intuitive illumination, joy and tranquility descend upon her. She accepts her own insignificance in the universe because she now understands that there is some purpose in life. This insight, she says, has endured and comforted her ever since:

> I have tried to wear no blinkers. I have not held a veil before my eyes, that I might profess that cruelty, injustice, and mental anguish were not. I have tried to look nakedly in the face those facts which make most against all hope—and yet, in the darkest hour, the consciousness which I carried back with me that morning has never wholly deserted me; even as a man who clings with one hand to a rock, though the waves pass over his head, yet knows what his hand touches.

In May, 1920, Cronwright came to England. He was shocked at the change in Olive, now a feeble old woman though at moments still able to summon up the enthusiasm and charm of her early years. He spent only a few weeks with her. In August she sailed for South Africa, where he planned to rejoin her after several months. Among those seeing her off at Waterloo was Havelock Ellis, and she sailed happy, going home at last. She landed at Cape Town and settled there, near her brother Will's family and many friends. Her health was reasonably good, and she appeared cheerful. Death came suddenly and quietly during the night of December 10, 1920. She was buried in a cemetery near Cape Town temporarily. In August, 1921, Cronwright arranged for her reinterment at Buffel's Kop, the summit of a mountain high above Krantz Plaats, the farm homestead where they had lived just after their marriage. A lonely, windswept plateau, it was one of her favorite spots, and she had expressed a wish to be buried there. Beside her were buried her baby, who had lived less than one day, and a beloved dog, Nita.

Her legacy was *The Story of an African Farm,* a striking, though certainly not an immortal, novel. But she also left behind a memory of intense idealism, a naive but passionate humanitarianism that epitomizes the best of late Victorianism. She was far too much the iconoclast to fit into any social or artistic niche: her reputation survives, modestly but persistently, not so much for achievement as for endeavor. Where religious faith had failed her, where genuine artistic creativity had eluded her, and where even her personal relationships had been perhaps less than successful, the polemical novel had provided her with a medium of expression and an opportunity to air her strongly held convictions to a public groping for guidance and illumination. Like Waldo's Stranger who appears briefly but, for Waldo, significantly, she leaves her readers with an old brown volume. "You must not expect too much," the Stranger says casually of it, without bothering even to tell us its title, "but it may give you a centre round which to hang your ideas, instead of letting them lie about in a confusion that makes the head ache. We of this generation are not destined to eat and be satisfied as our fathers were; we must be content to go hungry."

Notes

1. This poem was first published in *The New Statesman*, March 15, 1930, p. 739. It was reprinted in *The Collected Poems of Roy Campbell* (London, 1949), p. 26.
2. Afterword to the Fawcett Premier Book edition of *The Story of an African Farm* (New York, 1968), p. 274.
3. The extremes are represented in Margaret Lawrence's *The School of Femininity* (New York, 1936) which devotes one chapter, "Olive Schreiner: Who Lay Listening to the Biological Drum Beating," of sheer gush to her, and in Jim Tully's article, "An Ex-Hobo's Tribute to Olive Schreiner," *Literary Digest International Book Review*, September, 1925, pp. 653-54: "She was greater than anything she ever wrote, greater as a woman than as a writer, a Jane Addams with a genius for writing." Floyd Dell discussed her and Isadora Duncan in a chapter in his *Women as World-Builders: Studies in Modern Feminism* (Chicago, 1913), calling her "one of the figures in modern literature and a spokesman for all women who have not learned to speak that hieratic language which is heard, as the inexpressive speech of daily life is not heard, across space and time." With Isadora Duncan, he writes, she has "shown the way to a new freedom of the body and the soul." A French writer, Paul Mantoux, said that before being a writer, she was "a conscience" (*A Travers l'Angleterre Contemporaine* [Paris, 1909], p. 89). And the novelist Phyllis Bottome wrote enthusiastically, "Olive Schreiner was not really an inhabitant of this world. She was a visitant and a messenger of the gods. Our ways of life astonished and almost deranged her . . . she gave unconsciously to the world the rare spectacle of a soul perfectly disin-

terested and passionately dedicated to the cause of the weak" (*Contemporary Review*, CXXV [January–June, 1924], 624–30).

4. *The Letters of Olive Schreiner, 1876–1920* (hereafter *Letters*), ed. S. C. Cronwright-Schreiner (London 1924), p. 227 (to Havelock Ellis).

5. *Thoughts on South Africa* (London, 1923), p. 15. This was originally published as a series of magazine articles between 1890 and 1892. The principal source for biographical material is *The Life of Olive Schreiner* (hereafter *Life*) by S. C. Cronwright-Schreiner (London and Boston, 1924). More recent studies are Vera Buchanan-Gould, *Not Without Honour: The Life and Writings of Olive Schreiner* (London, 1948); Marion V. Friedmann, *Olive Schreiner, a Study in Latent Meanings* (a psychoanalytical study of dubious reliability) (Johannesburg, 1954); D. L. Hobman, *Olive Schreiner: Her Friends and Times* (London, 1955); Johannes Meintjes, *Olive Schreiner: Portrait of a South African Woman* (Johannesburg, 1965).

6. *Life*, pp. 12, 245.

7. *Ibid.*, p. 255.

8. See his sketch in *Dictionary of National Biography*, 1912–1921. There is no separate entry for Olive Schreiner in *DNB* but a brief sketch of her life is included in this entry for her brother.

9. *Letters*, pp. 129, 361. See her comment in a letter to Mrs. Francis Smith in 1906: "If anyone showed me a lock of hair and said, 'That is Wordsworth's, I should look at it and pass on; if they said it was Shakespeare's or Shelley's, I should stroke it, and if it was Shelley's kiss it . . . but if it was Heine's I should carry it about with me wherever I went. I don't know why I love him so" (pp. 254–55).

10. *Life*, p. 67.

11. *Ibid.*, p. 41.

12. This youthful romance was first reported in Vera Buchanan-Gould's *Not Without Honour*, pp. 38–39. Misreading Olive's handwriting she identified the man as Julius Zaar. See Meintjes' *Olive Schreiner*, pp. 20–21.

13. See S. C. Cronwright-Schreiner's Introduction to *Undine* (New York, 1928).

14. *Life*, p. 98.

15. *Ibid.*, p. 110.

16. *Thoughts on South Africa*, Introduction, p. 19.

17. *Letters*, pp. 6–7.

18. In a letter to Ellis in 1884 she says that a well-known chest specialist, Dr. Coghill, said "that if I married I would be quite well. He sent his wife to talk to me. She told me her own case was exactly like mine . . . and she said that from the day she married she never knew she had a chest again" (*Ibid.*, pp. 29–30). In his *From Rousseau to Proust* (Boston, 1935), Ellis compared Olive's allergic asthma with Proust's condition: "In many features of mental and emotional character she was very far removed from Proust. But in pathological respects, as well as by a highly sensitised psycho-neurotic nature, she was nearly allied to him" (pp. 389–90).

19. *Life*, pp. 136–37.

20. *Ibid.*, p. 138. Mrs. Brown's reminiscences are in *Mrs. John Brown, 1847–*

1935: An Account of her Social Work in Lancashire and South Africa, of her Memories of Lancashire Folk, and of her Friendship with Olive Schreiner, ed. Angela James and Nina Hills (London, 1937).

21. *Letters,* p. 17.
22. There have been suggestions that Meredith helped materially in revising the novel, but Olive denied these strongly. She insisted that she had met him only briefly and had never discussed revisions of the book with him. See *Life,* pp. 153–56.
23. Henry Norman, "Theories and Practice of Modern Fiction," *Fortnightly Review,* XI (December, 1883), 882.
24. This episode was reprinted separately under the title "The Hunter" in her collection of allegories, *Dreams* (London 1890), and in an elaborately printed and decorated edition of these allegories, *So Here Then Are Dreams,* issued by Elbert Hubbard in 1901. The real-life counterpart for this Stranger, Olive said, was one Willie Bertram, a clergyman's son, whom she knew only slightly. He lent her a copy of Herbert Spencer's *First Principles,* a book that influenced her deeply. Just as she finished writing this part of the novel, in 1878, she learned of his death, which was probably by suicide (*Life,* pp. 80–83).
25. There is an echo of *Wuthering Heights* at the end of a scene in which Waldo has been beaten and locked up in the fuel house by Blenkins. Lyndall comes to comfort him: " 'Waldo,' she said, as she helped him to stand up and twisted his arm about her waist to support him, 'we will not be children always; we shall have the power too, some day.' She kissed his naked shoulder with her soft little mouth. It was all the comfort her young soul could give him."
26. *Life,* p. 156.
27. In his autobiography *The Unexpected Years* (New York, 1936, pp. 115, 119), Laurence Housman described the sensation the book caused in one provincial town:

> From the local circulating library came a form for the recommendation of books for the coming year. Innocent of offence we put down two books which were just then being much talked about—*John Ward, Preacher* and *Robert Elsmere,* and a better one which was then less known, *The Story of an African Farm,* and, supposing from its title that it was merely an account of colonial life in which anyone might find interest, they got it, and a few weeks later it went into circulation.
>
> Then followed explosion. We had gone back to London, but word of the scandal we had caused soon reached us. A father of a large family found his daughter, aged eighteen, reading it. Having read a few pages of it himself, he rushed off to the Vicar and the Headmaster to demand why they had permitted such poisonous stuff to enter the Library, and they, in turn, finding my father's recommendation list was responsible for it, came to him to know what he meant by it. Thus charged with responsibility for a thing about which he knew nothing, he asked for the book and read it, and was horrified to find himself tarred with the brush of so odious a production.
>
> His letter denouncing it, and us, might also have been written

had we let loose on the community a book as free of speech as *Lady Chatterley's Lover* or James Joyce's *Ulysses*. And though I was able truthfully to say that it had been recommended to us in a sermon, that did not excuse us from the guilt of having passed the recommendation on.

* * *

The Story of an African Farm has now become a little old-fashioned and troubles nobody; but I can still hear the tone of vengeful relish with which a lady of respectable intelligence told me how having read it she "took it in the tongs and put it in the fire." She had not held it in the tongs while reading it; but, when the reading was over. the tongs became the symbolic instrument of her virtuous disgust.

28. *Life*, pp. 170–71, 212.

29. *Essays by Mrs. Havelock Ellis,* II (Berkeley, N. J., 1924), 41.

30. *"Their Trackless Way": A Book of Memories* (New York, 1932), p. 131.

31.   Worse still the book definitely put *Thelma's* nose out of joint and all Marie's friends raved ecstatically and talked a great deal about intellect and power and sense of tragedy. She read the book in private, came to the conclusion that it was not half as good as her own works, and immediately conceived a loathing for this unknown who had so casually, so cruelly wrested the laurel wreath from her brow (Eileen Bigland, *Marie Corelli, The Woman and the Legend* [London and New York, 1953], p. 99).

32. *Works and Days: From the Journal of Michael Field,* eds. T. and D. C. Sturge Moore (London, 1933), p. 193.

33. Roger Lhombreaud, *Arthur Symons, a Critical Biography* (Philadelphia, 1964), p. 144.

34. Hobman, *Olive Schreiner,* p. 1.

35. Stephen Winsten, *Salt and his Circle* (London, 1951) , p. 13. In a letter to Clement Shorter, January 9, 1891, Shaw wrote: "I was inexpressibly shocked by your disparagement of Olive Schreiner's volume [probably *Dreams*] in the *Star.* You ought to walk to South Africa and back with peas in your shoes by way of penance. What were you dreaming of? The book is a treasure" (*Collected Letters, 1874–1897,* ed. Dan H. Laurence [London, 1965], p. 281).

36. *Contemporary Portraits: Fourth Series* (New York, 1923), p. 294.

37. *Letters,* p. 75. Moore's opinion of *The Story of an African Farm* was fairly neutral: "I found it sincere and youthful, disjointed but well-written descriptions of sand-hills and ostriches sandwiched with doubts concerning a future state, and convictions regarding the moral and physical superiority of women: but of art nothing; that is to say, art as I understand it,—rhythmical sequence of events described with rhythmical sequence of phrase" (*Confessions of a Young Man,* Ch. X).

38. *Everyman Remembers* (New York, 1931), p. 108.

39. *My Days and Dreams* (New York, 1916), pp. 86, 226.

40. In the collected *Letters of Olive Schreiner* are many letters that Ellis turned over to Cronwright-Schreiner. These were so butchered in cutting

that they are of very limited value. One of Ellis' biographers, Arthur Calder-Marshall, shrewdly observed that neither Cronwright nor Ellis did her service in that edition: "Olive's letters, dashed off on the spur of anxiety or transient emotion, appear hysterical and often fatuous. To print them was as unfair as to take a tape-recording of a casual conversation and then broadcast it as a public debate." (*The Sage of Sex* [New York, 1959], pp. 103–104). Wishing them destroyed was not a matter of prudery on Olive's part so much as a sensible realization that some of the letters, read out of context, would give a distorted image—as indeed they do.

41. In *My Life* Ellis said that Olive "disliked" the review (which had appeared in the *Indian Review*). "She said it reminded her of a man in South Africa with a horse for sale, who, after admitting a long list of appalling defects in the animal . . . wound up by declaring emphatically: 'But it's a damned fine horse!' " Ellis said that he could not altogether accept it "as fine art or as sound doctrine" but in general he had high praise for it: "What delighted me in *The African Farm* was, in part, the touch of genius, the freshness of its outlook, the firm splendour to its style, the penetration of its insight into the core of things" (*My Life: Autobiography of Havelock Ellis* [Boston, 1939], p. 226) . It has recently been suggested that Ellis' one novel, *Kanga Creek: An Australian Idyll* (1922, but based on his life as a schoolteacher in the brush in 1878), might have been influenced by *The African Farm*. See John Heuzenroeder, "Havelock Ellis' Australian Idyll," *Australian Literary Studies*, III (1967), 3–17.

42. *My Life*, p. 229.

43. In her letters to Ellis, Olive discussed her sexual problems freely, often seeking his medical as well as his psychological advice. He valued her confidences, but did not hesitate to use some of the material in his own psychosexual studies, apparently with her approval. The most candid expression of Olive's sex life appears in a case history in his *Studies in the Psychology of Sex*, I (1942) ("The Sexual Impulse in Women"), Appendix B, "The Development of the Sexual Instinct," History IX. Though not identified, the subject is unmistakably Olive:

> The subject belongs to a large family having some neurotic members; she spent her early life on a large farm. She is vigorous and energetic, has intellectual tastes, and is accustomed to think for herself, from unconventional standpoints, on many subjects. Her parents were very religious, and not, she thinks, of sensual temperament. Her own early life was free from associations of a sexual character, and she can recall little now that seems to be sexually significant in this respect. . . . Her activities went chiefly into humanitarian and utopian directions, and she cherished ideas of a large, healthy, free life, untrammelled by civilization. She regards herself as very passionate, but her sexual emotions appear to have developed very slowly and have been somewhat intellectualized. After reaching adult life she has formed several successive relationships with men to whom she has been attracted by affinity in tem-

perament, in intellectual views, and in tastes. These relationships have usually been followed by some degree of disillusion, and so have been dissolved. She does not believe in legal marriage, though under fitting circumstances she would much like to have a child.

She never masturbated till the age of 27. At that time a married friend told her that such a thing could be done. She found it gave her decided pleasure, indeed, more than coitus had ever given her except with one man. She has never practised it to excess, only at rare intervals, and is of the opinion that it is decidedly beneficial when thus moderately indulged in. She has sometimes found, for instance, that, after the mental excitement produced by delivering a lecture, sleep would be impossible if masturbation were not resorted to as a sedative to relieve the tension.

Spontaneous sexual excitement is strongest just before the monthly period.

Definite sexual dreams and sexual excitement during sleep have not occurred except possibly on one or two occasions.

She has from girlhood experienced erotic day-dreams, imagining love-stories of which she herself was the heroine; the climax of these stories has developed with her own developing knowledge of sexual matters.

44. *My Life,* p. 230.
45. *Letters,* p. 44.
46. *Ibid.,* pp. 55, 56, 117, 119, 60–61.
47. *Life,* pp. 169, 180.
48. *Letters,* p. 168.
49. *Ibid.,* p. 183.
50. J. G. Lockhart and C. M. Woodhouse, *Rhodes* (London, 1963), p. 20.
51. *Life,* pp. 279–80. Her italics.
52. A "non-official" invasion of Dutch territory by an English company under Dr. Leander Starr Jameson, a close associate of Rhodes.
53. Felix Gross, *Rhodes of Africa* (London, 1956), p. 310.
54. *Life,* p. 232.
55. *Ibid.,* p. 252.
56. *Letters,* p. 217.
57. *Life,* p. 271.
58. *Ibid.,* p. 275.
59. *Thoughts on South Africa,* p. 361. Her italics.
60. *Closer Union* (Cape Town, n.d. [1908]), pp. 25–26.
61. "Recent Books: French and English," *Blackwood's Edinburgh Magazine,* CLXI (April, 1897), 479.
62. *Spectator,* February 27, 1897, pp. 303–305.
63. *Letters,* pp. 69, 160, 146–47.
64. *Life,* p. 316.
65. *Ibid.,* p. 354.
66. *Testament of Youth: An Autobiographical Study of the Years 1900–1925* (New York, 1925), p. 41.
67. See above, note 43.
68.   Mrs. Bland ("E. Nesbit") was so kind to me before I left London. I don't think I should have got away without her. She came the last

morning to finish packing my things and see me off. Do you know, she's one of the noblest women. I can't tell you about her life, because I mustn't, but it's grand. The last night she lay by me on the bed and drew me very close to her and pressed her face against mine, and, do you know. I have felt it ever since. I am going to get better . . . (*Letters*, [to Ellis, October 22, 1888], pp. 143–44).

Doris Langley Moore, in *E. Nesbit: A Biography* (London, 1933), quotes this letter and several others exchanged between them. She comments: "It is a pity that my information on the friendship of these two women, admirably suited to each other in temperament and outlook, is extremely meager. Nothing further appears in my records but a post card from Matjesfontein, S. A., in 1890, saying, '. . . It's just to tell you that I never forget you. Please send me a line' " (p. 114).

69. I have such a strong feeling for Louie. When she put her arm around me on the sofa I wanted to cuddle close up to her, but I was ashamed. I liked it. I have such an odd feeling for her. You know when I tell you people have loved me or anything of that kind you must not tell anyone. Love that has been given to you is too sacred a thing to be talked of to anyone (don't you think so?) except just to the person who is like part of you and will feel it as you do (*Letters* [to Ellis, June, 29 1884], p. 23).

70. "The most important event of my childhood was the birth of a little sister, and my love for her has shaped all my life. I sometimes think my great love for women and girls, *not* because they are myself but because they are *not* myself, comes from my love to her" (*Letters* [to Mrs. Francis Smith, October 22, 1907], p. 274).

71. *Ibid.*, pp. 280–81, 88–89, 102.

72. *Life*, p. 185.

73. Hobman, *Olive Schreiner*, p. 63.

74. Arnold Bennett complained that there was too much "propaganda" in *From Man to Man*, though he admired the novel and conceded that it "demands, extorts laudation." Nevertheless, this is not the kind of complaint one would have read of *African Farm* in 1883: "A hundred pages might be cut out of the book, still leaving the story intact. When the two chief propagandists open their mouths they talk just like Olive Schreiner writes: which fact does not make for convincingness" (*The Savour of Life* [London, 1928], p. 308).

75. Preface, *From Man to Man* (New York, 1926), pp. xxvi–xxvii.

76. The best critical appreciation of *From Man to Man* (and a sound evaluation of the *African Farm*) is by Margaret A. Fairley, "The Novels of Olive Schreiner," *Dalhousie Review*, IX (July, 1929), 168–80.

77. *Letters*, p. 12.

78. *Ibid.*, p. 38.

79. Preface, *From Man to Man*, p. xxviii.

At the present moment two things about the Christian religion must surely be clear to anybody with eyes in his head. One is, that men cannot do without it; the other, that they cannot do with it as it is.
—Matthew Arnold, Preface, God and the Bible (1875)

I had set out on a journey, with no other purpose than that of exploring a certain province of natural knowledge; I strayed no hair's breadth from the course which it was my right and my duty to pursue; and yet I found that, whatever route I took, before long, I came to a tall and formidable-looking fence. Confident as I might be in the existence of an ancient and indefeasible right of way, before me stood the thorny barrier with its comminatory notice-board—"No Thoroughfare. By order. Moses." There seemed no way over; nor did the prospect of creeping round, as I saw some do, attract me. True there was no longer any cause to fear the spring guns and man-traps set by former lords of the manor; but one is apt to get very dirty going on all-fours. The only alternatives were either to give up my journey—which I was not minded to do—or to break the fence down and go through it.
—T. H. Huxley, Preface,
Science and Christian Tradition (1893)

". . . if you take four out of five of the more thoughtful and instructed men of the day, you will find that not only have they no faith in a personal God or a personal immortality, but the very notions of such things seem to them absurdities."
"Yes," said Mr. Herbert, "it was once thought a characteristic of the lowest savages to be without a belief in a future life. It will soon be thought a characteristic of the lowest savages to be with one."
—W. H. Mallock, The New Republic, Ch. III (1877)

3.

Light on a Darkling Plain:
Mrs. Humphry Ward

I

It is a telling comment on Victorianism that one of its leading family dynasties was not Marlborough, Medici, Borgia, Fugger, or Rothschild, but Arnold. The founder of this line was not a warrior, a statesman, a banker, or a patron of the arts, but a clergyman and schoolmaster. Though some of his descendants practiced the arts of criticism, poetry, and fiction, not one of them deviated from the family mission of public service and education. Teaching was with them an ethical imperative. Matthew Arnold wrote:

> There is a view in which all the love of our neighbour, the impulses toward action, help and beneficence, the desire for removing human error, clearing human confusion, and diminishing human misery, the noble aspiration to leave the world better and happier than we found it—motives such as are called social—come in as part of the grounds of culture, and the main and pre-eminent part (*Culture and Anarchy*, Ch. I).

The Arnolds even married within that tradition—W. E. Forster (husband of Jane Arnold), liberal politician and reformer whose Education Bill of 1870 established a national system of elementary schools in England; Leonard Huxley (husband of Julia Arnold), son of the scientist and polemicist in the cause of science, Thomas Henry Huxley; Thomas Humphry Ward (husband of Mary Augusta Arnold), Oxford tutor, editor and art critic; G. M. Trevelyan (husband of Janet Ward), historian and Oxford professor. Down into the twentieth century their offspring have pursued the course of education, formally or informally, by lecturing, teaching, and writing.

The Arnolds were not a royal dynasty, but early and permanently associated with them was a cachet of *noblesse oblige*. In a bourgeois, secular society they represented an ideal—the cultivated mind and conscience, the aristocracy of learning, dedicated public service and ethical conduct, the religion not so much of the Book as of the book. What is curious to us today about their careers is their enormous popular success and influence in their own times. Every modern society has produced its share of educators, critics and social reformers, but in Victorian England they enjoyed a unique prestige. Measured in practical terms, their power was probably negligible. Rather than influencing social action, they registered or reflected certain significant trends in public opinion, most especially the zeal for self-improvement and, in the old Calvinist-Utilitarian spirit, the recognition that since self and society were mutually dependent, social reform was morally as well as practically imperative upon the individual.

The Arnolds reflected more. Not only did their collective effort epitomize the positive, energetic, progressive thrust of Victorian society. Simultaneously it reflected the doubt, confusion, and frequently the despair of their age. The complacency of the Establishment, the sublime dogmatism of the Evangelicals, the healthy but often mindless vigor of Kingsley's "muscular Christianity," were notably absent with them. Instead there was a sensibility of conscience that in some members of the family led to painful religious conflict, in others to morbid melancholy, and in still others to outright protest and action. Oddly enough, it was a female Arnold, Mary Augusta, later Mrs. Humphry Ward, who proved the most effectually active of the crusading Arnolds. No rebel, certainly no iconoclast, indeed as staid and genteel a figure as Victorian society ever produced, she wielded a more powerful influence on the religious thinking of her day and achieved more concrete social reform than did her grandfather Thomas Arnold of Rugby fame or her uncle Matthew. No creative thinker or artist in her own right, she was endowed only with high intelligence, fervent moral conviction, and a warm feminine sympathy for the sufferings—intellectual, spiritual and practical—of others. The Victorians often confused such talents as these for genius, but in no era are they to be underestimated.

Her medium was the novel. Through it she reached a wider audience than Matthew Arnold reached through poetry and criticism. He was the artist, she merely the polemicist. He has endured, she is today unread—and no one can question the justice of that verdict. What one does question today is the reason for her popularity as a novelist in her own time. The publishing phenomenon of *Robert Elsmere,* that record-smashing best-seller of the late 1880's in both England and America, is mystifying to the modern reader of the novel. One can account for most best-sellers, of the period—Marie Corelli, Hall Caine, M. E. Braddon —on grounds of their vulgarity and sensationalism. But *Robert Elsmere* and the dozen or so novels that Mrs. Ward produced after it, almost all of them financial successes if not best-sellers, are neither vulgar nor sensational. To explain their popularity one must look not at the novels themselves so much as at the public who bought and presumably read them.

Mrs. Ward's understanding of the psychology of her readers was based to some extent on a shrewd, businesslike insight into public taste. But it was also the result of her wholehearted identification with that public. Her attitude, to be sure, was condescending. The strain of Arnold in her kept her always figuratively on the lecture platform, a level above the mass of her readers. But even if slightly *de haut en bas,* she was one with her readers and their middle-class aspirations. Readers recognized in her high-mindedness and didacticism not a patronizing contempt for their ignorance, but an earnest respect for their desire for enlightenment and self-improvement. She complimented them by considering them capable of absorbing profound issues of theology and philosophy, learned disquisitions on history and literature, long debates on politics and social reform. The shopkeeper, the housewife, the romantic young girl, may have choked a little on passages like this one from *Robert Elsmere,* but they swallowed them down bravely and went on:

> To plunge into the Christian period without having first cleared the mind as to what is meant in history and literature by "the critical method," which in history may be defined as the "science of what is credible," and in literature as "the science of what is rational," is to invite fiasco. The theologian in such a state sees no obstacle to accepting an arbitrary list of documents with all the strange stuff they may contain, and declaring them to be sound historical material, while he applies to all the strange stuff of a similar kind surrounding them the most rigorous principles of modern science. Or he has to make believe that the reasoning processes exhibited in the speeches of the Acts, in certain passages of St. Paul's Epistles, or in the Old Testament quotations in the Gospels, have a validity for the mind of the nineteenth century, when in truth they are the imperfect, half-childish products of the mind of the first century, of quite insignificant or indirect value to the historian of fact, of enormous value to the historian of testimony and its varieties (Ch. XXIV).[1]

Perhaps the highest tribute one could pay Mrs. Ward was made by a critic who disliked her work intensely, William Lyon Phelps: "She has a well-furnished and highly developed intellect; she is deeply read; she makes her readers think that they are thinking." [2] And thinking they were. We have come to recognize more clearly today the profound ethical-moral-intellectual revolutions that were stirring up the later years of Victorianism. Our faulty conception of the age as one of stuffy, rigid, smug conservatism is being sharply revised. We know now that thinking Englishmen in the last century were keenly aware of the crumbling away of the foundations of their religious faith and of the challenges to the established social order rising everywhere. Their zeal for education reflected their desire to understand the swiftly changing world around them. Not all reacted in such despair and panic as W. H. Mallock's Mr. Leslie in *The New Republic:* ". . . in the views of the world at large there have been great changes; and these, I say, have come on us with so astonishing quickness that they have plunged us into a state of mental anarchy that has not been equalled since mental order has been known . . . . All society, it seems, is going to pieces" (Ch. III). But all *reacted,* in some fashion or another.

It was Mrs. Ward's genius to have seized precisely the issues of most burning public interest—religion, politics, social reform —and to have framed these in the relatively attractive form of fiction. She added the piquancy of story to the statistics of parliamentary Blue Books, the rhetoric of the pulpit, and the recondite speculations of the learned journals. The Master of Balliol, Benjamin Jowett, admired *Robert Elsmere* but wrote off its success as "really due to what everybody else is thinking." [3] The grand old man Gladstone, though alarmed at the religious skepticism of the novel, praised its earnestness and sincerity and recognized that it was "eminently an offspring of the time . . . [which] will probably make a deep, or at least a very sensible impression, not however among mere novel readers, but among those who share, in whatever sense, the deeper thought of the period." [4] Even its most disapproving critics, who found absolutely no literary or artistic merit in the book, grudgingly conceded, as did Rowland Prothero in the *Edinburgh Review* (April, 1892), that "she gave utterance—however hesitating and uncertain the voice—to some indeterminate, inarticulate, but widespread feeling that needed expression."

Such a comment as this last, indeed, epitomizes critical reaction to all of Mrs. Ward's novels. Her books said what her readers wanted to hear—not so much smugly confirming their prejudices and preconceptions as airing their questions, marshaling pertinent evidence and information, and finally guiding but not pushing them to a more rational, enlightened position. Mrs. Ward's readers knew that, although more learned than most of them, she was "one of us." And she in turn knew that she could count on their sympathetic response and cooperation. More than twenty years after the first great success of *Robert Elsmere,* in a preface to the Westmoreland edition of the novel, she wrote:

At a moment when the particular ideas put forward have a high degree of life and significance for a great many people, the public in a sense cooperates in the book. Such a novel as "Robert Elsmere" is entirely related to a particular time and milieu; and those who are drawn to read it, unconsciously lend it their own thoughts, the passion of their own assents and denials. Some happy chance bestows on a novel this suggestive, symbolic character; and the reader's eager sympathy, or antagonism, completes the effort of the writer.

Furthermore, Mrs. Ward's novels appealed to the essential idealism of her nineteenth-century readers. Her settings were always roughly contemporary, even when she drew on historical materials for her plots (the Lady Caroline Lamb-Byron relationship in *The Marriage of William Ashe,* the life of the painter George Romney in *Fenwick's Career,* the rivalry between Julie de l'Espinasse and Mme du Deffand in *Lady Rose's Daughter,* the marriage of Lord and Lady Holland in *Eltham House*). The English society that they portrayed was sufficiently realistic in detail—precise geographical setting and minute description of clothes, furniture, and customs—but its image was highly idealized and reflects a widespread ambivalence—the desire to see England as simultaneously the guardian of a proud old aristocratic tradition and the leader of vigorous progressive reform. Her most sympathetic characters are crusaders but not rebels. They fight valiantly to correct, improve, ameliorate, but they cherish their old country houses, they marry within their social class, and they have no intentions of upsetting tradition. Even her most ambitious middle-class readers relished Mrs. Ward's romantic nostalgia for the past. They delighted in passages like this one from *The Marriage of William Ashe* describing a costume ball where all the guests are dressed as figures from English history:

It is said that as a nation the English have no gift for pageants. Yet every now and then—as no doubt in the Elizabethan mask—they show a strange felicity in the art. Certainly the dance that followed would have been difficult to surpass even in the ripe days and motherlands of pageantry.

To the left, a long line, consisting mainly of young girls in their first bloom, dressed as Gainsborough and his great contemporaries delighted to paint those flowers of England— the folds of plain white muslin crossed over the young breast, a black velvet at the throat, a rose in the hair, the simple skirt showing the small pointed feet, and sometimes a broad sash defining the slender waist. Here were Stanleys, Howards, Percys, Villierses, Butlers, Osbornes—soft slips of girls bearing the names of England's rough and turbulent youth, bearing themselves tonight with a shy or laughing dignity, as though the touch of history and romance were on them. And facing them, the youths of the same families, no less handsome than their sisters and brides—in Romney's blue coats, or the splendid red of Reynolds and Gainsborough (Ch. X).

At the same time, however, her readers were moving with the currents of change and progress. Inside the drawing rooms of stately old country houses her aristocratic characters debate politics; then they go forth to Parliament, to settlement houses in the slums, to the cottages of the workers in the fields or the miners—legislating reform, nursing, teaching. Some of her most romantic heroes, like Aldous Raeburn in *Marcella* and Sir George Tressady, are descendants of those young aristocrats in Disraeli's novels who were impelled almost religiously by a sense of their duty to society. Her heroine Marcella may have sounded girlishly naive to some contemporary readers, but she spoke for a good many of them: "The time has come for a wider basis. Paternal government and charity were very well in their way—democratic self-government will manage to do without them!"

Time and experience mellow but do not substantially alter these views. Enlightened social reform, Mrs. Ward tells her readers—with their warm approval—is not only a practical necessity but a religious obligation. Man ultimately serves God best by serving his fellowmen. Thus Raeburn, now Lord Maxwell and leader of his political party reasons:

The vast extension of the individual will and power which science has brought to humanity during the last hundred

years was always present to him as food for a natural exultation—a kind of pledge of the boundless prospects of the race.
On the other hand, the struggle of society brought face to
face with this huge increment of the individual power,
forced to deal with it for its own higher and mysterious
ends, to moralise and socialise it lest it should destroy itself
and the State altogether; the slow steps by which the modern
community has succeeded in asserting itself against the
individual, in protecting the weak from his weakness, the
poor from his poverty, in defending the woman and child
from the fierce claims of capital, in forcing upon trade after
trade the axiom that no man may lawfully build his wealth
upon the exhaustion and degradation of his fellow—these
things stirred in him the far deeper enthusiasms of the moral
nature. Nay more! Together with all the other main facts
which mark the long travail of man's ethical and social
nature, they were among the only "evidences" of religion a
critical mind allowed itself—the most striking signs of something "greater than we know" working among the dust and
ugliness of our common day. Attack wealth as wealth, possession as possession, and civilisation is undone. But bring
the force of the social conscience to bear as keenly and ardently as you may, upon the separate activities of factory
and household, farm and office; and from the results you
will only get a richer individual freedom, one more illustration of the divinest law man serves—that he must "die to
live," must surrender to obtain (*Sir George Tressady,* Ch.
VII).

Granted the hunger of Mrs. Ward's public for knowledge
and enlightenment, it is still difficult to reconcile such passages
as these with the facts of best-sellerdom. This was, to be sure, a
public that devoured other equally weighty novels. J. H. Shorthouse's formidably erudite *John Inglesant,* that fictitious adult
education course in seventeenth-century English theology, was
another best-seller contemporary with *Robert Elsmere.* But Mrs.
Ward's high rank among popular novelists over the next three
decades was not won by scholarship alone. It was the result of
her instinctive grasp of her public's tastes and desires—for knowledge, for comforting reassurance of their social and political con-

victions, but, equally, for entertainment. She entertained her readers fundamentally in the same ways as did her less highly respected literary colleagues: only with the difference that she shunned their overt vulgarity and shrillness, their flamboyance and exaggeration. Her education, her good taste, her Arnoldian sense of mission saved her from their excesses, but not from their subject matter. After *Elsmere* her novels show a steadily increasing attention to elements of popular best-sellerdom—licit and illicit love, intrigue, family secrets, "fast" upper-class society, adultery, illegitimacy, sordid slum poverty, graphic details of physical suffering, deathbeds, morbid states of mind.

This is not to suggest that Mrs. Ward was succumbing to the contagions of Zolaism, which she honestly deplored.[5] She continued, without a trace of hypocrisy, to affirm the values of her bourgeois Victorian society; the wicked are punished; the innocent who sin through error or accident must suffer; marriage vows are sacred. Perhaps unconsciously, out of sheer innocence, Mrs. Ward made the best of both worlds. On the other hand, observing her keen intelligence and her lively interest in society, it is difficult to believe that she was not perfectly conscious of what she was doing. She was marketing her product. But she was also faithfully and diligently guiding that public *up* to her standards. She was the observer and recorder of the present, but also the guardian of tradition. By reading her novels in chronological order, one can trace the development of English moral sensibilities from Victorianism through World War I.

In *Robert Elsmere* she sprinkled just enough delicate touches of romance to refresh the reader in intermissions from the heady theological passages that form the bulk of her novel. Once she had tasted fame with *Elsmere,* however, Mrs. Ward courted her public more openly. Her next novel, *The History of David Grieve,* introduced a rebellious young girl who goes off to live in the wild bohemia of Paris and is sufficiently corrupted to tease the thrill-seeking public and sufficiently punished to satisfy the proper Victorian. From there on Mrs. Ward proceeded cautiously but steadily, growing more daring as her society grew more "modern." In 1903, in *Lady Rose's Daughter,* she introduced a heroine who is illegitimate, determined to run away with a man who will not marry her, yet who ends not in tragedy but as the wife of a duke. Mrs. Ward acknowledged that her heroine's rescue from disgrace was a defect in the book, but significantly she calls it an artistic rather than a moral mistake—"a certain treachery to the artistic conscience."[6] As for the "sin" of the heroine's mother, Lady Rose, who leaves a cold, straitlaced husband for another man, Mrs. Ward seeks moral support in the best literary precedents: "Colonel Delaney [the husband] made the penalties of it as heavy as he could. Like Karennine in Tolstoy's great novel he refused to sue for a divorce, and for something of the same reasons. Divorce was in itself impious, and sin should not be made easy."

Not all her heroines are so lucky, but their fates are often more interesting for their melodrama than for their morality.[7] The intrigue-filled story of another illegitimate young girl is introduced into the theological novel *The Case of Richard Meynell* (1911), obviously to leaven and spice the solemn material of the book. After being tricked into a false marriage by a scoundrel, this unfortunate girl wanders off in a snowstorm, falls over a precipice, and dies in agony. The heroine of *The Testing of Diana Mallory* (1906), spotlessly virtuous herself, suffers bitterly for the sins of her mother, a gambler and a murderess. Certainly Mrs. Ward's most appealing heroines from the point of view of the literary marketplace, are her impetuous, headstrong beauties who destroy themselves but win the author's, and presumably the reader's, pity and forgiveness. Typical of these is the charming but neurotic Kitty Ashe in *The Marriage of William Ashe* (1905). Kitty is an Edwardian "golden girl," a kind of ancestor to those beautiful, reckless heroines in F. Scott Fitzgerald a generation later. We deplore her destructiveness, but the author loves her and wants her readers to share that love. Kitty travels in a "fast" set, the Archangels (obviously modeled on the glittering and exclusive "Souls," that informal club of which Lord Curzon, Arthur James Balfour, and Margot Tennant were members). She smokes cigarettes and flirts outrageously. All this her handsome, rich, adoring, politically ambitious husband accepts tolerantly. But when she writes a novel exposing his political secrets, he finally leaves her. Her "sin" however, is nothing so innocuous as novel-writing. Distraught and betrayed by a jealous rival, she runs away with another man—a satanic, Byronic figure—and she pays amply. The lover treats her brutally, and she dies, painfully and penitently, of tuberculosis.

The pattern in its broadest outlines is too clear-cut to be merely accidental and unconscious. Mrs. Ward knew well enough that she was writing on the level of women's magazinery. Her heroines' clothes are from Worth, described down to the last ribbon and bit of expensive lace. Their jewels, their furs, their coiffures—all conform to a conventionally romantic scheme. The doors of smart Mayfair townhouses and fine old country houses are opened wide for her readers: the furnishings, the pictures on the walls, the menus, the smallest details of social behavior—nothing that would intrigue and delight the "common" reader escapes her camera eye. She courted that reader persistently, even attempting to enlarge her public by dramatizing some of her novels and by writing one original play. Characteristically, she plunged into the theater with vigor and worked as conscientiously at her plays as at her novels. But for the most part her efforts were disastrous. *Eleanor,* one of her most popular novels, was both a critical and a financial failure on the London stage in 1902, although Mrs. Ward had worked with a competent playwright, Julian Sturgis, on the dramatization, and it had a well-known cast that included Marion Terry and Elizabeth Robins. Undaunted, she wrote to the actress Eleanor Robson (Mrs. August Belmont) that "with all its harangues and the fatal flaw of Manisty's character [it] was very nearly a business success . . . and that simply because of its naturalness and truth of dialogue and feeling." [8] The original play *Agatha* (1903), a melodrama about a young girl's discovery of her illegitimacy, was written in collaboration with the professional playwright Louis N. Parker. It opened in New York with Eleanor Robson in the leading role, and (Parker recalled in his autobiography) "was greeted with every token of respect, like any other funeral." [9] Mrs. Ward made one last effort to capture the stage, dramatizing *The Marriage of William Ashe* in collaboration with Margaret

Mayo in 1905. This play had something of a run in stock companies in the United States, but its London production in 1908 closed after three weeks.

In all these attempts to woo the public Mrs. Ward displayed a curious mixture of vanity, shrewdness, and naïveté. There is something almost disarming in her sublime faith in her work, a trust and self-confidence that made it possible for her to stand, on the one hand, as the guardian and mentor of an idealistic, earnest public and, on the other, as a purveyor of sex and sensafionalism. Mrs. Ward's heroes and heroines are full of "rushing passions" and "trembling yearnings." But all is described in respectable literary language, with none of the shrillness and grammatical solecisms of Marie Corelli or M. E. Braddon. The young and innocent reader could not be corrupted by Mrs. Ward; the more worldly reader could make of her what he would: "Falloden's sense approved her wholly: the white dress; the hat that framed her brow; the slender gold chains that rose and fell on her gently rounded breast; her height and grace. Passion beat within him" (*Lady Connie,* Ch. IV).

Such a passage indicates the limits of Mrs. Ward's pre-Freudian innocence; her novels abound with similar ones. Human passion was exalted to romantic stereotype. Relations between the sexes, though at times represented as unhappy, were more often idealized and seen through a haze of romantic convention. Even more romantically idealized were relations between women. A good deal of the passion felt by Mrs. Ward's female characters is sublimated in relationships that modern readers would immediately designate as lesbian. To Mrs. Ward, however, these served as decorous outlets for her characters' passions while, at the same time, they were not only proper but even poetic and elevating. Such relationships flourished both in fiction and in real life in the nineteenth century. George Eliot, Mrs. Browning, Dinah Mulock Craik, and Jane Carlyle had circles of adoring female friends and disciples. Mrs. Ward herself, apparently fulfilled in her marriage and in motherhood, had ardent female admirers. What her novels reflect, therefore, is far more romantic convention than sexual perversion or repression.[10]

Nevertheless, one must acknowledge that the total effect of

such implied, latent, or merely accidental sexuality helped to sell her books. One of her greatest popular successes, for example, was *Eleanor* (1900), a vastly ambitious novel. Its purpose was nothing less than to portray the whole "revolution" of modern Italy, a country that Mrs. Ward had adopted in her prosperity as a second home and loved deeply. To an extent, she succeeds in her purpose. She surveys with exhausting thoroughness the total condition of Italy at the end of the nineteenth century (with a guidebook tour of the campagna thrown in to emphasize the contrasts between the ancient and the modern world)—the war in Abyssinia, the civil struggles, the battle within the Roman Church between modernism and conservatism. To heighten and render palatable her quite profound exposition, she weaves it into a love triangle involving an aging and sickly widow Eleanor, her intellectual cousin Edward Manisty, who is writing a book on Italy, and an innocent young American visitor, Lucy. Eleanor is brilliant, sensitive, grieving over a tragic past but clinging to life because she loves her cousin and is helping him with his book. She recognizes Lucy as a rival long before the younger girl or Manisty is aware of their mutual attraction. Desperately, Eleanor takes Lucy away to a remote village in the mountains. For a while the women live alone, Lucy nursing and worshiping the older woman: "The two fell into each other's embrace. Lucy, with the maternal tenderness that should have been Eleanor's, pressed her lips on the hot brow that lay upon her breast, murmuring words of promise, of consolation, of self-reproach, feeling her whole being passing out to Eleanor's in a great tide of passionate will and pity" (Ch. XII). Ultimately, Eleanor realizes the wrong she is doing, brings the lovers together, and dies in tearful but happy self-sacrifice.

What is most striking about *Eleanor* to the modern reader— and what begins to emerge as a recurring motif in Mrs. Ward's novels—is an emotional debauch innocent in intention, no doubt, but profoundly disturbing in its implications. At the root of her most serious and elevated fiction there is a sickly morbidity that undeniably appealed to a proper middle-class reading public. The simple pathos of the popular Victorian deathbed scenes is missing, but in its place there is an obsession with disease (many of her characters die gratuitously of painful, lingering illnesses) and suffering. "How ill she is," a character observes of Eleanor, "and how distinguished!" At the climax of the novel, in a passionate plea to Lucy to marry the man they both love, Eleanor lets her dressing gown fall from her shoulders:

> She showed the dark hollows under the wasted collar-bones, the knife-like shoulders, the absolute disappearance of all that had once made the difference between grace and emaciation. She held up her hands before the girl's terrified eyes. The skin was still white and delicate, otherwise they were the hands of a skeleton.
>
> "You can look at *that*," she said fiercely, under her breath—"and then insult me by refusing to marry the man you love, because you choose to remember that I was once in love with him" (Ch. XXV).

Mrs. Ward produced her own version of Gothic horror. Her learning, her serious intentions and keen intelligence gave her novels their critical distinction in their time, but there were other attractions about them. In accounting for her popularity, therefore, one must measure not only the particular qualities of the Victorian public—their earnestness and eagerness for knowledge—but the general nature of readers seeking thrills and forbidden delights. Consciously or unconsciously, Mrs. Ward exploited both sources to the fullest and reaped rich rewards.

II

Robert Elsmere was Mrs. Ward's second novel. She was thirty-seven at the time of its publication, mother of three children, wife of a member of the editorial staff of the London *Times,* and herself already a writer of some experience, having published many solid critical articles in *Macmillan's Magazine* and other periodicals, a highly respected translation of Frederic Amiel's *Journal Intime,* sketches of medieval Spanish kings and ecclesiastics in Bishop Wace's edition of Smith's *Dictionary of Christian Biography,* and, on the lighter side, a novel, *Miss*

Bretherton, and a book for children, *Milly and Olly.* But *Elsmere* was a single stroke of good fortune. Overnight it brought her fame and money. It was not merely a popular best-seller, but a novel that stirred intellectual circles everywhere. Its serious, conscientious, honest presentation of heated religious controversies was admired even by those whe deplored the author's "free thinking." It is Mrs. Ward's best novel, bringing together her talents for scholarship, orderly presentation and intelligent analysis of ideas, and reasoned polemicism. It is also her most interesting novel, because it faithfully represents a past era of intellectual history. One *trusts* Mrs. Ward as a register of her times, however little one *enjoys* her as a novelist.

Elsmere is also significant as a document in the autobiography of Mrs. Ward. Not an autobiographical novel, it is nevertheless a revealing portrait of both the life and the mind of its author. Like most less than first-rate novelists, Mrs. Ward had a very limited imagination. She never rose above literal reality of scene. Even when she used historical materials, as we have already noted, she set her stories in the present. She studied and observed prodigiously and never wrote a line of description or exposition that could not have been fully documented. *Elsmere* is a work of the imagination only to the extent that it is cast in the form of a novel. Many of its characters have been identified. Only one of these, Professor Grey (the Oxford philosopher T. H. Green to whose memory she dedicated the book), was actually modeled from life, but Mrs. Ward could not deny that there were many resemblances to identifiable people.[11] The whole impulse of the novel was a lecture that she had heard at Oxford in 1881 attacking the modernists in the church. She was so aroused that she dashed off a pamphlet in rebuttal, then spent the next three years developing and dramatizing these arguments in her novel.

But *Elsmere* reflects more than intellectual experience. It is also the expression of Mrs. Ward's childhood and young womanhood, and it brings together the three main streams of influence and activity that shaped her life: Oxford (both as a social community and as a center of learning), religious thought, and social reform. Her hero's youthful mind is stimulated in the lecture halls and libraries of the university; his religious faith is challenged and transformed into a new Christian ethic practiced as he moves from the shelter of the Church of England into the harsh realities of social work in the London slums. This does not precisely describe the course of Mrs. Ward's life, but it does reflect its general outlines. In specific detail it mirrors the crises in the lives of her parents, the philosophy of Green, who influenced her so strongly at Oxford, and the remarkable work that she was to do later in establishing settlement houses for the London poor.

Mary Augusta Arnold was the eldest daughter of Thomas, second son of Dr. Thomas Arnold of Rugby, that celebrated educator who shaped a whole generation of Victorian intellectuals —Arthur Hugh Clough, Arthur Stanley, and not the least by any means, his own sons, Matthew, Thomas, and William. William went out to India as Director of Public Instruction of the Punjab and died at thirty-one, but not before producing one interesting novel based on his experiences, *Oakfield, or Fellowship in the East* (1855.)[12] It is a somber book in which the hero leaves a happy, sheltered Oxford environment, driven by a vague melancholia that gradually ripens into painful religious skepticism:

> In some things I still love the Church of England;—the gentlemanly element in it . . . of its ordinances and rituals, —so satisfying to one's mere taste . . . but when I think of its wretched sectarian spirit . . . of its profession, so magnificently exalted, and its practice, so often standing in the way of, and even persecuting, the Truth, I shudder at the thought of yielding myself to it (Ch. II).

Matthew's achievement needs no chronicling here, save the observation that, like his brothers, he was deeply troubled by religious doubts. Thomas was the most seriously disturbed of the three. He vacillated painfully between reliance on authority and independence, embraced Roman Catholicism as a convert, then abandoned it to return to the Church of England, then reconverted and remained in the Catholic Church until his death.

It is ironic that the elder Arnold, who had so unflinchingly met the challenges of the nineteenth century to Church and tradition, should have produced three sons who were almost overwhelmed by them. Matthew, hewing closest to his father's line, worked out his "secular religion" by rejecting dogma and practicing his faith in "culture," in educating and refining the sensibilities of the English public. His outlook was infinitely more complex than his father's, but they shared the same spirit. Both were public educators. What James Martineau wrote of the father he might equally have observed of the son: "Though Arnold's great work lay at Rugby, and he achieved it in a way which was soon felt in every public school in England, his sympathies were not collected there; they were interwoven with society at every fibre, and bled with the wounds of humanity everywhere." [13]

Physically, Mary Arnold is said to have resembled her uncle Matthew more than she resembled her father.[14] Spiritually, too, she seems to have had a greater affinity with him and with the grandfather who had died nine years before her birth. Yet she always had sympathy for her father, with his "spiritual face" and "his gentle, hesitating ways," tolerating with no trace of bitterness his vacillations and the many practical difficulties that they caused his family. With a warmth far more apparent in her life than in her writing, she respected his troubled, idealistic conscience, although she did not, to any large extent, understand it. She described him as a young man:

Moved by a young and democratic despair of the conditions of life, social and political, in the Old World, Thomas Arnold, like Philip Hewson in the "Bothie of Tober-na-Vuolich"—his partial portrait, indeed, at the hand of his dear friend, Arthur Clough,—went out, in 1847, to seek for "simpler manners, purer laws" in the Colonies.[15]

Thomas Arnold settled first in New Zealand, but having no success in farming, he moved on to Tasmania as an inspector of schools. There he met, and in 1850 married Julia Sorrell, a descendant of one of the governors of Tasmania and, distantly, of a Spanish Protestant family who had fled to France and then to England in search of religious freedom. The staunch Huguenot strain in Julia was sorely tried by her marriage. In 1856 Thomas Arnold was received into the Roman Catholic Church in Hobart Town, Tasmania, and shortly thereafter, because he was a Catholic, he was relieved of his official appointment. The reasons for Arnold's first conversion are obscure. In his autobiography, *Passages in a Wandering Life*, he says only that for ten years his mind "had been in a welter of uncertainty on the subject of religious truth." [16] As a youth at Oxford he had been indifferent to the Oxford Movement. He had rooms in the High Street, directly across the road from St. Mary's, where Newman was at that time preaching his epoch-making sermons; only once did he bother to go to hear Newman, and he was unimpressed. But years later, on the other side of the world, he felt the call. The ironies of his conversion were many—most particularly the fact that the elder Arnold had vehemently opposed the Oxford Movement. Newman himself appreciated this irony, writing to Thomas of his conversion: "How strange it seems! What a world this is! I knew your father a little, and I really think I never had any unkind feeling toward him. . . . If I ever said a harsh thing against him I am very sorry for it. In seeing you, I should have a sort of pledge that he at the moment of his death made it all up with me." [17]

At the time of his conversion, Thomas and Julia Arnold had three young children—Mary, born June 11, 1851, and two sons, William and Theodore. Jobless and homeless, the family made the long, difficult journey back to England and threw themselves upon the generosity of the Arnold clan, who responded warmly. The elder Dr. Arnold's widow was living at Fox How, a substantial grey stone farm house in the Lake Country of Westmoreland, which her husband had built for his family. Though not the castle of a royal dynasty, it had awe-inspiring associations for the Arnolds, who worshiped literature as others worshiped royalty. This was Wordsworth country. The old poet himself had been dead six years when Thomas and his family returned to England, but his spirit, and the memory of his friendship with the elder Thomas and his visits to Fox How, were fresh. Mary Arnold's grandmother, her uncle Matthew, and her aunt Jane also had lively recollections of visits from Charlotte Brontë and Harriet Martineau. Here too Mary's father had long visits from his boyhood friend, the poet Clough. Literature, education, and service to the poor and less fortunate of the neighborhood were part of the air that little Mary breathed at Fox How. And the countryside itself left its mark on her—a delight in nature that is reflected in the lengthy but impressively faithful descriptive scenes of her novels, the most popular of which are set in this region.

Unhappily, Fox How was not to be the family's permanent home. As a Catholic, Thomas Arnold was severely restricted in his opportunities for employment. For five years they lived in Dublin, where he taught English literature at the new Catholic University of which Newman was the first rector. In 1862 he received an appointment as classical master at the Oratory in Edgbaston, Birmingham, now working directly under Newman. The family was poor and insecure. Following the custom in religiously mixed marriages, the boys were reared in their father's faith; Mary remained Protestant. Like many girls of her class and generation, she received a schooling, rather than an education, that was at best useless and at worst fostered a child's natural ignorance.[18] Her first school had at least the virtue of association with the family of her father's friend Clough. It was a small, genteel establishment in Ambleside, run by Clough's spinster sister Anne. Here Mary had relative freedom to ramble in the countryside she loved and to tell stories of her own invention to her classmates. At nine she was sent to a more formal "school for young ladies" in Shropshire—all Spartan discipline and bourgeois snobbery. Accepted at lower fees because of her family's prestige, she suffered the agonies of chilly rooms, poor food, and the bitter knowledge of her social and financial inferiority to her classmates.

Small wonder then that her father's break with Rome in 1865—as difficult to account for as his initial conversion—and his subsequent establishment at Oxford as a tutor and editor meant liberation and a new world for her. Fourteen, impressionable,

hungry for learning, she slipped into Oxford life, she wrote, "as
a fish into water." Although she lived there only some fifteen
years, in a sense she never left it. Her attachment to the university was as much sentimental as it was intellectual. Oxford's
beauty and antiquity, its identification with the Establishment,
with the proudest traditions of English history and culture, fundamentally appealed to her Arnoldian conservatism. But simultaneously its thriving intellectual activity—the still recent memory of Newman, the brilliant scholarship of Jowett and Pattison,
the treasures of the Bodleian—stimulated that other, almost contradictory, Arnoldian spirit of restless, persistent industry and
self-improvement. She attended lectures and eagerly soaked up
dinner-table conversations:

> There was in me, I think, a real hunger to learn, and a very
> quick sense of romance in things or people. But after sixteen,
> except in music, I had no definite teaching, and everything
> I learned came to me from persons—and books—sporadically,
> without any general guidance or plan. It was all a great voy-
> age of discovery, organized mainly by myself, on the advice
> of a few men and women very much older, who took an
> interest in me and were endlessly kind to the shy and shape-
> less creature I must have been.[19]

Reading independently in the Bodleian, she worked up a mastery of Spanish literature sufficient to impress even the visiting
French critic Hippolyte Taine. She was a solemn, earnest young
girl, whose friends described her as "handsome" rather than
pretty. But she was no Dorothea Brooke seeking a Casaubon.
Her marriage in 1872 to Thomas Humphry Ward was as romantic as any girl in her circumstances might have hoped for. Young,
a clergyman's son, and a fellow of Brasenose College, he had already distinguished himself for scholarship and for wit, having
contributed to a slender volume of local college humor called
The Oxford Spectator (1869). Years later, when Mrs. Ward's
novels brought her great wealth, a story was circulated about
their romance. The American Constance Fenimore Woolson reported it in a letter to a friend:

There is a pretty story told of her. She fell in love with Ward, and nearly broke her heart about him. For she had no money at all—in England a sine qua non; I mean that money is—and as he had none, his friends were thoroughly opposed to his saddling himself with such heavy responsibilities, young as he was. . . . Finally he did marry "poor Mary," as people were calling her. And now behold his reward! [20]

They began life in a modest house in Oxford where they entertained a small but select group of friends and neighbors— the German philologist Max Müller and his family, Walter Pater and his sisters, the Pattisons, Jowett—in rooms "aesthetically" decorated with Morris wallpaper and filled with small art objects that Ward, a connoisseur and later art critic for the *Times,* was already beginning to collect. Babies came quickly, and the Wards supplemented his meager teaching income with writing assignments. He began editing the monumental English Poets series, on which she assisted him, and contributed articles to the *Saturday Review.* Mrs. Ward, who had launched her literary career with stories in childhood and a three-volume novel at seventeen, now turned industriously to nonfiction, writing for the *Saturday Review,* the *Dictionary of Christian Biography,* and—with the confidence and experience of a young mother of three—a pamphlet on infant feeding which she distributed in the Oxford slums. In what little spare time she had she organized programs of adult education for women, helped to raise money for the establishment of a women's college at Oxford, and had her first taste of the social welfare work to which she later gave much of her energy.

Altogether it was a useful, happy existence—an Arnold ideal of service and intellectual activity. The only blot was Thomas Arnold's return, in 1876, to Catholicism. He had distinguished himself at Oxford for his teaching and for his excellent edition of the English sermons of the medieval church reformer John Wyclif and was on the point of being named to the Oxford Professorship of Early English when he made his decision, once again plunging his family into social and financial embarrassment. A year later his wife developed cancer, and although she survived for several years, she suffered horribly. These blows darkened Mrs. Ward's happiness but could not obscure the generally bright promise of her life. Their financial position improved considerably in 1881, when Humphry Ward joined the staff of the London *Times*. They moved to London, rented an old but cheerful house in Russell Square, and settled into an even busier life than they had had at Oxford. Mrs. Ward's friend John Morley, then editing *Macmillan's Magazine,* invited her to contribute critical essays which he called "causeries," and from 1883 to 1885 this fledgling Sainte-Beuve published a number of pieces on English, Spanish, and French literature. Her uncle Matthew provided advice and encouragement. From France, meanwhile, she was receiving direction from the critic Edmond Scherer. Her Oxford associations continued, Jowett, Pattison, and Mandell Creighton all visiting and corresponding with the Wards in London.

Out of this background then of family experience, of religious crises, and of scholarship and criticism, *Robert Elsmere* emerged. In a sense, all of Mrs. Ward's life up to the writing of the novel had been preparation for it. Inside the Bodleian she had studied medieval Spanish Catholicism, an age of literal, unquestioning faith in saints and miracles. Outside, in the lecture halls and the drawing rooms of the masters' houses, she had listened to the debates of contemporary English religious thinkers:

Darwinism was penetrating everywhere; Pusey was preaching against its effects on belief; Balliol stood for an unfettered history and criticism, Christ Church for authority and creeds; Renan's *Origines* were still coming out, Strauss's last book also; my uncle was publishing *God and the Bible* in succession to *Literature and Dogma,* and *Supernatural Religion* was making no small stir. And meanwhile what began to interest and absorb me were *sources—testimony.* To what—to whom—did it all go back, this great story of early civilization, early religion, which modern men could write and interpret so differently? [21]

This is the question that led to Robert Elsmere's ultimate break with established religion. It was the question of the day—in which names of archeologists, historians, comparatists, and textual critics like Strauss, Baur, and Renan stirred excitement and controversy everywhere. What these scholars and critics challenged was not merely an abstract philosophical-theological concept, but the very nature of a Christian's belief. Darwin and other scientists had already undermined the rational base of faith. Now the spiritual bases were under attack. The issues of *Robert Elsmere* were, therefore, of burning importance to its readers.

What fascinated Mrs. Ward was the way in which an intelligent, sensitive, religiously motivated man might react to this challenge. In shaping such a character in her fictional hero Robert she drew on three examples from life—her father, the Swiss philosopher Amiel, and the Oxford philosopher T. H. Green. In her father Mrs. Ward had observed the most tragic and dramatic example, a man whose decision not only led him out of his church but drew him into another, even more authoritarian, church, with all its unhappy consequences for his family. In Amiel, whose *Journal Intime* she translated in 1885, she found the intellectual who simply withdraws from the struggle and becomes the alienated, disengaged, "superfluous man." Her uncle Matthew, not without sympathy for a man so similar to Senancour and Maurice de Guérin, nevertheless found the *Journal* "a study of mental pathology." His Arnoldian sense of duty to society was repelled by Abiel's confession: "The life of thought alone seems to me to have enough elasticity and immensity, to be free enough from the irreparable; practical life makes me afraid." Very likely Amiel touched too close to the root nerve of Matthew Arnold's own fears.

His niece, however, had a healthier, less troubled outlook. During her impressionable Oxford days she had also been exposed to the teachings of the liberal-idealist philosopher Thomas Hill Green.[22] In his ethical humanism, theology rejects dogma, ritual, and miracle for practical, useful action in society. His students did not go off into deserts to commune with the Holy Spirit; they went instead into the slums to found settlement houses. For this they were no less Christian—but they were "modern." They translated faith into deeds, private individual despair into principled public action, humanitarianism, and progress. Even the doubting, melancholy Amiel ultimately confessed to a personal religion, and here Mrs. Ward found his affinity with Green:

> Conscience and the moral progress of the race—these are his [Amiel's] points of departure. Faith in the reality of the moral law is what he clings to when his inherited creed has yielded to the pressure of the intellect, and after all the storms of pessimism and necessiterianism have passed over him. The reconciliation of the two certitudes, the two methods, the scientific and the religious, "is to be sought for in that moral law which is also a fact, and every step of which requires for its explanation another cosmos than the cosmos of necessity." [23]

At Oxford, in 1881, Mrs. Ward attended the Bampton Lecture delivered by the Reverend (later Bishop) John Wordsworth, grandnephew of the poet, on "The Present Unsettlement of Belief." A partisan of the conservative Oxford group centered in Christ Church, Wordsworth attacked the liberals for their "sins" of intellectual arrogance and unbelief:

> I sat in the darkness under the gallery. The preacher's fine ascetic face was plainly visible in the middle light of the church; and while the confident priestly voice flowed on, I seemed to see, grouped around the speaker, the forms of those, his colleagues and contemporaries, the patient scholars and thinkers of the Liberal host, Stanley, Jowett, Green of Balliol, Lewis Nettleship, Henry Sidgwick, my uncle, whom he, in truth—though perhaps not consciously —was attacking. My heart was hot within me. How could one show England what was really going on in her midst? Surely the only way was through imagination; through a picture of actual life and conduct; through something as "simple, sensuous, passionate" as one could make it. Who

and what were the persons of whom the preacher gave this grotesque account? What was their history? How had their thoughts and doubts come to be? What was the effect of them on conduct? [24]

The immediate result of this outburst of passion was a pamphlet, "Unbelief and Sin," that Mrs. Ward dashed off and distributed through an Oxford bookseller. When they learned that the printer had broken the law by neglecting to put his name on the pamphlet, it was withdrawn. By then *Robert Elsmere* had been conceived, although she did not begin writing the novel until 1885. Distractions of family life and illness (she was troubled all her life and frequently disabled with writers' cramp, the symptoms sounding much like bursitis) slowed her work on the book, which also proved to be far longer than she had planned. After writing a few chapters she submitted it to Macmillan's, which had published her first novel, *Miss Bretherton*. In one of those many examples of publishers' clouded crystal balls, they rejected it "on the ground that the subject was not likely to appeal to the British public." [25] George Murray Smith (of Smith and Elder), who had published the novels of Charlotte Brontë a generation earlier, scented promise and offered a modest advance of £200. The novel was published in three volumes in February, 1888, and within a month Smith knew that he had made a brilliant investment.[26]

One edition followed another; the demand could not be satisfied. The first edition (only 500 copies) sold out by the end of March, the second and third by mid-April, two more in May, two in June; 5,000 copies of a new "popular" edition were bought up in July, 7,000 in August, 4,000 a month for the rest of the year. In the United States it proved a bonanza, but not, unfortunately, for the author and original publisher—because the International Copyright Law was not enacted until 1891. Except for a small sum Macmillan gave her for the American rights and £100 from another American publisher, Lowell, she realized nothing on a book that by March, 1889, had sold some 200,000 copies in the United States. Marketing history was made in the rush to distribute the novel; price wars and tie-ins were introduced (a soap company offered *Robert Elsmere* and Gladstone's rebuttal, "Robert Elsmere and the Battle of Belief," a pamphlet, free with the purchase of a bar of soap). The actor William Gillette rushed a dramatized version to the Boston stage, and an anonymous hack wrote a sequel to the novel, advertising it with more enterprise than integrity: *"Robert Elsmere's Daughter*—a companion story to *Robert Elsmere*—by Mrs. Humphry Ward." 27

If the English reception of the novel was somewhat more restrained, it was no less remarkable. Like many popular novels, *Elsmere* profited even by adverse criticism. The shock and indignation with which some of the clergy received it did more to encourage sales than did any amount of advertising. And when the former Prime Minister Gladstone devoted a lengthy essay in *The Nineteenth Century* to answering its attack on revealed religion, its stature was enormously increased. The theologians dissented; the more sophisticated literary critics yawned and mocked (Oscar Wilde called it *Literature and Dogma* with the literature removed, and the *Saturday Review* dismissed it as tedious), but the public liked it.

Like her fellow Victorian novelists, Mrs. Ward knew the importance of story-telling, of capturing and engaging the reader's attention through a line of sustained narrative. Like her contemporaries, too, she had a healthy respect for the love story. *Elsmere* is a solemn presentation of the most serious intellectual and moral issues of the day. Nevertheless, it begins as an innocent, pretty romance; it is liberally laced with genteel love-making. Since her main plot deprived her of the most standard formula—her hero and heroine marry early in the book—she introduced (gratuitously, in the opinion of many critics of the novel) a subplot involving a romance between the heroine's sister Rose, a gifted violinist, and the Oxford tutor Langham. It is a feeble romance, Langham being a melancholy skeptic, an *enfant du siècle,* and Rose ultimately marries another man. But it demonstrates Mrs. Ward's awareness of the need for constant leavening of her weighty intellectual matter.

The opening sections of the novel, in particular, emphasize domesticity, idyllic rural scenes, and the general sweetness of

Biedermeier. The Leyburns—widowed mother and her daughters, plain spinsterish Agnes, flighty Rose, and saintly Catherine —live in the Westmoreland country that Mrs. Ward knew and loved. They had settled here much as the elder Thomas Arnold had settled his family at Fox How. The father, an evangelical scholar and headmaster of a school, is now dead, but his spirit is felt deeply by his children, especially the eldest, Catherine, who had shared his evangelical faith and continues to practice it by nursing the poor and sick in the neighborhood and generally exuding quiet piety. She serves, therefore, as a natural foil for the ardent young clergyman Robert Elsmere, fresh out of Oxford, who comes to the region on a brief visit, meets and falls in love with her, and ultimately wins her. The seeds of their future conflict are planted early. Robert is an intellectual, a philosopher and scholar; Catherine is an intuitive, emotional woman whose faith is unquestioning. Nevertheless they are drawn together by fundamental spiritual ties, as well as by physical attractions (Mrs. Ward makes much of Catherine's stately beauty and Robert's youthful good looks):

> These two people . . . were perhaps always overserious, oversensitive. They had no idea of minimizing the common experiences of life. Both of them were really simple, brought up in old-fashioned simple ways, easily touched, responsive to all that high spiritual education which flows from the familiar incidents of the human story, approached poetically and passionately (Ch. XIX).

The novel thus begins with what seems a conventional happy ending. It moves on to a marital crisis provoked not by the usual causes but by religion. "Catherine, could you ever have married a man that did not believe in Christ?" her sister asks. "Never, Rose! To me it would not be marriage." The man Catherine marries believes in Christ, but his belief is seriously altered by the discoveries, scientific and secular, of his time—mainly the rejection of miracles and the literal interpretation of the Bible. To Mrs. Ward's credit as a thinker, though not to her credit as a novelist, Robert's "deconversion" is carefully and logically analyzed. From the outset we know him to be a warm and emotional man as well as an intellectual—prone to human ties of love, family, and friends. Significantly, although the process of Robert's gradual alienation from the Church is intellectual, it is prodded at every stage by some human influence. It begins with his hero-worship of the brilliant Oxford philosopher Henry Grey (T. H. Green). Up to this time the sensitive young student had felt no particular religious calling—but he attends one of Grey's much heralded lectures or "lay sermons," with their emphasis on ethics, the practical morality of life in modern society:

> It was the speaker himself, and the occasional passages in which, addressing himself to the practical needs of his hearers, he put before them the claims and conditions of the higher life with a pregnant simplicity and rugged beauty of phrase. Conceit, selfishness, vice—how, as he spoke of them, they seemed to wither from his presence! How the "pitiful, earthly self" with its passions and its cravings sank into nothingness beside the "great ideas" and the "great causes" for which, as Christians and as men, he claimed their devotion.
>
> To the boy sitting among the crowd at the back of the room, his face supported in his hands and his gleaming eyes fixed on the speaker, it seemed as if all the poetry and history through which a restless curiosity and ideality had carried him so far took a new meaning from this experience. It was by men like this that the moral progress of the world had been shaped and inspired; he felt brought near to the great primal forces breathing through the divine workshop; and in place of natural disposition and reverent compliance, there sprang up in him suddenly an actual burning certainty of belief (Ch. V).

Grey and Oxford, at that time fired with a new, post-Newman "wave of religious romanticism," have their effect on this young student, as later another man, the icy, brilliant Squire Wendover, will have his effect. But even before he comes under

Wendover's negativistic influence, Robert's religious faith is challenged. When his tutor calls religion "a respectable mythology," Robert replies firmly, "Christian theology is a system of ideas, indeed, but of ideas realized, made manifest in facts." At this stage he is not even momentarily disturbed by Langham's question, "How do you know they are facts?" He confidently cites "Christian evidences." A few years later, however, he reads *The Origin of Species* and proclaims it "a revelation." Then, in the course of study for a book he wants to write on French history, he reads Church chronicles and biographies of the medieval saints, "pushing his imaginative, impetuous way through them." He is struck by the "embryonic processes of thought and morals," the "bizarre combinations of ignorance and knowledge," the naïveté of the mind that lacks science. It was all, he concludes, superstition, "a tissue of marvels." When finally he comes under the influence of the free-thinking Squire Wendover, who introduces him to the German and French archeologists and textual scholars, he is ripe. Gladstone and other critics of the novel were wrong when they objected that Mrs. Ward had made Robert's loss of faith too sudden, portraying him as simply an "easy victim" of Wendover's coldly analytical skepticism. Nor can she be faulted seriously for making Robert's break with the Church so agonizing for him. Here again she anticipated by emphasizing his sensitivity, his deep emotional commitment to his faith and to his parish duties, and mainly his passionate love for his wife. When at last he faces his demon, wrestles with it, and emerges convinced that "miracles do not happen" and that Christ is a symbol not a "man-God," his first thought is for her: "Oh God! My wife—my work!"

Where Mrs. Ward erred, however, was in her failure to dramatize Robert's experience. His soul-shattering journey out of the Church of England is described largely by a bibliography with a series of illustrative quotations. Mrs. Ward wanted to create drama—she sprinkled her pages with italics and exclamation points, her characters suffer and sob and gasp. But she set the scene for Robert's crisis in a library and never really moved beyond the shelves. Robert takes the visiting Langham on a tour of Wendover's library:

"These are the Tracts, all the Fathers, all the Councils, and masses, as you see, of Anglican theology. Now look at the next case, nothing but eighteenth century! . . . And there again . . . are the results of his life as a German student."

"How long was he there?"

"Ten years at Berlin and Heidelberg. . . . But that bookcase fascinates me. Half the great names of modern thought are in those books."

And so they were. The first Langham opened had a Latin dedication . . . signed "Fredericus Gulielmus Schelling." The next bore the autograph of Alexander von Humboldt, the next that of Boeckh, the famous classic, and so on. Close by was Niebuhr's "History," . . . here were most of the early editions of the "Leben Jesu," . . . and similar records of Baur, Ewald, and other members of the opponents of the Tübingen school (Ch. XIV).

The great "seduction," the subtle influence of the Mephistophelean Wendover, is a formal, rhetorical marshaling of quotations, introduced stiffly by the author: "We may quote a few fragmentary utterances taken almost at random from the long wrestle of the two men, for the sake of indicating the main lines of a bitter after-struggle." It is no more dramatic than the erudite essay Mrs. Ward published in *The Nineteenth Century* (March, 1889), "The New Reformation: A Dialogue," in answer to Gladstone's review of her novel. Here two men, formerly fellow students, debate the same issues, one speaking as a loyal clergyman in the Church of England, the other, just returned from Germany, speaking as an independent. Into this dialogue, Mrs. Ward recalled in her memoirs, "I was able to throw the reading and the argument which had been of necessity excluded from the novel." Anyone reading that massive novel today might well wonder what she had excluded.

Once the novel stumbles as it does in this potentially gripping climax, it inevitably fails in the resolution—Robert's adjustment to secular life as a lay clergyman, a social worker and adult educator, bringing to the working classes a Christian ethic based on understanding and education rather than mere dogma.

He rejects any compromise—unlike the young clergyman Richard Meynell who, a generation later, marries Robert's daughter,
breaks with dogma, but remains within the Church to work for
his principles. When Grey suggests a similar course to Robert
he rejects it handily, but he does accept the philosopher's advice:

> But take heart . . . It is the education of God! Do not ima-
> gine it will put you further from Him! He is in criticism,
> in science, in doubt, so long as the doubt is a pure and
> honest doubt, as yours is. . . . The leading-strings of the past
> are dropping from you; they are dropping from the world,
> not wantonly or by chance, but in the providence of God.
> Learn the lesson of your own pain—learn to seek God, not
> in any single event of past history, *but in your own soul*—
> in the constant verifications of experience, in the life of
> Christian love (Ch. XXVII).

Putting this theoretical ethic into practice, Robert goes to London, establishing a settlement house not unlike the one Mrs.
Ward established, where he preaches a "New Brotherhood of
Christ," as the organization comes to be known. "My friends,"
he says to a crowd of London workmen,

> the man who is addressing you tonight believes in *God,* and
> in *Conscience,* which is God's witness in the soul; and in
> *Experience,* which is at once the record and the instrument
> of man's education at God's hands. He places his whole
> trust, for life and death, "in God the Father Almighty." . . .
> He believes in an Eternal Goodness—and an Eternal Mind
> —of which Nature and Man are the continuous and only
> revelation (Ch. XL).

The strain of labor in the slums ultimately breaks Robert's
health and he dies of tuberculosis, leaving behind his widow and
child and the New Brotherhood, which "still exists and grows."
The final note is pathetic rather than triumphant. The whole
novel, in fact, hardly colorful at the outset, fades into a dim
twilight. The only drama of the last portions is Catherine's.

From her first reaction of shock and horror at her husband's break with orthodoxy, through her stubborn, numbed loyalty to him in the first days of their London residence, to her final resigned acceptance of his stand, she is far more realistic and believable a human being than her husband. With her Mrs. Ward achieves some depth and shading of character and a degree of ambivalence. Much as her husband's decision appalls her, she cannot conquer her love for him. In her first shock she rushes wildly into the countryside. Robert finds her—guilty and self-accusing for her desertion of him as much as she is self-righteous in her own unquestioning faith. She exclaims:

> Oh, how I loathed myself! That I should think it could be God's will that I should leave you or torture you, my poor husband! I had not only been wicked toward you—I had offended Christ. . . . I will never give up hope, I will pray for you night and day. God will bring you back. You can not lose yourself so. No! no! His grace is stronger than our wills. But I will not preach to you—I will not persecute you—I will only live beside you—in your heart—and love you always (Ch. XXIV).

In spite of her affirmation of love, Catherine is human enough to feel dismay and disapproval of her husband's actions. Though she remains loyal to him, she is silent, cold, and distant. At last, however, she learns of the good that Robert's work has achieved and witnesses his profound spiritual influence upon a dying man. Then she returns to him both in body and in soul: "Henceforward to the end Elsmere and his wife were lovers as of old." She never shares his views, but she learns to respect and tolerate them:

> No—she was not unhappy. Something, indeed, had gone forever out of that early joy. Her life had been caught and nipped in the great inexorable wheel of things. It would go in some sense maimed to the end. But the bitter, self-torturing of that first year was over. Love, and her husband, and the thousand subtle forces of a changing world had con-

quered. She would live and die steadfast to the old faiths. But her present mind and its outlook was no more the mind of her early married life than the Christian philosophy of today is the Christian philosophy of the Middle Ages. She was not conscious of change, but change there was. She had, in fact, undergone that dissociation of the moral judgment from a special series of religious formulae which is the crucial, the epoch-making fact of our day (Ch. XLVI).

No character in *Robert Elsmere* has real humanity, but Catherine, confused, unhappy, finally resigned to tolerating if not embracing a new view of the world, is far more representative of Mrs. Ward's age than is Robert Elsmere. Described once as "a Dinah Morris in society," Catherine survives into the twentieth century, carrying her fervent faith into a sequel published in 1911, *The Case of Richard Meynell*. She is not the center of this story, which describes the struggles of an Elsmere of the next generation who wages his spiritual battle within the Church, however, rather than leaving it. Now mother of a grown daughter, who in the end marries the hero Meynell, Catherine still has to struggle to accept the new attitudes of the Broad, Modernist Church. At last, as in the earlier novel, she does passively accept them, to the extent at least of admiring Meynell for his nobility and self-sacrifice in the several moral-ethical crises of the novel and welcoming him as a son-in-law. But her quiet death at the end of the novel suggests weary resignation to the inevitable rather than positive affirmation.

The zeal that fired *Robert Elsmere* carried it over passages of lofty theological debate, high-flown discussions of biblical textual criticism and exegesis. Whatever the novel lacked in drama and sustained narrative interest, it had the energy of the author's strong convictions, her lively sense of the immediacy of her subject, its relevance to her readers. But the reading public of 1911 was substantially different from Elsmere's audience of 1888, and of this almost everyone—critics and public alike—was aware, except, apparently, Mrs. Ward herself. For one who had in the past been such a sensitive barometer of public interests, Mrs. Ward showed herself curiously obtuse here. Possibly she was misled by the specialized interests of the society in which she traveled. She continued to be vitally concerned about religious questions, especially Modernism, the "new Christianity." Her Catholic friends in France and Italy were witnessing profound changes in their national churches. In 1903 Brunetière asked her permission to publish a French translation of *Robert Elsmere* in his *Revue des Deux Mondes*. The subject of the novel, he explained, would have been of little interest to his readers in 1888, but "there was now so much affinity between them and the problems and debates which Modernism had been forcing on French Catholicism that . . . 'it had become worth his life to publish it.' " [28]

In the next few years she continued reading avidly in the literature of Modernism—Bergson, William James, Father Tyrrell. She attended debates at Oxford and went out of her way to listen to sermons of ardent young liberal clergymen. Her enthusiasm is reflected everywhere in the novel but, unhappily, it is fatal. Where in *Elsmere* she managed at least to suggest the essential conflict in dramatic terms, in *Meynell* there is simply no integration of theme with plot. She writes with fervor and conviction but produces only the text of sermons and pages of theological debate not even thinly disguised as dramatic dialogue:

> "You think you can take what you like of a great historical religion and leave the rest—that you can fall back on its pre-suppositions and build it anew. But the pre-suppositions themselves are all crumbling. 'God'—'soul,' 'free-will,' 'immortality'—even human identity—is there one of the old fundamental notions that still stands, unchallenged? What are we in the eyes of modern psychology—but a world of automata—dancing to stimuli from outside? What has become of conscience—of the moral law—of Kant's imperative—in the minds of writers like these?"
>
> He pointed to two recent novels lying on the table, both of them brilliant glorifications of sordid forms of adultery.
>
> Meynell's look fired.
>
> "Ah!—but let us distinguish. *We* are not anarchists—as those men are. Our claim is precisely that we are, and

desire to remain, a part of a *Society*—a definite community with definite laws—of a National Church—of the nation, that is, in its spiritual aspect. . . .

"Then why all this bother?"

"Because the conditions must be adjusted from time to time! Otherwise the church suffers and souls are lost—wantonly, without reason. But there is no church—no religion without some venture, some leap of faith! If you can't make any leap at all—any venture—then you remain outside— and you think yourself, perhaps, entitled to run amuck—as these men do!" He pointed to the books. "But *we* make the venture!—*we* accept the great hypothesis—of faith!" (Ch. XII).

The melodramatic episodes of the plot—the intrigue of village gossip, a young girl's discovery of her illegitimacy, her tragic death—are ladled out with a heavy hand and never blended with other ingredients. The pallid romance of saintly, twenty-six-year-old Mary Elsmere and the noble-spirited forty-four-year-old Meynell makes the Catherine-Robert Elsmere relationship seem, by contrast, passionate. *The Case of Richard Meynell* was Mrs. Ward's last pronouncement in fiction on religious matters. The church novel, which had flourished so vigorously in the nineteenth century, was finished by 1911, and Mrs. Ward moved on to new issues. But between *Elsmere* and *Meynell* she made two other weighty contributions to this genre, both well received in their time.

The first of these was *The History of David Grieve*, published in 1892, four years after *Elsmere*. Unlike so many of her contemporaries who flooded the market with their work, grinding out novel after novel in a desperate pursuit of income, Mrs. Ward was relatively independent. *Elsmere* had been a staggering and totally unexpected financial success. Thanks to it she became famous and rich overnight, able to indulge every taste and desire—long holidays in Italy, the purchase of a fine old country house ("Stocks"), generous support of a settlement house in London. She was also able to devote more than three years of thought and study to her next novel, *David Grieve*. Largely on the basis of *Elsmere's* reputation, the new novel proved even more rewarding financially. In all Mrs. Ward realized more than £20,000 on it. Thanks to the new International Copyright she received £7,000 from the American and Canadian rights alone. Some 80,000 copies were snatched up in England within the first two years of publication.[29] Nevertheless, the novel was a disappointment. Some hailed it as a worthy successor to the work of George Eliot, as the best English novel since *Middlemarch*. Others were simply overwhelmed by its tremendous length.[30] Still others were offended or dismayed by Mrs. Ward's clumsy attempts at naturalism—her subplot involving life and free love among the artists of the Barbizon school in France.

A kind of secular *Robert Elsmere, The History of David Grieve* continued to explore the theme of man's faith. But here, instead of an upper-class theologian and clergyman, the hero is of working-class background, self-educated. His problems are domestic rather than theological. Still, Mrs. Ward's purpose was to show the *testing* of a man who discovers that he cannot lean on the easy props of conventional, revealed religion. *Grieve* seems almost a deliberate effort to correct the faults of *Elsmere*. The latter, for all its popularity, was too slow-moving, too rarified and intellectual. As if to make up for this failing, in the new novel Mrs. Ward introduced considerably more passion, stark suffering, and violent action. It is packed with lurid and morbid detail. Its most sensational episodes are the Paris scenes —David's "Storm and Stress" love affair with a Parisian artist and the adventures of his sister, the wild and promiscuous Louie, who becomes an artist's model, mistress, and later wife of an impoverished artist, and eventually commits suicide. Pandering equally to popular tastes are scenes involving the brutal treatment of the orphaned Grieve children by their miserly aunt and the painfully graphic account of the death from cancer of David's young wife.

The most interesting and uncharacteristic passages of the novel are the Manchester working-class scenes: David's struggles to establish himself in the book business, his friendship with "Daddy" Lomax, an eccentric free-thinker who runs a vegetarian restaurant. Though awkwardly written, they reflect careful research and observation.[31] Also noteworthy is the realistic detail of the country scenes, again closely observed and sensitively described. There are some interesting vignettes of country folk—for example, the brief sketch of the old parents of David's father, Sandy, who has left home and achieved a modest success as a cabinet-maker:

> The letter in which he announced it [his good fortune] to his father reached the farm just as the last phase of his mother's long martyrdom was developing. The pair, already old—James with work and anxiety, his wife with sickness—read it together. They shut it up without a word. Its tone of jubilant hope seemed to have nothing to do with them, or seemed rather to make their own narrowing prospects look more narrow, and the approach of the King of Terrors more black and relentless, than before. Jenny lay back on her poor bed, with the tears of a dumb self-pity running down her cheeks, James's only answer to it was conveyed in a brief summons to Sandy to come and see his mother before the end (Bk. I, Ch. IV).

By far the largest part of the book is typical of Mrs. Ward's lecture-platform didacticism: informative educational talk, factual detail. A *bildungsroman* tracing the hero's development from childhood to maturity, it is more a bio-bibliography than a biography. David, an orphan, receives only the most rudimentary schooling. His meek uncle Reuben and his stingy, domineering wife Hannah conceal from the boy the fact that his father had left a little money, so David labors on their farm, hungry for learning but unable to go to school. He gets some help from a sympathetic clergyman, Mr. Ancrum, but most of his education comes from voracious and undirected reading—first he manages to pick up books such as *Paradise Lost* and Josephus' *Jewish Wars;* then, after a visit to Haworth (into which Mrs. Ward incorporates a lecture on the careers of the Brontës, for whose novels she wrote the excellent Prefaces, a few years later, in the "Haworth Edition"), he begins to read novels such as *Shirley* and *Nicholas Nickleby:*

By a natural transition the mental tumult thus roused led to a more intense self-consciousness than any he had yet known. In measuring himself with the world of "Shirley" or of Dickens, he began to realise the problem of his own life with a singular keenness and clearness. Then—last of all—the record of Franklin's life,—of the steady rise of the ill-treated printer's devil to knowledge and power—filled him with an urging and concentrating ambition, and set his thoughts, endowed with a new heat and nimbleness, to the practical unravelling of a practical case (Bk. I, Ch. VII).

Primarily, however, *David Grieve* is a religious novel. Like Elsmere, its hero, Grieve, goes through various crises of faith. As an ignorant youth he comes under the influence of fanatical evangelicism:

They had no connection with any recognised religious community, but the members of it had belonged to many—to the Church, the Baptists, the Independents, the Methodists. They were mostly mill-hands or small tradesmen, penetrated on the one side with the fervour, the yearnings, the strong formless poetry of English evangelical faith, and repelled on the other by various features in the different sects from which they came—by the hierarchical strictness of the Wesleyan organisation, or the looseness of the Congregationalists, or the coldness of the Church. They had come together to seek the Lord in some way more intimate, more moving, more effectual than any they had yet found; and in this pathetic search for the "rainbow-gold" of faith they were perpetually brought up against the old stumbling-blocks of the unregenerate man—the smallest egotisms, and the meanest vanities (Bk. I, Ch. IX).

David attends services in which the congregation is aroused to religious hysteria. He gets carried away; losing control of himself he gets drunk and is involved in a brawl. Ashamed and embittered, he resolves for the rest of his life to resist such emotional excesses. He runs away from the farm and settles in Manchester, where he struggles for a living and reads Voltaire, Diderot, Mill, and Locke, moving from rationalism to skepticism to agnosticism. Later in life he keeps a journal recording his religious development. Like Elsmere he rejects "miracles" and "legends": "I have passed of late into a conception of Christianity far more positive, fruitful, and human than I have yet held. I would fain believe it the Christianity of the future. But the individual must beware lest he wrap his personal thinking in phrases too large for it" (Bk. IV, Ch. I).

Recognizing the importance of science, he reads the German textual critics and rejects the "maintenance of the older prepossession" of the Church of England clergy:

> That the spiritual principle in nature and man exists and governs; that mind cannot be explained out of anything but itself; that the human consciousness derives from a universal consciousness, and is thereby capable both of knowledge and of goodness; that the phenomena and history of conscience are the highest revelation of God; that we are called to co-operation in a divine work, and in spite of pain and sin may find ground for an infinite trust, covering the riddle of the individual lot, in the history and character of that work in man, so far as it has gone—these things are deeper and deeper realities to me. They govern my life; they give me peace; they breathe me to hope. But the last glow, the certainties, the *vision,* of faith? Ah! me, I believe that He is there, yet my heart gropes in darkness (Bk. IV, Ch. IV).

In David's spiritual development various extremes of religious belief are illustrated—the narrow Low Church fundamentalism of Purcell, father of the girl David marries; the extreme High Church pietism of Dora Lomax, who loves David and renounces him in an act of nunlike self-sacrifice; the mysticism of the ascetic clergyman Ancrum.

It is this Ancrum who saves David from despair and suicide when he returns to England after his stormy Wilhelm Meister Paris experiences. Gradually David recovers his spirits, makes a success in business as a publisher, and marries Lucy, a pretty but shallow young girl. His later life is melancholy in spite of his business successs. His wife cannot share his intellectual and spiritual interests. His main joy is his little son, Sandy. His sister Louie, more unbalanced than ever, destroys herself in a violently melodramatic episode. In the epilogue David, now a widower, is reconciled to life, devoting himself to his work and his child:

> It seemed to him that he had been "taught of God" through natural affection, through repentance, through sorrow, through the constant energies of the intellect. Never had the Divine voice been clearer to him, or the Divine Fatherhood more real. Freely he had received—but only that he might freely give. On this Christmas night he renewed every past vow of the soul, and in so doing rose once more into that state and temper which is man's pledge and earnest of immortality since already, here and now, it is the eternal life begun.

Apart from the extravagant praise of her loyal friends—Jowett, who wrote that it was "the best novel since George Eliot"; Meredith Townsend, who called "the consistency of the leading characters . . . wonderful"; and Walter Pater, who found in it "a mellower kind of art [than in *Elsmere*]—a more matured power of blending disparate literary gifts in one"—nobody seemed to like *David Grieve* except the public. Even Mrs. Ward acknowledged that it was "didactic in some parts and amateurish in others." [32] For some time after its publication she avoided the "religious" novel, turning to political subjects in *Marcella* and *Sir George Tressady,* and experimenting in naturalism, with which she had flirted in the opening episodes of *Grieve,* in a short, bleak tragedy of country life, *The Story of Bessie Costrell* (1895). But the lure of religious controversy was irresistible, and in 1898 Mrs. Ward returned to it in what many regarded as her best novel, *Helbeck of Bannisdale.*

In this book she reversed the conflict of *Robert Elsmere,* transferring the profound religious piety to her hero, a Catholic, and the doubting spirit to the heroine. But *Helbeck* is not the bookish-academic debate that, in essence, *Elsmere* is. Ten years later, more experienced in the craft of fiction, she was able to dramatize the issues as she had failed to do in the earlier novel. The conflict between Alan Helbeck and Laura Fountain is strong because both are more sharply characterized and because little is introduced to distract the reader from the central theme of the novel. Except for one lurid incident involving a workman's death in a foundry accident, there is no overt melodrama. The heroine's suicide at the end is treated with relative restraint. In general, Mrs. Ward succeeds in integrating her scene—a crumbling old Tudor house, the wildly beautiful Westmoreland country—with the moods of her leading characters. The reader is for once spared travelogue commentaries, and the lectures on theology and church history are for the most part appropriately motivated and less obtrusive than in most of her novels.

The chief interest of the novel is Mrs. Ward's sympathetic portrait of the devout Catholic Helbeck. Here she drew upon her own knowledge of her father's religious history. Though herself closer in spirit to her rebellious, skeptical heroine, she was nevertheless able to present the Catholic point of view with creditable honesty. Some years after its first publication, she wrote that her greatest satisfaction had been her father's praise of the book: "I had said nothing to hurt that Catholic sensibility, at least, which I most dreaded to hurt, nothing consciously unjust to his side of that great controversy in which from my youth up I had been able to follow him, without in the smallest degree chilling the strong affection between us which grew up with life, and knew no forced silences." [33]

Both Laura and Helbeck are sensitive and intelligent, keenly aware of their all but irreconcilable religious conflict. The daughter of a Cambridge lecturer in "an obscure scientific subject," she has been brought up with no religious training and with a positive contempt for ritual and superstition. When her father dies, she reluctantly accompanies her ailing stepmother back to her old family home of Bannisdale, where the stepmother's brother, Alan Helbeck, maintains a long family tradition of Catholicism. At first Laura is contemptuous of his religious observances and watches the celebration of mass in his private chapel with scorn:

A wave of the most passionate repulsion swept through her. What a gross, what an intolerable superstition!—how was she to live with it, beside it? The next instant it was as though her hand clasped her father's—clinging to him, proudly, against this alien world. Why should she feel lonely?—the little heretic, left standing there alone in her distant corner. Let her rather rejoice that she was her father's daughter (Bk. I, Ch. III).

But Laura is an ardent, beautiful young girl, attracted to Helbeck's romantic good looks and gentle manners, just as he is attracted to her. Mrs. Ward neglects no opportunity to spice the religious debate with passages of conventional love story. Laura's golden hair, white neck, youthful grace, and slender figure are described at great length. In the ruggedly beautiful Westmoreland country she is awakened to physical passion: "The north spoke to her, and the mountains. It was like the rush of something passionate and straining through her girlish sense, intensifying all that was already there. What was this thirst, this yearning, this physical anguish of pity that crept back upon her in all the pauses of the day and night?" Helbeck, who is close to forty, has lived an almost monastic life, and Laura's presence stirs him to memories of the past:

It was the emergence of something hidden and passionate; and it awoke in himself a strange and troubling echo—the passing surge of an old memory long since thrust down and buried. How fast his youth was going from him! It was fifteen years since a woman's voice, a woman's presence, had mattered anything at all to him (Bk. II, Ch. I).

Once again then Mrs. Ward's readers got their mixture of romance and theology, their entertainment and their education. The principal crisis of the day—the conflict between the freethinking skeptic and the seeker after certainty—was reduced to a conventional love story. It is a measure of Mrs. Ward's integrity, however, that she offered no easy solutions to the dilemma. Instead, she recognized that neither side had the answer. Laura's position, she makes clear, is the rational one; but, like most of us, Laura needs stronger emotional props:

> She represented forces of intelligence, of analysis, of criticism, of which in themselves she knew little or nothing, except so far as they affected all her modes of feeling. . . . But when in this new conflict—a conflict of instincts, of the deepest tendencies of two natures—she tried to lay hold upon the rational life, to help herself by it and from it, it failed her everywhere (Bk. IV, Ch. III).

Helbeck has the security of his faith, but he learns in the end—by losing Laura—that he can make no compromises and that there is no real place for him in the modern world. Mrs. Ward's spokesman in the novel is a minor character, a Cambridge professor who places the conflict of the lovers in the perspective of the revolution of modern life—"a vast transformation of moral ideas. . . . Beside the older ethical fabric—the fabric that the Church built up out of Greek and Jewish material—a new is rising. . . . And the net result in the best moderns is at once a great elaboration of conscience—and an almost intoxicating sense of freedom" (Bk. V, Ch. I).

Helbeck and Laura are innocent victims of this "vast transformation," largely because neither of them has learned what Robert Elsmere learned from the fictional Professor Grey and Mrs. Ward learned from the real Professor Green—that God is immanent, not in ritual and dogma, but in the institutions of human society: "His witness grows with time. In great books and great examples, in the gathering fulness of spiritual utterance which we trace through the history of literature . . . in the moralising influences of civil life . . . one spirit still speaks—there God's sunshine is shed abroad. . . ." [34]

III

In *Lady Rose's Daughter* (1903) Mrs. Ward describes the developing social conscience of Jacob Delafield, a young man of an aristocratic family, who has come under the influence of his liberal Oxford professors:

> In the first place, he was conscious, like many other young men of his time, of a strong repulsion toward the complexities and artificialities of modern society. As in the forties, a time of social stir was rising out of a time of stagnation. Social settlements were not yet founded, but the experiments which led to them were beginning. Jacob looked at the life of London, the clubs and the country-houses, the normal life of his class, and turned from it in aversion. . . . And he meanwhile found himself hungry to throw aside these tamed and trite forms of existence, and to penetrate to the harsh, true, simple things behind. His imagination and his heart turned towards the primitive, indispensable labours on which society rests—the life of the husband-man, the labourer, the smith, the woodman, the builder; he dreamed the old, enchanted dream of living with nature; of becoming the brother not of the few, but of the many (Ch. XIII).

The liberal idealism that swept Oxford in the 1870's and '80's had its influence in life much as Mrs. Ward described it in her fiction. Social reform became the new evangelicalism, regenerating the spirit of the reformer as much as—if not more than—it corrected the evils of modern industrial society.[35] A quarter of a century earlier Thomas Arnold had instilled a philosophy of Christian Socialism into his pupils at Rugby. Green too had been educated at Rugby. Although Dr. Arnold was dead by that time, his teaching continued to dominate the school: "Christianize the nation and introduce the principles of Christianity into men's social and civil relations." [36] Subtilized and refined by his studies in the German idealist philosophers, Green's philosophy extended Arnold's teachings beyond sectarianism into the wider area of human conscience. In his work Mrs. Ward found the answers both to the religious and to the social dilemmas of her day. When Robert Elsmere left the Church to establish his New Brotherhood of Christ in the London slums, he was putting that philosophy into practice. In much the same way Mrs. Ward herself established the Passmore Edwards Settlement in London. The Oxford influence was pervasive: a Benjamin Jowett Lectureship, a library named in memory of T. H. Green (who had died in 1882), and a former student of his appointed warden of the institution.

The first public announcement of the new movement stated its "Elsmerian ideals" in unmistakable terms: "To provide a fresh rallying point and enlarged means of common religious action for all those to whom Christianity, whether by inheritance or process of thought, has become a system of practical conduct, based on faith in God, and on the inspiring memory of a great teacher, rather than a system of dogma based on a unique education." [37] Initially the purpose of the organization was religious education. Ultimately it became a social welfare center. Mrs. Ward was the energetic guiding spirit. She recruited lecturers (Mrs. J. R. Green, widow of the Oxford historian, on English history; Beatrice Potter, soon to marry Sidney Webb, on cooperatives; Stopford Brooke on English poetry), addressed meetings, raised money. In 1894 her appeals for funds brought a windfall. J. Passmore Edwards, philanthropist and founder of public libraries, offered £4,000 for a building. The Settlement that was completed in 1897 in Tavistock Square was named in his honor.[38] It grew rapidly. By 1904 some 1,700 children, most of them with working mothers who were not at home during the day, were coming regularly for after-school recreation. They were offered gymnastics, story-telling, music drills, the use of a library, and lectures in history. There were lectures and recreational facilities for working-class adults as well, but the really significant accomplishments were with the children. Probably Mrs. Ward's greatest single achievement was her program of education for crippled and invalid children, for whom no public education had been available. Largely due to her vigorous campaigns, the London County Council and later the House of Commons established local, then national schools for handicapped children. The Arnold family tradition of public service had perhaps never before produced such impressive results.[39]

In all her social work Mrs. Ward remained very much the lofty Lady Bountiful. Although she appeared frequently at the

Settlement House to pat the children on the head, she was happier negotiating with statesmen and philanthropists, writing impassioned letters to the *Times* and novels like *Marcella* and *Sir George Tressady,* in which the issues of social reform are debated in the drawing rooms of the rich. She had always delighted in the "issue-y" novel. It was therefore deeply gratifying for her to discover that the public shared her interests. If by the mid-1890's religion was dwindling as a topic of burning interest, politics was certainly in the ascendant. Marxism, socialism, and Fabianism were becoming staples of popular literature—as H. G. Wells, Bernard Shaw, and other writers were discovering. *Marcella* (1894) and its sequel *Sir George Tressady* (1896) were financial and critical successes. Reviewers were generally enthusiastic. Gladstone, eighty-five and going blind, nevertheless managed to read *Marcella* "with great pleasure and an agreeable sense of congeniality." Beatrice Webb, while disclaiming any powers as a literary critic, called *Tressady* "the most useful bit of work that has been done for many a long day. You have managed to give the arguments for and against factory legislation and a fixed standard of life with admirable lucidity and picturesqueness—in a way which will make them comprehensible to the ordinary person without technical knowledge." [40]

The "ordinary person" to whom Mrs. Webb referred swallowed the education in political economy along with large gulps of romance and melodrama. Both novels are amply fattened with conventional matter: in *Marcella* a beautiful headstrong heroine who impulsively rejects an adoring aristocratic suitor, Aldous Raeburn, and comes to mature self-knowledge only after self-sacrificing work as a nurse in the slums of London; a brutal murder by poachers; much fashionable upper-class dialogue. In *Sir George Tressady* readers are offered a matronly but still beautiful Marcella, a veritable Egeria, manipulating the political destinies of England by her charm and her influence on her still adoring aristocratic husband Raeburn, now the leader of his political party; and a noble-spirited young hero who has marital troubles and dies tragically in a mining disaster. Both novels are "dressed" and "furnished" in meticulous detail. The cold statistics of the parliamentary Blue Books are bedecked in sables and lace. Incongruous as this formula may appear to the modern reader, it evidently suited Mrs. Ward's readers.

On social issues, as on religious ones, she grasped the temper of the times with unfailing accuracy. She wrote not as an opportunist exploiting popular interests, but as one who shared these interests with her public. Essentially conservative, she followed the traditional Arnold family line of progressive liberalism and humanitarianism, accepting, even welcoming, the challenges of the new era, but doing so in a spirit of enlightened, constructive compromise. Radicalism and violence were destructive, but they could be averted if they were anticipated by intelligent reform. Marcella flirts dangerously with radicalism—both in ideology and in the person of an attractive radical politician. He proves to be of weak character, while the fundamentally conservative but liberal-thinking Raeburn proves strong and noble. Sir George Tressady also moves from conservatism to liberalism: in so doing he confounds the confused and often insincere radicals. Reform, Mrs. Ward preaches, is restorative, not radical. It restores tranquility, faith, fellowship—the solid values of an older England that have become lost in the materialistic flux created by the Industrial Revolution.

Consistent with this outlook, Mrs. Ward strongly opposed the Women's Suffrage Movement. In the long run her opposition cost her much respect among the younger generation, for on suffrage, unlike other popular issues, Mrs. Ward chose the losing side. In her own time, however, she was allied with a genuinely liberal and enlightened group. The violence and hysteria that characterized so much of the suffrage movement—arson, bombings, riots, hunger strikes—and the shrillness of its leaders alienated many people who would otherwise have been sympathetic.[41] But Mrs. Ward's opposition was grounded on the more basically conservative conviction that women *were* different from men. While they might claim equality of rights and civic responsibilities in community activities like school boards—they had no place in the rough-and-tumble world of politics. As early as 1889 she drafted "An Appeal against Female Suffrage," which had among its signers Lady Randolph Churchill, Mrs. T. H. Green, Mrs. Leslie Stephen, Mrs. Arnold Toynbee, Beatrice Potter, and

Eliza Lynn Linton—and proclaimed women's rights to citizenship but not the parliamentary vote: "to admit women to the ordinary machinery of political life would inflame the partnership and increase the evils already so conspicuous, of that life, would tend to blunt the special moral qualities of women." [42]

In a phrase like "the special moral qualities of women," Mrs. Ward betrays the essential romanticism of the Arnolds. The "New Woman" of the 1880's was not her Egeria, her ideal of a beautiful, elegant matron dispensing wisdom and charity in a lace-trimmed tea gown. As Mrs. Ward portrayed her some years later in Gertrude Marvell, in her antisuffragette novel *Delia Blanchflower* (1915), she was neurasthenic, fanatical, and destructive. Gertrude is an extreme example, who seeks and achieves a ghastly martyrdom, dying in a fire she has set in one of the great old houses of England to "dramatize" her cause. But even where less fanatic, the New Woman is dangerous:

> So women everywhere—many women at any rate—were turning undiscriminately against the old bonds, the old yokes, affections, servitudes, demanding "self-realization," freedom for the individuality and personal will; rebelling against motherhood and lifelong marriage; clamouring for easy divorce and denouncing their own fathers, brothers and husbands, as either tyrants or fools; casting away the old props and veils; determined, apparently, to know everything, however ugly, and to say everything, however outrageous (Ch. I).

As one who was herself actively engaged in social welfare work, pushing for parliamentary action on many reform measures, Mrs. Ward was in a seemingly inconsistent position. She was so much aware of this that in 1908 she founded the Women's Anti-Suffrage League, an organization "for bringing the views of women to bear on the legislature without the aid of the vote." Until the outbreak of World War I she devoted much time to writing polemics and to speaking in her cause. She was effective, to some extent at least, in blocking the suffrage legislation that came before Parliament in 1912, but in the long run all that she achieved was the enmity of the growing numbers of suffrage sympathizers. When war came, Mrs. Ward threw herself into new activities, but she continued to fight her losing antisuffrage battle until her final defeat in 1918.

Still the conscientious chronicler of her times, however, Mrs. Ward made a valiant attempt to record the victorious New Woman sympathetically in her fiction. One of her last novels, *Cousin Philip* (1919; published in the U.S. as *Helena*) introduces the new "Girl of the Period," who smokes cigarettes, drives a motor car, and calls her men friends by their first names. The heroine declares:

> I want to have my life to myself a bit. I'm like the miners and the railway men. I'm full of unrest! I can't and won't settle down just yet. I want to look at things—the world's like a great cinema show just now—everything's passing so quickly you can hardly take breath. I want to sample it where I please. I want to dance—and talk—and make experiments. (Ch. VI).

For all her boldness this heroine ultimately settles down to marriage with a young man of her own upper class. He has embarked on a political career in which, presumably, she will assist him—but decorously, in a tea gown.

Nowhere did Mrs. Ward display her zeal for public service more energetically than in World War I. As with her antisuffragism, her war fervor struck many of the younger generation as misguided. In the hindsight of the 1920's, the horror and futility of war by then so amply demonstrated, Mrs. Ward's glorification of the British cause, her propaganda to win American sympathy and to bring America into the war, appeared absurd and even tragic. Looking back—more objectively, one hopes—today, however, one is struck by the stamina and spirit of a woman in her mid-sixties, in poor health, with every excuse to retire gracefully, who plunged into the most exhausting war work—visited hospitals, factories, munitions plants; traveled to the trenches in France; stood within three-quarters of a mile of actual combat;

and wrote three volumes of war reporting, as well as some half-dozen novels. Her reaction to the war was deeply personal and emotional, not only because her son Arnold was fighting but because she was aware of the cataclysmic nature of this war, its threat to the very civilization of Europe. In January, 1916, Theodore Roosevelt, whom she had met when he was president in 1908, wrote her:

> The War has been, on the whole, well presented in America from the French side. We do not think justice has been done to the English side. . . . I wish that some writer like yourself could, in a series of articles, put vividly before our people what the English people are doing. . . . What I would like our people to visualize is the effort, the resolution and the self-sacrifice of the English men and women who are determined to see this war through. . . . There is not a human being more fitted to present this matter than you are. I do hope you will undertake the task.[43]

Such an appeal was irresistible—on grounds of sheer human vanity, perhaps, but equally as an appeal to that social conscience that loomed so large with Mrs. Ward. The three books she wrote —*England's Effort* (1916), *Towards the Goal* (1917), and *Fields of Victory* (1919)—are mixtures of straight war reporting and propaganda, distinguished only for the enthusiasm and mastery of detail which they reveal. Always a diligent recorder of her observations, she was a good reporter and served her cause well.

The rigors of wartime activity did not apparently shorten Mrs. Ward's life. She followed the peace negotiations and postwar economic developments with keen interest and wrote one last novel, a mystery story with a wartime background, *Harvest* (1920). If her last years were clouded with disappointment—the failure of her antisuffragism, the decline in her reputation as a novelist—they were nevertheless happy on the whole. She had the satisfaction of seeing the practical results of her crusade for play centers, for in 1917 and again in 1919 the government voted public money for their support. In 1918 her long battle for special schools for handicapped children was won when the

House of Commons added a clause to the new Education Bill establishing such schools throughout England. Her private life was tranquil. Her daughter Dorothy was a devoted companion; her daughter Janet married G. M. Trevelyan and took a lively interest in her mother's social work; her son Arnold was elected to Parliament. In March, 1920, her husband underwent a serious operation but made a good recovery. Her own health, however, began to fail rapidly, and she died in London on March 24, 1920. She was buried in the churchyard at Aldbury, the village seat of her country house Stocks, with tributes from many dignitaries of church and state, not least of which was a telegram from King George and Queen Mary: "Their Majesties believe that Mrs. Humphry Ward's distinguished literary achievements, her philanthropic activities, and her successful organizations to promote the health and recreation of children will endear her memory to the hearts of English-speaking people." [44]

IV

In her autobiography, which she wrote in the midst of World War I, *A Writer's Recollections,* Mrs. Ward recalled that when she and her husband moved to London from Oxford in 1881, George Eliot had just died, and that the decade which followed saw the passing of Browning, Carlyle, and Tennyson. In the intervening years, she observed, the whole world had changed. That former world "looks to us now as the Elysian fields looked to Aeneas as he approached them from the heights —full not only of souls in a blessed calm, but of those also who had yet to make their way into existence as it terribly is, had still to taste reality and pain." [45] Mrs. Ward's career spanned the era from Victorianism to modern times. She kept pace with progress and change, yet we read her today more as a Victorian than as a modern writer. Even in her lifetime more perceptive critics recognized her as "old-fashioned." She was a contemporary of Henry James, Joseph Conrad, and D. H. Lawrence,[46] but—even apart from the absurdity of comparing her to novelists like these —she seems to have existed in another world entirely. As a practicing novelist she could only manufacture a marketable product, suitable to the needs of the day, as stale the next day as yesterday's loaf of bread. Thus even while she kept pace with change, shortening her heroine's skirts, turning carriages into motor cars, introducing telephones and electric lights in her country houses, her work was so superficially modern that it was outdated almost as soon as it appeared.

In the epilogue to her autobiography Mrs. Ward surveyed the current literary scene. Her highest praise was for George Meredith and Henry James. Somewhere lower, but still in an honored position, she names Hardy, Conrad, Stevenson, Kipling, and Arnold Bennett. But she had little praise for H. G. Wells, dismissing him as a journalist rather than an artist—lively and topical but lacking in both charm and substance. Ironically, her critical assessment of Wells might, with only slight alteration, have been written of herself: "Mr. Wells seems to me a journalist of very great powers, who has inadvertently strayed into the literature of imagination." [47] If ever a writer strayed into the literature of imagination it was Mrs. Ward. Not a professional journalist, she nevertheless performed the major functions of a journalist, reporting her observations, interpreting the current scene to the widest possible public. She chose to pass for a novelist, writing a kind of fictitious journalism—heightened by the conventions of popular fiction and colored by romance. But basically her work was undigested and unimaginative. It never occurred to Mrs. Ward that she was not an artist. Even if she had confronted that possibility, it probably would not have disturbed her, for she was serene in her self-confidence, her sense of mission and artistic seriousness. She was proud that her works were called "novels with a purpose." Citing her uncle Matthew's comment on poetry as "a criticism of life," she argued that art, the novel, cannot have "a divine and irresponsible isolation." Her novels met her criteria, and she put herself confidently into the company of Rousseau, Goethe, and Sand as writers who use art "as the torch for exploring life." [48]

Her exalted sense of the importance of her work was strengthened by the response *Robert Elsmere* received on its publication. Its admirers—not the least of them Tolstoy, who called her the greatest living English novelist—were almost hysterical in their enthusiasm. What impressed Mrs. Ward particularly was that even its detractors treated it with respect. A work that could command the energies of Gladstone—albeit in disagreement—and the serious attention of Lord Acton, Richard Holt Hutton, Jowett, Pattison, and men of like stature—was not to be dismissed as a mere entertainment. Having thus launched her career with a "prophetic" book, it is little wonder that she felt a sense of special purpose in all her later writing. Not long after the publication of *Elsmere* she wrote to an old friend, the religious novelist Felicia Skene, of her desire to begin a new book:

> But it is very difficult to make a fresh start while I feel the old book penetrating every day as it were, deeper and deeper, and touching human life more keenly. I wish sometimes I could quite forget it! The strain of feeling is often too much, and it is kept up by constant letters and reviews, especially from America, which every week brings. It is not good for one mentally or morally, and it is not good for work.[49]

No novel of hers after *Elsmere* quite matched its reception, but most of them made enormous amounts of money and many received flattering critical attention. Her fame as a novelist, her high social standing as an Arnold and the wife of a former Oxford tutor who had become a respected critic and editor, and her growing influence as a polemicist in social reform—all combined to create an image so bright and lofty that Mrs. Ward the human being was overshadowed by Mrs. Ward the public figure. Interviewers stressed her great-lady manner, her dignity and queenly presence ("One cannot help feeling that he is in the presence of a distinguished person"[50]). The young American novelist Gertrude Atherton, visiting London in 1895, saw her as "the Queen of Literature. The word 'great' was applied as freely then as now, and few doubted that Mrs. Ward was as great (and immortal) as Mr. Gladstone and others proclaimed her. She took herself with portentious seriousness, and so did her readers on both sides of the Atlantic."[51]

Inevitably Mrs. Ward invited ridicule as well as respect.[52] No one so thoroughly identified with the Establishment could have escaped it. And she was additionally handicapped by totally lacking the saving grace of a sense of humor. Much has been written about her humorlessness, her ponderous, overwhelming earnestness. Actually, she tried to introduce flashes of humor into most of her work—light conversation, high-society wit, the innocent babbling of children, the earthy natural talk of country folk. Her efforts were painfully transparent and clumsy. Even where drawn closely from life (David Grieve's little son was modeled on her nephew Julian Huxley[53]), her children are baby-talking monsters, her society wits are self-conscious bores, and her country folk are dialect-ridden clods. A feeble exception, perhaps, is a pious evangelical old lady whom the heroine of *Marcella* visits in a London slum:

> She held up a little paper-covered tract worn with use. It was called "A Pennorth of Grace or a Pound of Works?" . . . "I do love a track!" said Mrs. Jervis pensively. "That's why I don't like these buildings so well as those others, Em'ly. Here you never get no tracks; and there, what with one person and another, there was a new one most weeks" (Bk. III, Ch. VII).

Even her daughter concedes in her biography of Mrs. Ward that "like all those who possess the ardent temperament, the will to move the world, [she] worked first and foremost by the methods of direct attack rather than by the subtler shafts of humour," and she quotes her mother writing a little pathetically to a friend in 1911: "*Am* I so devoid of humour? I was looking at *David Grieve* again the other day—surely there is a good deal that is humorous there."[54] If Mrs. Ward found humor there, she proved the charge against herself.

Nevertheless, she was maligned or at least unjustly mocked for her deficiency. Frank Harris dismissed her as "simply a Goddess who dispensed judgment and weak tea and throned it over the minds of men . . . a prim little governess body without a spark even of talent . . . an intolerable pedagogue in petticoats writing interminable prosy tales of nobodies while devoting her wealth to uplifting the working classes." [55] More damaging perhaps was his quoting her uncle Matthew's alleged comment on *Elsmere:* "Have you read it? I've not; to tell the truth I'm afraid to . . . she's a little—heavy, don't you think? I would not say— tedious?" [56] But Harris is not a reliable witness. As Bernard Shaw observed to him in 1908:

One could not ask you to meet Mrs. Humphry Ward. You may say: "God be praised for that! I never wanted to meet Mrs. Humphry Ward." All the same, you cannot have a career in London as a journalist unless you can be trusted to take Mrs. Humphry Ward in to dinner and to leave her under the impression that you are either a very respectable or a very charming man.[57]

Much as he scoffed at Mrs. Ward, Shaw had a healthy respect for her. He had benefited by her hospitality several times, staying as a guest in a cottage on her country estate, and he knew the value of her social work.

The writer whose opinion Mrs. Ward valued, probably above all others, was Henry James, who was a lifelong and devoted friend. Her daughter Dorothy took a photograph of them strolling the grounds at Stocks some time close to World War I [58] —two dignified elderly people, apparently engrossed in profound thought or conversation. Mrs. Ward, biting her index finger in intense concentration, is elegantly gowned, with a large tulle-trimmed hat and a fur boa; James wears spats, striped trousers, dark jacket, and a large-brimmed hat. A heavy chain stretches across his ample middle, and he carries a cane. The photograph suggests a charming mixture of intimacy and formality, a spirit of mutual esteem and confidence. Their friendship dated back to the Wards' first years in London, when James visited them in Russell Square and submitted to being climbed on by five-year-old Janet Ward, who fell asleep in his lap.[59] Over the years he visited and corresponded faithfully, writing long, patient, sympathetic comments on her books. He spent time with the Wards at their villa in Italy, sharing their love for that country and impressing them with his great knowledge of Italian art and history. Finally, he shared Mrs. Ward's ardent support of the Allied effort in the war, and his adoption of British citizenship shortly before his death was a gesture that moved her deeply.

On the more purely artistic side, however, one often wonders at James's toleration and even encouragement of Mrs. Ward's writing. She is not the only instance where he became involved in an almost-Jamesian situation: a sharp conflict between his ethics and his aesthetics. Numerous literary ladies, most notably Vernon Lee,[60] pained and embarrassed him by forcing their work on him for judgment. Ever the gentleman-cavalier, he was often forced to squirm and almost perjure himself, praising the ladies' efforts while he tried to teach them something about the art of the novel. Ironically, some of his best criticism of the novel was inspired by one of Mrs. Ward's worst novels, *Eleanor*. She sent him proofs of the book, seeking his advice on her American character Lucy. His comments on Mrs. Ward's failure to focus on a single character as a "center" are the basis for his now classic observation on point of view:

> And may I say (as I *can* read nothing, if I read it at all, save in the light of how one would *one's self* proceed to tackling the same *data!*) just two other things? One is that I think your material suffers a little from the fact that the reader feels you approach your subject too *immediately*, show him its elements, the cards in your hand, too bang off from the first page—so that a wait to begin to guess *what and whom the thing is going to be about* doesn't impose itself: the antechamber or two and the crooked corridor before he is already in the Presence. The other is that you don't give him a positive sense of dealing with your subject from its logical centre. This centre I gathered to be, from what you told me in Rome (and one gathers it also from the title), the consciousness of Eleanor—to which all the rest (Manisty, Lucy, the whole phantasmagoria and drama) is presented by life. I should have urged you: "Make that consciousness full, rich, universally prehensile and *stick* to it—don't shift

—and don't shift *arbitrarily*—how otherwise, do you get your unity of subject, or keep up your reader's sense of it?" To which, if you say: "How then do I get *Lucy's* consciousness?," I impudently retort: "By that magnificent and masterly *indirectness* which means the only dramatic straightness and intensity. You get it, in other words, by Eleanor." "And how does Eleanor get it?" "By *everything!* By Lucy, by Manisty, by every pulse of the action in which she is engaged and of which she is the fullest—an exquisite—register. Go behind *her*—miles and miles; don't go behind the others, or the subject—i.e. the unity of impression—goes to smash." [61]

Neither hypocrisy nor diplomacy dictated James's comments on Mrs. Ward's novels so much as respect for her intelligence and goodwill. He was frank enough to criticize what he genuinely disliked—her naturalistic *Story of Bessie Costrell* ("I find, for myself, your best in your dealings with data less simple, on a plan less simple"), her tendency to introduce conventional "third volume-y" happy endings. Of her first novel, *Miss Bretherton* (1884), its somewhat Jamesian plot involving a beautiful young actress and a restrained scholarly hero who does not realize that he loves her until almost too late, James wrote to her:

I wish that your actress had been carried away from Kendal altogether, carried away by the current of her artistic life . . . one doesn't feel her, see her, enough, as the pushing artist, the *cabotine!* She lapses toward him as if she were a failure, whereas you make her out a great success. No!—she wouldn't have thought so much of him at such a time as that—though very possibly she would have come back to him later.[62]

And although he praised *Robert Elsmere* ("The book has great and rare beauty and interest of a high order"), he disliked the romantic subplot and pointed out candidly that she often failed to *represent* character ("your people are not simply enough seen and planted on their feet") and that she did not always maintain artistic objectivity toward her characters. Of her portrait of

Robert, for example, he observed: ". . . one fears a little sometimes that he may suffer a sunstroke, damaging if not fatal, from
the high oblique light of your admiration for him." [63]

James was far too great an artist himself to confuse Mrs.
Ward's polemics for art. The qualities that he singled out of her
work for special notice are those of the intellect: "Knowledge,
curiosity, acuteness, a critical faculty remarkable in itself and
very highly trained, the direct observation of life. . . ." [64] Beyond
these, Mrs. Ward had nothing but industry and self-confidence.
It was enough to make her in her day a rich, famous, and influential woman. It is enough to make her even in our day a figure
worthy of attention and respect.

Notes

1. In 1885, Mrs. Ward outlined her plans for the yet unwritten *Robert
   Elsmere* to her friend Lady Bell and asked her opinion: "I said I
   thought the story most interesting," Lady Bell recalled.

   > But I was foolish enough and ignorant enough to add that I was
   > not sure that the main issue of the book, the question of believing
   > and doubting, would interest the general public. She stood still . . .
   > and looked at me with astonishment—and said with a fervour and
   > conviction that I have remembered so often since, "But surely there
   > is nothing else so interesting in this world!" (*Landmarks* [London,
   > 1929], p. 98).

2. *Essays on Modern Novelists* (New York, 1910), pp. 205–206.
3. Amy Cruse, *After the Victorians* (London, 1938), p. 31.
4. " 'Robert Elsmere' and the Battle of Belief," *Nineteenth Century*, XXIII
   (May, 1888) , 766 ff.
5. See her essay "Recent Fiction in England and France," *Macmillan's
   Magazine,* L (August, 1884), 250–60. Reviewing a group of French novels
   (Feuillet, Ohnet, Daudet, Cherbuliez), she concludes that the French
   influence "is a cause for alarm; we see in it a menace to the sense of
   beauty, to the power of conscience, and to all the sweeter and finer elements of imagination."
6. Preface to Westmoreland edition, Vol. XI. This handsome collected edition of Mrs. Ward's novels (to 1911) with her introductions, was published in the United States by Houghton Mifflin, 1909–1912, and in
   London by John Murray in 1911.
7. See Arnold Bennett's comment:

   > I have invented a destiny for Mrs. Humphry Ward's heroines. It is
   > terrible, and just. They ought to be caught, with their lawful male

protectors, in the siege of a great city by a foreign army. Their lawful male protectors ought, before sallying forth on a forlorn hope, to provide them with a revolver as a last refuge from a brutal and licentious soldiery. And when things come to a crisis, in order to be concluded in our next, the revolvers ought to prove unloaded. I admit that this invention of mine is odious, and quite un-English, and such as would never occur to a right-minded subscriber to Mudie's. But it illustrates the mood caused in me by witnessing the antics of those harrowing dolls (*Books and Persons: Being Comments on a Past Epoch, 1908–1911* [New York, 1917], p. 52).

8. A.L.S., September 8, 1903, Special Collections, Columbia University. For John Oliver Hobbes' correspondence with Mrs. Belmont, see below, pp. 268–69, n. 8.

9. *Several of My Lives* (London, 1928), p. 206. *Agatha* was privately printed in 1903. One sample of the dialogue will explain its total failure; the hero is speaking to a woman who is threatening blackmail:

> Ford: You miserable woman.
> Mrs. Bob: Oh, hard words won't get rid of me!
> Ford: I have only to lift my finger—and you go to penal servitude!

10. The Victorians' conception of love between those of the same sex cannot be fairly understood by an age steeped in Freud. Where they saw only beautiful friendship, the modern reader suspects perversion . . . we must avoid reading back interpretations that could never have been suspected when they were written (Gordon S. Haight, Introduction to *Edith Simcox and George Eliot*, by K. A. McKenzie [Oxford, 1967], p. xvi).

Mrs. Ward herself observed, in describing an intensely emotional scene between two women: "The tender and adoring friendship of women for women, which has become so marked a feature of our self-realising generation, had passed Letty by. She had never known it. Now . . . she seemed to be trembling within reach of its emotion" (*Sir George Tressady*, Ch. XXI). In her last novel, *Harvest* (1920), two women join forces to run a farm: "They had met at college, taken their farm training together, and fallen in love with each other. . . . Each had been attracted by the loneliness of the other, and on leaving college nothing was more natural than that they should set up together" (Ch. II). One of the most interesting portraits of such a friendship is in George Meredith's *Diana of the Crossways* (1884), where the heroine is deeply devoted to an older woman. After quoting one especially ardent passage from a letter Diana writes to her ("I long for your heart on mine, your dear eyes. . . . My beloved. . . . It is not compassion I want. I want you"), Meredith comments: "They had often talked of the possibility of a classic friendship between women, the alliance of a mutual devotedness men choose to doubt of" (Ch. VII).

11. See her unpublished letter to [Stephen] Haweis, London, May 8, 1888, in the Lowell Collection, Houghton Library:

> The only portrait in Robert Elsmere is that of Professor T. H. Green. This is patent to all who know Oxford, and I meant it to

be so. But with regard to Elsmere I never had the idea of J. R. Green [the historian] in my head. The only real person who may have helped me with him is Kingsley, whose life, a very favourite book of mine, suggested some of the *colouring* of the country parish part—nothing else. . . . The London life has nothing to do with J. R. Green. Towards the end I became aware that people might say there was a certain likeness between his death and Elsmere's, but by that time my own conception of Elsmere's fate—arrived at quite independently—was so fixed that I could not alter it.

The Squire is in no sense a portrait of [Mark] Pattison, whose real nature was essentially different. And Langham is merely an attempt to realise, under English forms, some traits—the most forbidding ones—of men like Amiel and Senancour, with whom I had naturally been occupied during my translation of Amiel's Journal.

That there are details and descriptions taken from real life in the novel goes without saying. But as I said before the only portrait in it is that of W. T. H. Green. There is a sketch among the minor characters—to be perfectly true—of a person now dead and known to a small circle. But this concerns no one but myself. Langham, Elsmere, the Squire, are the results of my own thoughts, feelings and interests and nothing else.

She reiterated this disclaimer and gave further details of the origins of the novel in her preface to the Westmoreland edition of *Elsmere*.

12. The hero of *Oakfield*, like its author, died young, his health ruined by the rigors of the Indian climate. The book makes no attempt to glorify colonialism. Rather, it emphasizes the emptiness and futility of army life. E. M. Forster wrote a sympathetic appreciation of the novel, which he described as "a strange, quixotic, disillusioned work . . . It is so sincere, and it states so fearlessly truths which are unwelcome to the governors and the governed . . ." ("An Arnold in India," *The Listener* [October 12, 1944], pp. 410–11, reprinted in Forster's *Two Cheers for Democracy*).

13. "The Life and Corrsepondence of Thomas Arnold, D. D.," *Essays, Reviews and Addresses*, I (London, 1890), 71.

14. Margaret Woods, "Mrs. Humphry Ward: A Sketch from Memory," *Quarterly Review*, CCXXXIV (July–October, 1920), 47–60.

15. Preface to *William Thomas Arnold, Journalist and Historian*, by Mrs. Humphry Ward and C. E. Montague (Manchester, 1907).

16. The instability and meakness of my proceedings I do not mean to palliate or underestimate. The only plea I can urge is, that I acted in good faith, and that the taint of self-interest never attached to what I did. With folly, weakness, obstinacy, pliancy I may be charged, and more or less justly; but no one can say that any one of my changes was calculated with a view to worldly advantage (*Passages in a Wandering Life* [London, 1900], p. 186).

17. Quoted in Mrs. Ward's *A Writer's Recollections*, I (New York and London, 1918), 28. Many years later, in her novel *The Case of Richard Meynell* (1911), Mrs. Ward has an elderly bishop of the Church of England comment, in the more modern ecumenical spirit, on the trial of the crusading modern clergyman Meynell:

Herbert, just before I was born there were two great religious leaders in England—Newman and Arnold of Rugby. Arnold died prematurely, at the height of bodily and spiritual vigour; Newman lived to the age of eighty-nine, and to be a Cardinal of the Roman Church. His Anglican influence, continued, modified, distributed by the High Church movement, has lasted till now. Today we have been listening again, as it were, to the voice of Arnold, the great leader, whom the liberals lost in '42. Arnold was a devoutly orthodox believer, snatched from life in the very birth-hour of that New Learning of which we claim to be the children. But a church of free men, coextensive with the nation, gathering into one fold every English man, woman and child, that was Arnold's dream, just as it is Meynell's. . . . And yet though the voice, the large heart, the fearless mind ,and the broad sympathies were Arnold's some of the governing ideas were Newman's. As I listened, I seemed . . . to see the two great leaders, the two foes of a century ago, standing side by side, twin brethren in a new battle, growing out of the old, with a great mingled host behind them (Ch. XXI).

18. In *A Writer's Recollections*, I, 133 ff., Mrs. Ward comments on the progress in education for girls since her own childhood:

Poor teaching, poor schoolbooks, and, in many cases, indifferent food and much ignorance as to the physical care of girls—these things were common in my school-time . . . it was not till I went home to live at Oxford in 1867, that I awoke intellectually to a hundred interests and influences that begin much earlier nowadays to affect any clever child.

See also the opening chapters of her novel *Marcella*, where her young heroine's unhappiness at school reflects her own experience.

19. *Ibid.*, I, 137. She has a charming account of her meeting with George Eliot and George Henry Lewes at the Pattisons', pp. 144–48.

20. Quoted in *The House of Harper*, ed., J. Henry Harper (New York, 1912), p. 486.

21. *A Writer's Recollections*, I, 220.

22. For a valuable discussion of Green's philosophy and his influence on Mrs. Ward, see Melvin Richter, *Politics of Conscience: T. H. Green and His Age* (London, 1964).

23. Preface to her translation of *Amiel's Journal* (The Home Library, New York, n.d.), pp. l–li.

24. *A Writer's Recollections*, I, 224–25.

25. Janet Penrose Trevelyan, *The Life of Mrs. Humphry Ward* (hereafter *Life*) (London, 1923), p. 50.

26. *Life*, pp. 74–75. For a summary of the sales history and reception of the novel, see Basil Willey, "How 'Robert Elsmere' Struck Some Contemporaries," *English Association Essays and Studies*, X (1957), 53–68. *Elsmere* remained in print until the 1930's. The only recent edition is a paperback Bison Book (Lincoln, University of Nebraska, 1967), edited and with an introduction by Clyde de L. Ryals.

27. *Life*, p. 76.

28. Introduction to Westmoreland edition of *Robert Elsmere*.

29. For accounts of sales see *Life*, p. 95; S. Nowell-Smith, "Firma Tauchnitz,"

Book Collector, XV (Winter, 1966) , 435–36; and an unpublished letter by Mrs. Ward in the Fales Collection, New York University, to Campbell Clarke, November 16, 1892: "According to my latest reports its circulation has not risen above 100,000 copies in the various copyright editions of England, America and the colonies, so I cannot but feel that it has found many friends in spite of the severe attacks that have been made upon it."

30. George Gissing commented:

> You will see from the Athenaeum that Mrs. Ward's new book promises to repeat the success of "Robert Elsmere." I have not read it. . . . Her method is *precisely* what mine was when I wrote "Workers in the Dawn." Of course she has a mature mind and wide knowledge; but artistically I believe she is at the very point I had reached, after study of George Eliot, some ten years ago. Her books are enormously long, and she develops with great labour the intellectual advance of every character.

Six months later, having read the novel, Gissing wrote: "I think it is better than the reviews led me to expect. But of terrific length . . ." (*Letters of George Gissing to Edward Bertz, 1887–1903,* ed. Arthur C. Young [New Brunswick, N. J., 1961], pp. 145, 159).

31. See her unpublished letter, September 17, 1888, in the Houghton Library, addressed to an unidentified bookseller, in which she asks for half a dozen or so biographies:

> . . . of a class I am now anxious to collect—viz. working class biographies or autobiographies of the present century. I want anything which will throw light on those processes and incidents of self-culture by which men like Thomas Cooper, or William Lovett, or Daniel Macmillan rose to knowledge and success in their different ways. . . . Manchester life in particular I should like some record of—some which would enable me to grasp the development of a boy of great gifts sprung from the Derbyshire moors and living the life say of a bookseller's assistant in Manchester. Will you kindly regard this letter as private?

Mrs. Ward became acquainted with Manchester life at firsthand through visits to that city, where her brother William was on the staff of the *Manchester Guardian.*

32. *Life,* pp. 99–100; *A Writer's Recollections,* II, 136–37. Owen Seaman, the *Punch* humorist, has a delightful parody of Mrs. Ward in *Borrowed Plumes* (London, 1916, pp. 115–25). Part of it refers directly to *David Grieve:*

> He was cognisant of a recrudescence of feeling in favour of the strait tenets of his childhood's orthodoxy. . . . Almost involuntarily he found himself reviewing the processes, now logical, now arbitrary, by which he had arrived at his present tolerance of the principles of Christian Science, qualified by an obscurantist Pantheism. His early unreasoning acceptance of U. P. dogma; his tentative excursions in Kant, followed by a sudden and glorious emancipation from the school of Peebles; his reaction from the strain of the larger Secularism under the Pagan teaching of Barbizon and La Bohème;

then, at first sight of the Eternal City, his *volte-face* from the doctrines of the Latin Quarter to those of the Latin fathers.

33. Introduction to the Westmoreland edition of *Helbeck of Bannisdale*. In *A Writer's Recollections*, I, 29, Mrs. Ward describes her mother's inability to reconcile herself to Thomas Arnold's conversion:

> My poor mother felt as though the earth had crumbled under her. Her passionate affection for my father endured till her latest hour, but she never reconciled herself to what he had done. There was in her an instinctive dread of Catholicism. . . . It never abated. Many years afterward, in writing *Helbeck of Bannisdale*, I drew upon what I had remembered of it in describing some traits in Laura Fountain's inbred, and finally indomitable, resistance to the Catholic claim upon the will and intellect of men.

34. T. H. Green, *Works*, ed. R. L. Nettleship, III (London, 1889), 248.

35. Richter, *Politics of Conscience*, pp. 13–15.

36. Quoted by Basil Willey in "Thomas Arnold," *Nineteenth Century Studies* (New York, 1949), p. 55.

37. *Life*, p. 82.

38. Before the building was finished Edwards had donated £14,000. The Duke of Bedford sold them the Tavistock Square land at less than market price. See *Life*, pp. 120–21, and *A Writer's Recollections*, II, 148–49.

39. "She did for the industrial classes what her grandfather did in other fashion for the boys of the middle and upper classes. . . . This is her earthly monument" (London) *Times Educational Supplement*, April 1, 1920: obituary article on Mrs. Ward.

40. *Life*, p. 117; *A Writer's Recollections*, II, 165–66.

41. For example, Henry James's reaction in a letter to Mrs. Ward May 6, 1914, commenting on the mutilation by a militant suffragette of Sargent's portrait of him hanging in the Royal Academy:

> Figure me as a poor thing additionally impaired by the tomahawk of the savage. . . . Surely indeed the good ladies who claim as a virtue of their sex that they can look an artistic possession of that quality and rarity well in the face only to be moved bloodily to smash it, make a strange appeal to the confidence of the country in the *kind* of character they shall bring to the transaction of our affairs. Valuable to us that species of intelligence! Precious to us that degree of sensibility (*Letters*, ed. Percy Lubbock II [New York, 1920], 366–67).

42. *Nineteenth Century*, XXVIII (June, 1889), 781–85.

43. *Life*, pp. 269–70. Her visit to America in 1908 was the basis for a novel, *Marriage à la Mode* (1908; published in England as *Daphne*), which combines travel book with an attack on divorce, a practice she discovered to her horror much freer in America than in England. In the course of the novel her characters attend a reception at the White House and meet the President and his cabinet—all easily recognizable. Of Roosevelt she writes fulsomely, ". . . the reincarnation of forces primitive, overmastering and heroic. An honest Odysseus! toil-worn and storm-beaten, yet still with the spirit and strength . . . of a boy . . . a rugged figure . . . breasting the modern world, like some ocean headland, yet not

truly of it, one of the great fighters and workers of mankind" (Ch. IV).

44. (London) *Times*, March 26, 1920; obituary article on Mrs. Ward.
45. II, 233.
46. U. C. Knoepflmacher draws some amusing but otherwise hardly signifi-
    cant parallels between Mrs. Ward's novel *Lady Connie* (1916) and D. H.
    Lawrence's *Lady Chatterley's Lover*. He cannot establish that Lawrence
    knew the novel. Indeed, other than the coincidence of the heroine's
    names, the novels have very little in common ("The Rival Ladies: Mrs.
    Ward's 'Lady Connie' and Lawrence's 'Lady Chatterley's Lover,'"
    Victorian Studies, IV [December, 1960], 141–58.
47. *A Writer's Recollections*, II, 244.
48. See above, Introduction, p. 13.
49. A. L. S., January 8, 1889, Fales Collection.
50. Charles S. Olcott, *The Lure of the Camera* (New York, 1914), p. 98.
51. *Adventures of a Novelist* (New York, 1932), pp. 233–34.
52. In her autobiography *The Fabric of Memory* (New York, 1957), pp.
    24–25, Mrs. August Belmont recalls visiting Mrs. Ward at Stocks along
    with Louis N. Parker to discuss her role in Mrs. Ward's play *Agatha:*

> Mrs. Ward herself was typically Victorian in appearance, tall and
> stately, with a genuinely pleasant, although somewhat overwhelming,
> personality. We were far from being inspired by *Agatha;* however,
> we were impressed by Mrs. Ward. When I inquired with interest
> how she wrote her books—did she wait for inspiration and then take
> up the pen—she replied, "Not at all. My family, of course, comes
> first. I give the household orders for the day; at nine-thirty I retire
> to my study, put my knees under the table, and stay there until
> time for lunch. Sometimes thoughts flow easily. Sometimes only a
> paragraph will be the morning's work." . . . As we left Tring behind,
> Louis N. Parker dispelled the awesome atmosphere when he chris-
> tened our hostess "Ma-Hump."

53. *Life*, p. 99.
54. *Life*, pp. 255–56.
55. *Latest Contemporary Portraits* (New York, 1927), p. 101.
56. *Ibid.*, p. 98.
57. *Frank Harris on Bernard Shaw* (London, 1931), p. 273.
58. The photograph is reproduced in *Life*, p. 252.
59. *A Writer's Recollections*, II, 16.
60. See below, Ch. V, pp. 305ff.
61. *Letters of Henry James*, I, 322–23. His italics.
62. *A Writer's Recollections*, II, 18–19.
63. Quoted in her introduction to *Robert Elsmere*, Westmoreland edition.
64. "Mrs. Humphry Ward," *English Illustrated Magazine*, IX (1892), 399–
    401. Leon Edel writes that some years later, when a friend asked James
    how he had come to write this article, he replied, "I have written no
    article on Mrs. Ward—only a civil perfunctory *payé* (with words be-
    tween the lines) to escape the gracelessness of refusing when asked." In
    spite of this comment, James reprinted the article the following year
    in his *Essays in London and Elsewhere* (*Henry James: The Middle
    Years* [Philadelphia and New York, 1962], p. 207).

*I believe I am a lover of souls, but people scare
me out of my wits: it is not that I am nervous—
I have only a sensation of being, as it were, in
"the wrong Paradise." I am not at home; I talk
about things which I do not believe in, to
people who do not believe me. I have become
constrained, artificial.*
—Letter to George Moore,
March 8, 1894 [1]

4

The Wrong Paradise:
John Oliver Hobbes

When the Victorians called a woman "clever," they paid her
a slightly left-handed compliment. Female intelligence, even in a
predominantly antifeminist age, was always recognized as a de-
sirable quality. Matched with wit and sufficient creative power
to produce some concrete achievement—for example, a novel or
a poem—the combination was altogether felicitous. To the extent, then, that it suggested a productive use of skill and talent,
"cleverness" was a compliment. But the word also suggested
something less flattering and less desirably feminine: smartness,
shrewdness, overconfidence, brittle social sophistication. Early in
the century we read that Jane Austen's Emma "is spoiled by
being the cleverest of her family." In Charlotte Yonge's novel of
1865, *The Clever Woman of the Family*, a heroine who "had
the palm of cleverness ceded to her ever since she could recollect,
when she read better at three years old than her sister at five . . .
[and] surpassed in acquirements and reflection all the persons

with whom she came in contact," is punished severely for her
self-assurance and pride. Cheated by a scoundrel and imposter,
she becomes indirectly responsible for the death of a child and,
after due suffering, agrees in the final chapter with her husband
that "such cleverness as that is a far more perilous gift than your
plodding intellectuality has even been." [2] And Charles Kingsley
patronizingly admonished his female readers: "Be good, sweet
maid, and let who will be clever."

It was one of the several unhappy ironies of Pearl Mary-
Teresa Richards Craigie's life that she was strikingly clever.
William Dean Howells, who respected and admired her work,
summed her up as "the very clever woman who had the caprice
of calling herself 'John Oliver Hobbes.' " [3] Only the evidence of
her published work remains today to testify to the ultimate
seriousness of her talent. The evidence of her biography tends
rather to support Howells—the rich, pretty, spoiled, and clever
young woman who capriciously scribbled plays and novels that,
thanks to her father's large fortune and her own charm and initi-
ative, were published and received with some fleeting success.

For a brief period at the turn of the century Mrs. Craigie
was a famous and, in some circles, a notorious woman. Her
novels sold well in England and America and were received with
respect and often acclaim by the critics. She contributed to the
first number of *The Yellow Book,* comfortably at home in the
literary company of Henry James, George Moore, and Max Beerbohm. Her work appeared in the 1896 Christmas issue of *Saturday Review* alongside Thomas Hardy's, and in the elegant and
exclusive *Anglo-Saxon Review,* published by Lady Randolph
Churchill (Mrs. Cornwallis-West). Between 1898 and 1900 three
of her plays (*The Ambassador, The Wisdom of the Wise,* and the
one-act *A Repentance*) were produced by Sir George Alexander
at the St. James Theatre, where only a few years earlier *Lady
Windermere's Fan* and *The Importance of Being Earnest* had
had their premières. Her first play, a one-act "trifle," *Journeys
End in Lovers Meeting* (1894), had Ellen Terry in the leading
role. At its première, a glittering charity matinee, Mrs. Craigie
sat in a box with the Princess of Wales (later Queen Alexandra)
and Henry Irving. She gave public lectures in England and the

United States on Dante, Tolstoy, Loyola, Balzac, and Brahms. Her public image was glamorous. She was rich, beautiful, exquisitely gowned, and—the supreme achievement of that era— "a woman with a history." Her reputation managed to survive a sordid divorce case, a conversion to Roman Catholicism, a barrage of gossip that linked her romantically with such eminent figures as Arthur James Balfour, Lord Asquith, and Lord Curzon, and—most remarkable—even the vicious scandal-mongering of George Moore.

In the light of such a triumphant career, it is difficult to account for the total oblivion into which Mrs. Craigie fell only a few years after her sudden and premature death. The answer rests, in part, with the period of the '90's itself and the ephemeral quality of so much of the work that it produced. The very gifts of wit, charm, wealth, and social position that she had were, ironically, those which thrust her into the center of the over-decorated, self-conscious, affected, and perverse literary society of her day. She had other gifts of a more substantial nature—religious sensibility, a keen analytical mind, solid scholarly and intellectual ability. Twenty or thirty years earlier these might have directed her into the kind of serious work that attracted George Eliot. This is not to suggest that John Oliver Hobbes might have been anything other than what she was, certainly not to suggest that she had anything like George Eliot's genius. But it does remind us that the peculiar course her career took was shaped by the Decadent movement of the '90's, that she cultivated her talents for witty epigram and fashionable aestheticism, rather than those other talents she had in equal measure.

John Oliver Hobbes chose her own direction. She never drifted aimlessly. Throughout her brief career, however, there is evidence that she wanted to move in other directions as well. Even while writing some of her gauziest little social comedies, she was wrestling with all manner of profound issues, religious and purely intellectual, reading philosophers and theologians, studying Greek and Latin, listening to Wagner (attentively but not appreciatively [4]), and playing Beethoven on the piano. She was not so much ambivalent as multidirectional. She had no conflict among her interests, no forced alternatives or choices. Her father's wealth made it possible, even easy, for her to have two worlds—or three or four had she wanted them. Her misfortune, indeed, was that in being able to have everything, she possessed or mastered nothing.

In the total assessment, Mrs. Craigie's literary career dwindles into some arch drawing-room comedies in the Oscar Wilde manner, a handful of novels and short stories, a few negligible essays and scraps of literary criticism. Her most striking characteristic is a gift for epigram, but this, like the other felicities of her life, was a dubious blessing. It gives her work a certain sparkle. It also quickly palls. The American novelist Gertrude Atherton, who hated her, put her into a novel, *Ancestors,* where she spouts epigrams: "The British aristocracy is to society what God is to the world—all sufficient, all merciful, all powerful." At this point her listener thinks: "And she would sacrifice Him and all his archangels for an epigram." A less vicious but equally damaging verse was circulated in 1894:

> John Oliver Hobbes, with your spasms and throbs,
> How does your novel grow?
> With cynical sneers at young Love and his tears,
> And epigrams all in a row.[5]

Her work is easily reduced to formula—a series of changes and variations on the perverseness of the human heart, the dialects of the spirit. In principle, of course, this is a theme with infinite possibilities. She treats it seriously and ambitiously at times, especially in her novel *The School for Saints* and its sequel, *Robert Orange.* But for the most part she merely plays with it in virtuoso exercises—love stories with fanciful and grotesque titles, faceless but impeccably mannered characters who talk brilliantly and act foolishly. She never learned to construct a story, and she confused diagramming for plotting. The reference in the verse quoted above to the "cynical sneers" in her love stories was suggested, probably, not so much by their cynicism as by their mechanical and contrived pattern. She will begin with one pair of lovers, align them carefully against another pair, introduce still other pairs, and then begin a change-partners quadrille, until by the end of the story we have quite lost sight of the original positions. All this is done in fashionable town and country houses with witty talk and polished manners, the author playing the role of puppeteer, manipulating her characters through their intricate but stiff-jointed movements. Her detachment makes her appear the cynic. Often, however, her pose is transparent. The cynicism is as affected and artificial as everything else in her work. Underneath it is the curious and painful vulnerability of a very unhappy woman.

No one should have been better aware of her failures than Mrs. Craigie herself. Her mind and literary tastes were far too good for her to fail to recognize her limitations. Perhaps it was merely the iconoclast pose, but more likely it was the genuine vigor of her intellect that led her to hail Henry Fielding for his earthiness and realism. She would rather, she confesses, read how his Amelia "pawned her best chemises and her trinkets to pay for Booth's gambling debts than be given a long unreal account of her obtaining, in a sweet conversation and a tea-gown, several thousand pounds from a Platonic admirer. The pawnshop exists; the millionaire Platonic admirer is yet to be found." [6] Similarly, she praises George Sand for her freshness and vitality: "We never suspect the burning pastille, the gauzy tea-gown, or the depressed pink light." [7] John Oliver Hobbes, we read in her biography, wore flowing "Watteau" gowns, lived in overfurnished rooms with stained glass lampshades, if not depressed pink lights, and "choice bibelots," [8] and spent much of her time in bed suffering from fatigue and illnesses that often defied medical diagnosis. It must have been apparent to her in moments of soul-searching that her failure in her own work was clearly not one of taste but of talent.

The literary reputation Mrs. Craigie sought was that of sophisticated wit. The personal pose she assumed was that of tragic muse. Though a pose, it was not particularly unnatural or affected. At worst she was socially ambitious and self-dramatizing. She was, however, much maligned by gossip and much put upon. To live up to her position meant to live down an American Low Church background, an aggressive father who had made his fortune selling patent medicine, a neurotic, eccentric mother, an unhappy marriage and a scandalous divorce, a religious conversion, and a reputation for cleverness that alienated scores of other self-conscious social climbers. Max Beerbohm, who knew her only slightly, had a typically acid comment on her: "The pretty and pleasant little woman of the 1890s was of all climbers the grimmest, of all wire pullers the most indefatigable and undiscourageable, and of all ladies who ever put pen to paper the most brazenly conceited." Max, his biographer tells us, had a genial prejudice against all women writers.[9] Nevertheless, it must be admitted that Mrs. Craigie convicts herself.

Whatever secret anxieties she may have had, Mrs. Craigie showed no trace of modesty about her writing. Her self-confidence was sublime. Her father recounts, for example, her difficulties in first getting her books published in America. He came with her to New York in 1892 to sell her second novel, *The Sinner's Comedy,* fortified with clippings of "exceptionally favourable reviews of her first book. . . . I accompanied her upon most of these visits, but, by her particular request, I did not attempt any negotiation: she preferred to state the case herself." They were turned down everywhere until they approached Cassell & Company, which published many British books and accepted this one. Even if Cassell had refused them, Mrs. Craigie was prepared to carry her siege to Boston: ". . . she never wavered for one instant in her conviction that she would get the book published, and upon satisfactory terms." Even later, when securely established on both sides of the Atlantic, she continued to use the hard sell with her publishers. She was a good business woman, possibly the result of her father's influence, and took a coolly professional attitude toward the publication of her work. She handled her business affairs efficiently, advised on how her books should be advertised, and followed her sales records carefully.[10] On editorial matters she was self-assured and firm. When Macmillan returned the manuscript of her first novel, suggesting revisions and a change of title, she refused to make any changes and sent the manuscript directly to Fisher Unwin, who accepted it for the Pseudonym Library. However, she declined to publish future novels in that series, which was identified with "light" literature. Instead she suggested to Unwin that he publish *The Sinner's Comedy* in a yellow paper cover, as French novels were usually issued, and sell it at half a crown. "I think it would attract more than the humdrum three-and-six-penny cloth. As to Terms. As I told you before I should be sorry if you suffered any loss on my account. Whether you paid me more for a longer book or not, would not deter me from spending a year on it if I felt it was necessary to the full development of my idea." She read her reviews closely, delighting in praise, bristling at criticism, but usually good-natured: "Please do not think I am 'peppery' under criticism: if a reader may not have his opinion of a book why write at all? I cannot resist, however, uttering a word of self-defense when a set of characters (who are described with the nearest approach to realism I have ever attempted) are called stagey." [11] To the public—and this included her publishers—she always appeared serene and secure: "I am absolutely certain that my *biggest* sales are for the future," she wrote Unwin in 1904:

> because some of my best ideas are far in advance of the present average reader. . . . I write from knowledge and that is why my method is so expensive; it is also why the books will ultimately have value. They have many faults, no doubt, but they are not twaddle. As psychological stuff they are sound, and as studies of modern English life, they are the truth.[12]

Her private image was quite another thing. Writing was a form of personal indulgence for Mrs. Craigie as, indeed, her whole life was an indulgence; her ill health, her religion, her philanthropy,[13] probably even her unhappy marriage, are expressions of it. In 1898 her mysterious malady—fits of total exhaustion and unconsciousness—was finally diagnosed as a form of epilepsy, *le petit mal*. She appeared to welcome the diagnosis as an excuse for a veritable debauch of self-indulgence—physical, spiritual, and intellectual. "This is why I need constant attendance." she wrote to Charles Lewis Hind:

and every sort of small luxury. That is why I can never be
sure of my mood. That is why I cannot walk some days for
fear of falling. That is why I am more sure of the reality of
the next world than this: and that is why I depend rather
on God for my support than on human beings—no matter
how kind: that is why my work must ever be, to a great extent, objective, or if you prefer it, insincere. Everything I
write as an author is, in a sense, a matter of acting—dramatic impersonation.

Such a condition permitted and even encouraged those qualities
of her work for which she was so often criticized—her seeming
detachment from human sympathies and emotions and her bland
assumption of intellectual superiority: "It has been complained
that I have not found my 'true' line. I am discovering it by
degrees. I am a writer of histories—some one must give me the
human nature and I will compose a commentary upon it. I am
not a lover of humanity. I like souls. I understand all sorts of
purely mental things. I am not good at the mere emotions." [14]
Like many another poseur, Mrs. Craigie eventually became
what she pretended to be. The tragic muse may have been an
inappropriate role for her, but it was not so absurd as it at first
appears. To trace the brief span of her life is to see a small-scale
drawing-room tragedy: a bright talent misspent and wasted, a
woman with every potentiality for happiness and success doomed
by her own gifts. Neither her art nor her religion provided any
lasting consolation. Only a few months before her death she
wrote: "My idea is that Christianity (in its very nature pessimistic
so far as this world is concerned) reconciles one to the squalor of
life." [15] Of the actual squalor of life Mrs. Craigie had very little
knowledge. But she was a bitterly unhappy woman when she
wrote those lines. For more than ten years she had uttered cries
of anguish in letters to her closest friends. In 1894 these cries had
a synthetic, theatrical note: "The silence of my life overwhelms
me. . . . I cannot face the loneliness of a crowded drawing room:
the host of mere acquaintances, the solitariness of the return. . . .
I try to forget myself in other people: I try to think only of
others, and never of myself. I choke my soul with work, and yet

—and yet!" Over the years, however, there is a deepening melancholy, a quieter but more compelling despair alternating with feverish outbursts of energy, social life, and writing. In March, 1906, she observed: "I am not morbid at all, but no one who knows me as well as I know myself could wish me to live. I am never free from acute mental suffering . . . it is the spectacle of life itself, the struggle to keep going, the eternal fight against discouragement, against stupidity, against cruelty." [16] One of John Oliver Hobbes' major weaknesses as a novelist was her inability to create believable characters. But in herself she created her best character—colorful, complex, and if not (as she would have wished) tragic, at least credibly pathetic.

The principal published source of our knowledge of Mrs. Craigie is the patchwork biography *The Life of John Oliver Hobbes* that her father put together a few years after her death —a collection of his fond memories, the tributes of a few admiring friends, and her letters. These last are so cut and patched, their receivers' names often concealed with X, Y, Z initials, that they distort the shadowy image that the book presents. Furthermore, her father's uncritical admiration for his talented daughter, his use of her most pretentious and inflated comments and the fulsome tributes of some of her friends, emphasize, probably unjustly, the stuffy, conceited, affected personality and completely obscures her humanity. Equally unsatisfying is the sympathetic but unrevealing portrait of her in Henry Logan Stuart's novel *Fenella* (1911). Stuart, an English-born American journalist, was a Catholic. He probably had not known Mrs. Craigie personally, but he appears to have read her father's biography and he certainly knew the outlines of her life. His character Althea Rees is the only daughter of a rich American, "a big, oldtime orating and banqueting type of American citizen," who buys a literary magazine, the *Parthenon,* to promote his daughter's literary ambitions. Her novels are noted for their brilliant talk and style and—after her conversion to Catholicism—for asceticism which "never strayed far from the purlieus and issues of Mayfair. . . . She had that affinity to the highly placed which is less snobbery, I believe, than a kind of perverse idealism." The circumstances of Althea's divorce appear to have been lifted from the *Times'* account of the Craigie divorce trial, and her unexpected death is described much as it is in the biography.

Most of the other writing about Mrs. Craigie is either uncritical and adoring, if it is the work of her friends, or malicious, if it is the work of her enemies. Ellen Terry, who acted in one of Mrs. Craigie's plays, wrote of her enthusiastically:

> Pearl Craigie had a man's intellect, a woman's wit and swiftness of apprehension. Brilliant she always managed to be, even in the dullest company, and well as she talked, she was never guilty of monopolising conversation. . . . Wonderfully tolerant, she would all the same not easily forgive any meanness or injustice that seemed to her deliberate. Hers was a splendid spirit.[17]

Lady Randolph Churchill remembered her as "A woman of great sympathies . . . a brilliant and clever conversationalist [who] could hold her own with all manner of men, and yet in the more frivolous company, which she often frequented and thoroughly enjoyed, she never talked over people's heads. She had the art of drawing everyone out and making them appear at their best." [18] Lord Curzon, eulogizing her at memorial ceremonies in 1908, hailed her as an extraordinary woman of "an intense and vivid personality, which pervaded her writings, irradiated her talk, and informed her life." [19]

It was Mrs. Craigie's misfortune that her enemies—Gertrude Atherton and George Moore in particular—were uncommonly articulate, and their accounts are more interesting than those of her friends. Mrs. Atherton draws a cruel fictional portrait of her in *Ancestors* (1907). It has, nevertheless, a certain basis in fact. As far as one may gather from her memoirs, *Adventures of a Novelist*, Mrs. Atherton knew her only slightly. They met once at a garden party, where Mrs. Craigie struck her simply as "a short, dark woman who would have been plain but for a pair of remarkably fine eyes." But Mrs. Craigie made the fatal error of snubbing her: she "even turned her back on me pointedly one night when she was receiving with the hostess at a literary party."

This was enough to trigger Mrs. Atherton's wrath. She accused Mrs. Craigie, American-born and therefore a rival sister-novelist, of jealousy—"until I appeared [she] had been the only American pebble on the literary beach"—and of seeing to it that *The Academy,* the literary weekly owned by Mrs. Craigie's father, constantly "slammed" her novels.[20] Vincent O'Sullivan, reviewing all this in his admirably objective account in *Opinions,* judged that Mrs. Craigie was far too well established and secure at this time to be jealous of the then relatively unknown Mrs. Atherton.[21] But the wound rankled. In *Ancestors* Mrs. Atherton portrayed her as a wealthy American, Julia Kaye, "astonishingly clever," given to epigram-making and snubbing young sister Americans who are visiting England. Aside from such details, nothing in the portrait is more than literary gossip, but after the venom is boiled out of the mixture, a residue of probability remains.

For example, Mrs. Atherton sketches Julia Kaye's parents as vulgar social climbers. They were in fact neither vulgar, nor, in the aggressive sense, climbers. But they were Americans of recent wealth, most of it acquired in what was then the socially dubious business of patent medicine manufacture. John Morgan Richards was certainly not the slum-reared peddler of *Ancestors* who makes a fortune by turning "the torch of his genius upon the fatal antipathies of vermin," in Mrs. Atherton's colorful prose. He was of a quite respectable background, born not in the slums but in the rather idyllic rural surroundings of Aurora, New York, in 1841, son of a Presbyterian clergyman, James Richards, and descendant of a venerable line of clergymen. Nor did he begin his career as a peddler—although "traveling salesman and advertising agent" may have meant as much to sensitive upper-class British society in the 1890's. His obituary in *Printer's Ink* (August 15, 1918) acknowledges that "his methods in those days were similar to those of the advance agent of a circus," and adds in tribute that when he came to England to promote his line of patent medicines, "he used the first pictorial poster advertising a trade article in Great Britain," thus being singlehandedly responsible "for the introduction of American advertising methods abroad." Mrs. Craigie benefited magnificently from her father's business success, but she was never able to live down the sources of his wealth: a line of Colgate products, Bromo-Seltzer, Mrs. Allen's Hair Restorer, and—the patent medicine that he almost immortalized—Carter's Little Liver Pills. Henry James once met Mr. Richards, having been discreetly informed beforehand of his primary business account. "Obsessed by this fact, Mr. James was wont to relate that when he entered the drawing-room at Lancaster Gate and was introduced by Mrs. Craigie to her father, he shook hands with the remark, 'How are you, Mr. Carter?' " [22]

Whatever cause of social embarrassment he may have been for her, Mrs. Craigie was deeply attached to her father. Their photographs show a striking resemblance—large square face, firm mouth, high cheekbones, sweet eyes, but photographed usually in a shrewd, penetrating stare. He was sympathetic to her work and proud of her success. In using his money to advance her career—if, in fact, that was the reason for his purchase of *The Academy*—he was also gratifying his own literary bent.[23] He wrote two books: *With John Bull and Jonathan: Reminiscences of Sixty Years of an American's Life in England and in the United States* (1906), a pompous and meandering autobiography, and *Almost Fairyland* (1914), an enthusiastic testimonial to the Isle of Wight, where the Richards family summered for many years. No doubt he was at times a trial to his cultivated and socially ambitious daughter, and she struggled to break away from him, taking chambers for herself once at the Albany and building a private cottage retreat some little distance from the family's palatial home on the Isle of Wight. But the fact remains that she turned to him in almost every crisis of her life, and, though financially independent, she chose to be with or near him until only a few hours before she died.

Mrs. Craigie had a less sympathetic relationship with her mother, a commonplace, rather simple-minded woman who, in later years particularly, carried her religious fervor and philanthropy to neurotic if not insane excesses. Nevertheless, she was not the crude social climber Gertrude Atherton portrayed as Julia Kaye's mother. Her maiden name was Laura Hortense Arnold, and she was born in Nova Scotia, where her grandfather had been a member of the colonial parliament. She met Richards in Boston, where they were married on December 31, 1863. An ardent churchwoman, she was active in charity work, arranged bazaars, and was given to spurts of evangelical fervor. A visitor described the elegant salon of 56 Lancaster Gate, the Richards' London house, where Mrs. Craigie lived after her divorce, as decorated with flowered wall paper, framed religious mottoes, a life-size statue of Joan of Arc, and a large placard on which was printed "What would Jesus say?" When Mrs. Craigie entered the room and found her guests staring at the placard, she explained quickly, "Oh, that's mother's." [24]

Pearl was their first child, born at the home of her maternal grandparents in Chelsea, near Boston, on November 3, 1867, and the only American-born member of what was to be a family of three sons and two daughters. Ten days after her birth her father was on his way to London on business, and within a few months he was permanently settled there. His wife and infant daughter joined him in February, 1868. Thus merely an accident of birth and time made Pearl Richards an American. She returned to the United States many times as a visitor, but she was by background, by education, and apparently by choice as loyally and unequivocally English as it was possible to be.

An only child for the first few years of her life, pretty and precocious, Pearl early became accustomed to being the center of admiring attention. The family was solidly prosperous and rapidly growing richer. They lived first in a furnished house near Kennington Gate; in 1870 they moved into a house in Tavistock Square, in then still fashionable Bloomsbury. Socially the Richards had not yet "arrived." According to Mrs. Atherton's cruel portrait of them in *Ancestors*, their social ambitions were thoroughly frustrated, and it was only by hard-nosed persistence that they finally won a precarious place in society. But the record, at least Mr. Richards' testimony, suggests more reasonably that their first years in England were typical of those of most newcomers in a closed society: "Outside business relations, we had no American friends to visit. An American colony had not then been founded in London and there were but few social engagements to tempt us away from home." [25]

Mrs. Richards occupied herself with philanthropic visits to

the orphaned children at neighboring Tavistock House, later to be the scene of Mrs. Humphry Ward's social work. Mr. Richards plunged actively into the affairs of the City Temple, a nonconformist church, and formed a close personal friendship with its presiding clergyman, Dr. Joseph Parker. In such an atmosphere of earnest good works Pearl grew up, a plump, cheerful, lively little girl who in winter dressed in boys' clothing because her father had decided that these would be a safeguard against the drafts and chills of a London house without central heating. She trotted alongside her mother carrying presents to the unfortunate orphans; she read hungrily; she scribbled stories for Dr. Parker's church newspaper; and she developed in a thoroughly conventional pattern—a good boarding school in Newbury, Berkshire, from 1876 to 1877, private day schools in London in 1878 and again from 1882 to 1886, and a school in Paris from 1880 to 1881. She was always allowed to read freely, to visit art galleries and theaters, and in general to indulge every taste and potential talent. In 1883 she returned to Paris to study music, having shown exceptional talent for the piano. Her most significant education, however, came from her independent reading—extensive, wildly varied, and completely undisciplined. Before she was seventeen, she writes, she had read "without method all the works—many of them many times over" of Shakespeare, Fielding, Thackeray, Dickens, George Eliot, Dante, Milton, Ouida, Rita, Harrison Ainsworth, and Rhoda Broughton. But it was not until she was past twenty, she says, that she could appreciate Balzac, Meredith, and Flaubert, and the philosophers Aristotle, Plato, and the German metaphysicals.[26] By May, 1886, the Richards family had achieved sufficient status to manage a presentation at Court for their pretty young daughter. Later that year she made her first trip to America to be a bridesmaid at the wedding of Julia Randall Drake, and less than a year later, in February, 1887, she became a bride herself, at Christ Church, Lancaster Gate, London.

Because of the unhappy outcome of this marriage, Mr. Richards says as little as possible about it in his biography of his daughter, and she says nothing at all in any of her published writings and very little in the letters that are extant. From the number of unhappy marriages in her novels one is tempted to draw unverifiable conclusions about her own marriage. Mrs. Atherton has an interesting and relatively fair version. Her heroine Julia, "an uncommonly clever little girl," resolves early in her life "to read her name in Burke." Educated with every advantage, she travels to India, where she meets a romantic young military officer, "heir to an ancient baronry, chivalrous, impressionable, and hard-up." They marry and live happily for five years, until his death. Nineteen-year-old Pearl Richards married a handsome young man with a faint resemblance to Mrs. Atherton's character. He was Reginald Walpole Craigie, twenty-nine, a clerk in the Bank of England, of a solidly respectable family. The military-India connection may have been the fact that he was the grandson of Colonel Craigie of the Bengal Military Board.[27] On their wedding trip to Cannes, Mrs. Craigie became seriously ill with a knee inflammation which forced their early return to England, where they lived with the Richards family for six months, until she recovered; then they took their own flat in Oxford Street.

The Craigies appear to have plunged gaily into London society. Attractive, rich, and well connected, they were received everywhere. According to one literary gossip column, he was a dapper young man-about-town, "very handsome and agreeable, with a splendid physique and—a passion for drink." [28] Taking such reports for what they are worth, the fact remains that for the first years of their marriage Mrs. Craigie apparently managed to keep pace with her husband's social activities. She recorded her lively doings in a series of sketches for a weekly, *Life*—pieces of art and drama criticism published under the title "The Note-Book of a Diner-Out" and the pseudonym "Diogenes Pessimus." These were intrinsically of so little value that some years later she refused an offer to collect them in a book. They served, however, as practice exercises for the witty society novels and plays that she was to write later. Besides, they kept her active mind engaged. Even in her early twenties Mrs. Craigie was not satisfied with the conventionally "good life," and in some respects she was even this early suspicious of its shallowness and frivolity. In 1889 she began taking courses in Greek and medieval literature with Alfred Goodwin and W. P. Ker at University College, London, pursuing these studies seriously and continuing them, though with many interruptions for travel and personal affairs, until 1902. She also worked hard at her writing. Essentially un-imaginative, she took the greatest pains to see, literally, whatever scene she described. She wrote slowly and carefully, polished and rewrote, spared no effort nor energy—nor, where necessary for travel and research, money.

In July, 1890, the Craigies joined her parents on the Isle of Wight, where the Richards had summered regularly since 1872. Here, on August 15, her son John Churchill Craigie was born. That autumn they returned to town, taking a house just outside London at High Barnet. The marriage was by now apparently doomed. Mr. Craigie remained the dashing young man-about-town. But his wife, preoccupied with motherhood now as well as literature, withdrew more and more from the fast set in which they had traveled. "She became very depressed," her father re-called, "and often, while her husband was engaged in town, she would come with her infant and the nurse, to spend the day with us." [29] By May, 1891, they had separated. The divorce was not granted until July, 1895, but there was no attempt at rec-onciliation during the intervening years. Gossip linked Craigie's name with very high society, commenting on "his being intimate with the new Duchess of York [who became Queen Mary] and her mother and brothers, odd as it may seem for royalty to recog-nize a simple bank clerk." Meanwhile his wife was reported to be living quietly with her father, "oftener seen swinging along country lanes miles from home than in a drawing-room." [30] As the injured party she had little difficulty in obtaining the divorce and winning custody of their child, but the experience was sordid and painful. The grounds were adultery and cruelty. Craigie denied the charges, pleading "condonation of his adultery and cruelty, if any; connivance of his adultery, if any; conduct on the part of his petitioner conducing to his adultery, if any." [31]

Mrs. Craigie was obliged to take the witness box and to give and hear testimony in a case that was covered by the newspapers and widely publicized. Her father and a nurse also testified. The

London *Times* reported: "The case is an extremely filthy one, and most of its details are utterly unfit for publication in a newspaper." If the details did not reach the newspapers, they certainly were circulated in the society in which the Craigies moved. The trial lasted two days, ending abruptly when Craigie, advised by his lawyer that he would have difficulty corroborating his testimoney, agreed to drop his defense. The jury thereupon found him guilty of adultery and cruelty, and the divorce was granted.

Although Mrs. Craigie had the satisfaction of winning her freedom and the custody of her child, she paid a formidable price in suffering. On the day she received her decree she wrote two letters to her closest women friends in response to their messages of sympathy. To Ellen Terry she wrote: "The strain has been very great. I can hardly realize the verdict at present. I feel that the trial is still going on—that it is going on for ever and ever! The sensation is hideous. But I have got my child." [32] She revealed herself even more candidly in a letter to Florence Henniker, sister of Lord Crewe and a minor writer herself:

> I must thank you for your words of sympathy. The ordeal on Wednesday was a severe one, but I have been shewn so much kindness & given so much encouragement that half its bitterness is already past. The thought of my child sustained me during the trial—the horror of which the *Times* only hinted at. I have seen other reports which were—from the circumstances of the case—garbled & inaccurate. For four hours & a half I was under cross-examination: I fainted once & yesterday after the verdict was given I was carried out of the court-room half insensible. I can only realize the result of the case today—& now in a vague sense only. I cannot help thinking that when a woman is in the position of *plaintiff* she should be spared such suffering. I felt so grieved for my parents who were present & could only think that if I had a son or a daughter so tortured under my eyes —I should die of sorrow. It nearly killed my father when I became insensible. He & my mother are simple people of the old school—homely, devoted to each other, living only for their family & kind deeds. It was death to me to see them in that courtroom listening to such desolating & revolting

facts of life as I had to tell. It was to spare them that I bore so much for four years in absolute silence. And yet it all had to be told! This is the irony of so-called self-sacrifice. It is too often made in vain—I am leaving town & hope soon to feel stronger.[33]

The law court had vindicated Mrs. Craigie by designating her the injured party, but it could not erase the scandal and the social stigma of divorce. There were those who, perhaps as much out of antagonism to her as loyalty to Craigie, defended him. A note in the American periodical *Bookman* in March, 1897, reported, ". . . a feeling is springing up that in the matter of the divorce suit brought by her against her husband, the latter received something less than even-handed justice. Mr. Craigie has some warm friends, who have stood by him from the first; and through them his side of the case is beginning to make its way into the minds of many who had formerly condemned him." More painful for Mrs. Craigie, however, than such rumors, must have been the fact that, having become a Roman Catholic in 1892, she was committed to a moral and spiritual position thoroughly and implacably in conflict with her practical situation. It made the prospect of remarriage unlikely, if not actually unthinkable. Furthermore, it prevented her from raising her son in her own faith. When she entered him in Eton in 1899 she wrote to his housemaster, Arthur Benson: "With regard to the boy's religious instruction: he may not be brought up as a Roman Catholic. I have the sole guardianship and custody of the child, but the English law is very decisive on *that* point." [34]

In the years between her separation from her husband in 1891 and her divorce, Mrs. Craigie became a novelist and playwright, producing her lightest, most frivolous work. Yet in this same period she was undergoing the most sobering and shattering kind of emotional conflict. Her writing reflects this experience only perversely and negatively, assuming a brittle tone as artificial and often as irritating as a high-pitched nervous laugh. Even the pseudonym under which she published reflected an arch pose. She made no attempt to conceal her identity or her sex, though she was occasionally amused at the surprise of her readers when they discovered who she was. She started using a pseudonym simply because her first book, *Some Emotions and a Moral,* was accepted by Fisher Unwin for publication in the Pseudonym Library series. But in calling herself "John Oliver Hobbes" she demonstrated once again the odd nature of her thinking: "I chose the name of John because it is my father's and my son's; Oliver because of the warring Cromwell; and Hobbes because it is homely." [35] Also, she observed that she was an admirer of the philosopher Hobbes, that his unyielding rationalism saved her from "maudlin sentiment," and that she selected Oliver because "it filled the mouth." No doubt she found a mask helpful. It hid nothing, but it presented a face to the world.

She was twenty-four when she wrote her first novel—a trifling yet not altogether uninteresting social comedy. Even this early, in her choice of a title, *Some Emotions and a Moral,* and character names (George Golightly, Godfrey Provence) she showed that preciosity so characteristic of the '90's and of all her work. Like many of her contemporaries she rebelled consciously, indeed self-consciously, against the technical conventions of the large, well-made Victorian novel. Without actually experimenting in new techniques, she lightly dismissed or made free with the old ones: the earnest but intrusive authorial point of view, the careful development of motivation, plot, and character, and the attention to detail and probability. Instead she offered witty dialogue and epigrams, characters who act impulsively and capriciously, a series of loosely related incidents rather than a plot. She delighted in abrupt switches of mood. Her comedies almost invariably introduce at least one episode of violent or sudden death—treated, however, so coolly and casually that the reader finds himself, like the author, totally detached from sympathy with the victim. In this first novel, for example, the hero, unhappily married and in love with another woman, discovers that his wife has been unfaithful to him (in spirit if not in deed) when he sees her frenzied reaction to the suicide of his best friend. *A Study in Temptations* (1893), one of her more cheerful stories where young true love finally triumphs, begins with a grim prelude in which a distraught young father plunges out of a window after learning of his wife's death in childbirth. In *The*

Sinner's Comedy (1892), an egoistic young man jilts his mistress so that he may marry for money. The mistress, already saddled with a worthless husband whom she cannot divorce because she is Catholic, then falls in love with an admirable clergyman but dies before she has any chance for happiness with him. The clergyman, incidentally, is loved by the wealthy young woman who is to marry the egoistic young man. Love and life are treated with a chilly detachment that serves to emphasize both their comic and their tragic irony. The selfish and shallow characters survive and prosper and are comically absurd. The sensitive and sincere characters are destroyed. "If the gods have no sense of humour," she concludes *The Sinner's Comedy*, "they must weep a great deal."

John Oliver Hobbes' first reviews were generally admiring, but her critics almost unanimously complained about her coldness, her cynicism, her flippancy and apparent inhumanity. To a degree such criticism pleased her, for it confirmed the image she was seeking to establish with the public. But she was enough of an artist—and enough of a businesswoman concerned with the sales of her books—to want to establish the ultimate seriousness of what she was writing. In posing as the cynic-satirist writing only to amuse, she was building a defense against really serious criticism of her fiction as art. Yet in introducing pathetic and dramatic episodes she was admitting that these "fantasias," as she sometimes called her stories, were more than they pretended to be. She was fully aware of the ambivalence of her attitude. In the preface to the second edition of *A Study in Temptations* she wrote:

A greater part of the book was composed under the strain of bad health, and all of it in circumstances of peculiar anxiety. If the author had written as he felt or thought, the result would have been far from amusing. And his sole aim has been to amuse. In times of illness, irritability, and grief, he has often cast about him for some light reading—simple yet not altogether meaningless, unreal yet not impossible; he has longed to draw a veil on actualities and see a shadow-life frisking on tiptoes, followed by a dance of sorrows and a merry-making of cares. He does not presume to say that he has fulfilled his own desire in the following pages, but the desire in question may explain their tone.

This seriousness of purpose in her writing, in spite of all its seeming frivolity, is suggested also by the novelists who influenced her and whom she consciously or unconsciously imitated. Among her contemporaries, George Meredith and Thomas Hardy had the greatest influence upon her. She was pleased, as well she might have been, when reviewers compared her to Meredith. In 1902 and 1903 Meredith exchanged some letters with her, and she visited him at Box Hill. An old man, mellow and gracious, he referred to her as "a vigorous young sister in the craft." [36] He could not have failed to recognize some of the more striking oddities of his *The Amazing Marriage* (1895) in her ambitious duo of novels, *The School for Saints* (1897) and *Robert Orange* (1900)—the high-minded heroine, who goes to Spain to join the cause of the Carlists; her husband, who is converted to Roman Catholicism and dies in religious orders. But such imitation evidently flattered Meredith more than it distressed him. More generally there are echoes of Meredith-ian language and tone in most of her novels—the sudden mixtures of tragic and comic moods, the indifference to conventional transitions, spirited characters who follow their impetuous hearts with no regard for convention or common sense. *The Serious Wooing* (1901), with its charming heroine who shocks society by running off to live with a Socialist lover, reminded W. L. Courtney of *Lord Ormont and his Aminta* (1894), "not by any slavish process of imitation . . . but in accordance with the free work of an artist inspired by a particular influence." [37] And, while there is no "slavish process of imitation," there is an unmistakable connection between Meredith's Sir Willoughby Patterne and Mrs. Craigie's "egoist," a smug young bachelor in *The Sinner's Comedy:*

He believed that Man was the measure of all things; that Man was Sir Richard Kilcoursie. His views on women were, perhaps, more remarkable for their chivalry than their reverence; that she could lose her youth was a blot on creation;

that she could lose her virtue made life worth living. As his nature was sensuous rather than sensual, however, the refinement of his taste did for him what the fear of God has hardly done for few. He waited for his Eve: she was to be Guinevere, not Molly Seagrim.

Like Meredith, Hardy respected Mrs. Craigie's talents. He met her in 1893 and called her "that brilliant woman"; in 1908 he attended the memorial services for her. His influence upon her work is less obvious than Meredith's, but in one novel it is striking.[38] This is *The Herb Moon,* where a Hardy-esque realism intrudes rather disconcertingly into a novel subtitled "a fantasia" that deals mainly with the misadventures and misunderstandings of a pair of lovers. In contrast to its predecessors, this novel begins in a simple rural setting with a deceptive air of naturalness—a drab, rather faded heroine tied to a hopelessly insane husband and quietly in love with a modest, self-effacing clerk in a cotton factory. The characters include a frank-speaking farmwife, some uneducated servants who talk in reasonably authentic-sounding country dialect, and—straight out of Hardy—a recruiting sergeant who gives a homely commentary on life, love, and soldiering. His function in the novel is purely decorative, but Mrs. Craigie handles him well enough to demonstrate that she was a faithful student of the master. Nevertheless, she is visibly more comfortable when she moves her heroine to London upper-class society as the companion of a wealthy, worldly old lady. The story has a conventionally happy ending with the death of the insane husband, freeing the heroine to marry the hero who, having heeded the recruiting sergeant, has become a distinguished military officer.

The element of Hardy that appealed most to Mrs. Craigie was not his rendering of scene, region, and local speech, but his stark philosophical fatalism. She considered *Jude* his greatest book: "Of course, it is *not* poetical and the bedroom scenes are profoundly unpleasant. But there is much in Greek tragedy—and comedy—equally forbidding." [39] Mrs. Craigie was fascinated by the morbid and the ugly. In her own writing she sometimes quite strikingly conveyed a sense of deadly corruption beneath a sleek, shining surface. Odd as it may seem in a writer who won fame for her wit, her vision of life was essentially grim. Emerging as a novelist during a period of intense personal suffering, she inevitably reflected and expressed bitterness and disillusion. Consider, for example, a short story she published in 1895, "The Worm that God Prepared," which describes in nasty detail the romance of an overaged and oversexed daughter of a snobbish, aristocratic father. Desperate to have a husband, the girl secretly marries the sickly son of a wealthy tradesman. Her father, hearing reports of a scandal in the young man's life and jealous of his daughter's interest in him, sneaks into his room at night and, finding him in bed with a woman, stabs them both, only to discover that he has killed his own daughter.

This, to be sure, is the most extreme example of Mrs. Craigie's weird and perverse taste. It is framed in the outlines of a fable—the ironies of fate demonstrated with an icy, relentless objectivity, as though the author expects us to join her in bitter laughter. Into otherwise unobjectionable novels she introduces many characters who are physically, morally, or mentally repulsive. The insane husband is happily off the scene and hidden in a sanatorium in *The Herb Moon*, but in *The Serious Wooing* a similar character appears in a flashback as he is being married to a beautiful young girl: "Shortclough was a *crétin* from the beginning. I can see him now as he looked on their wedding day —his swivel-eye rolling horribly, and that wobbly under-lip turned down as far as the chinline." Even when sane, some of her male characters have a peculiar physical and spiritual loathesomeness, especially when juxtaposed to the beauty and innocence of their wives. Wrexham Parflete, who in *The School for Saints* marries the exquisite seventeen-year-old, convent-bred Brigit, is both morally and physically contemptible. The hero of that novel, Robert Orange, reflects that "selfish, coarse-minded people usually married well. Men of the Parflete type found angels, and shrewd, vixenish women entrapped the very sons of God. The thought was sickening."

As Orange's observation indicates, Mrs. Craigie did not spare her own sex. Her female monsters have some of the same pernicious effects on their men as Hardy's Arabella had on Jude.

Anne Passer Delaware destroys the career and the life of a brilliant young doctor, Simon Warre, in *The Gods, Some Mortals, and Lord Wickenham* (1895):

> She had a nature of strong impulses, a defective education in weak principles, and that excitable temperament which needs every bodily satisfaction to keep it sane. In the absence of material aids there is only one intellectual gift which can save either men or women of this type from complete degradation, and that is a desire for romance, for refinement, for the poetic. And Anne was a stranger to this purifying influence. She had that appalling brutality of mental constitution which is more often found in creatures of delicate appearance and great nervous force than in those whose even health and robust air are the effect—less than the cause—of their tranquil spirit. Culture may do much, but nothing can alter the quality of one's moral fibre; if it be coarse, it must remain coarse, and although it may be spun into silk, it will be silk of harsh grain—unyielding, rough. Anne had no innate ideal of conduct to make her suffer when she fell beneath it; she lived by impulse—if a good one, it was well; if a bad one it was well also. She only felt remorse when an action turned to her disadvantage, or when some adverse judgment from a looker-on wounded her self-esteem. Vanity was all the conscience she possessed; and this, although Warre did not know it then, was why it was so utterly impossible to love her, so hard even to admit her beauty without an inward shrinking—a sort of shame (Ch. IX).

Because she demands it, Warre marries this creature, though he loves a sweet, refined girl. On their wedding day he discovers that she has had an affair with another man, and he never consummates their marriage. Finally she leaves him. He is now free to get a divorce—for which she has given him ample grounds—and to marry the girl he loves. But he refuses to act ("The soul and the manhood within him were dead") and goes off on a medical mission to the tropics where he contrives to work himself to death.

The personal implications of this novel are interesting. For the first but not the last time in her fiction, Mrs. Craigie identifies herself with her hero. She makes him a tragic, grief-ridden figure, beaten down in all his brilliance and promise by the selfishness of others. "I envy him," his friend Lord Wickenham remarks at the end of the novel, "although his body is one with the sands of the sea, and his grief was more than he could tell, and his life, in men's judgment, a failure." Questioned by the critic W. L. Courtney as to why she did not allow her hero to marry the girl he loved, she wrote (within months of her own divorce):

> He feared the scandal of a divorce, and the inevitable reproach attaching to remarriage. A divorced man or woman—no matter how innocent or how cruelly wronged—is *not* considered a good match. Many people would regard the marriage as illegal. . . . Poor Warre—over-worked, heartbroken, world-weary—could not ask a girl to endure social ostracism—or worse, social toleration. It may be that I should have made more of this in the book, but I feel the folly of such persecution so deeply that I feared I was not the person to write it at any length.[40]

In one of his unhappiest moments Simon Warre wanders into a Roman Catholic Church, where he finds solace simply by sitting quietly. He never thinks seriously of conversion. The heroine of *The Herb Moon* also drifts by chance into a Catholic Church and is deeply moved by the mass: "Her seat faced the high altar, and when she gazed upon the cross it seemed, not an emblem of sorrow, but the mysterious key to the city of eternal happiness." But at this moment in her life she is young and full of hope: "Her impetuous spirit paused at a plan of life which, in her judgment, made the pleasures of this world insipid." Years later she recalls the experience with a saddened spirit but makes no effort to join the church. Pearl Craigie, however, made the step which she did not allow her characters to make. She was received into the Roman Catholic Church on July 5, 1892, taking the baptismal names Mary-Teresa. Exactly what brought her into

a church so alien from the New England nonconformist background of her family, we shall probably never know. Although
she spoke of her religion freely and introduced it into many of
her novels, her decision was private. That she was attracted to
Rome was no more remarkable than the conversions of a number
of other writers of the "Decadent" group in the '90's—Ernest
Dowson, Aubrey Beardsley, Lionel Johnson—all aesthetic, sickly,
unhappy, deeply in need of intense emotional experience. Mrs.
Craigie's coversion came only one year after the shattering of her
marriage and certainly reflects a need for consolation. But it also
reflects a philosophical and intellectual need almost as pressing
as the more purely emotional one. According to one of her
spiritual advisers, Father Gavin, S.J.:

> she assured me that she read herself into the Church. After
> God and His grace, the change of Faith was due to her
> own study and reading. Her conversion . . . could not be
> ascribed to sermons, still less to the attraction and beauty of
> the Church's liturgy and public services. She became a
> Catholic by study and conviction and in obedience to her
> conscience.[41]

The analytic, self-examining urge was strong in her, in the
long run probably stronger than the purely spiritual one. "Has
it ever struck you," she once remarked to William Archer, "that
the Church of Rome, which alone among the Churches of Western Europe enjoins and enforces continual examination of conscience, is the real creator of modern analytical fiction? The
Fathers of the Church are the fathers of psychology. St. Augus-
tine, St. Thomas Aquinas, St. Bernard, and Abelard—where will
you find subtler soul-searching than in their writings?" Citing the
Catholic novelists—Stendhal, Balzac, Flaubert, Tolstoy, and Dostoevsky, she concluded that "analytic fiction has always flourished
in the neighbourhood of the confessional." [42]

Something, however, seemed to stand in the way, blocking
Mrs. Craigie's complete fulfillment in the church. Some of the
Catholic characters in her novels—notably Robert Orange—

achieve a far deeper and more satisfying faith than she herself appears ever to have had. The obstacle may have been this intellectual, analytical bent. She accepted the church as the best alternative or the last resort. "The more I see of life," she wrote in 1905, "the more I feel that the Church is *all* we have, and although much that is outward in it is strange and perplexing, it is also true that so-called *realities* will not bear argument and dissection. If we must have illusions, let the illusions be beautiful at least." [43]

Her problem may have been even more fundamental, rooted in the psychological complexities of her character. George Moore wrote two novels about a beautiful, talented, sensual woman who becomes a nun—*Evelyn Innes* (1898) and a sequel, *Sister Teresa* (1901). It has been suggested that Mrs Craigie was the inspiration and, in more literal detail, the source of these stories, especially since Evelyn Innes adopts the baptismal name of Teresa on entering the church. In view of Moore's reputation for exaggerating and distorting his material, and in view of the stormy course of his relationship with Mrs. Craigie, he is an unreliable witness. Nevertheless, we know that she wrote many letters to him in which she expressed herself freely on a variety of subjects, among them religion. Moore was shrewd enough to detect in her a conflict between sensuality and asceticism which he gives to his heroine Evelyn:

> the delicious terror and irresistible curiosity which she experienced on opening St. Teresa's Book of Her Life she had never experienced before. It was like rebirth, being born to a new experience, to a purer sensation of life. It was like throwing open the door of a small, confined garden, and looking upon the wide land of the world. It was like breathing the wide air of eternity after that of a close-scented room. She knew that she was not capable of such pure ecstasy, yet it seemed to her very human to think and feel like this; and the saint's holy rapture seemed as natural —she thought for a moment—even more natural even more truly human than the rapture she had found in sinful love (Ch. XXXV).

Mrs. Craigie no doubt looked with suspicion upon "rapture," holy or otherwise, but she was deeply concerned with sensuality. In order to assert her worldliness and sophistication, she was forced to take a firm stand:

> I do not like the ways of some Catholics, but I love the religion. They want me to join all kinds of things: I won't. I could be an early Christian or a Renaissance Christian; but I canot be a Philistine Christian or a Smart Christian or a Simian Christian. Much of this devotee-ism is unwholesome, perverted sensuality. I hate it. Honest sensuality is not for *me* personally, but it isn't nauseating.

These are the words of a mature woman-of-the-world, but her rejection of "honest sensuality" betrays a strong puritanical streak. She wrote in 1897 (probably to Moore) of a Jesuit priest under whom she was studying theology: "He has paid me the highest compliment I have ever received on my work. He says it is absolutely free from sensuality—and that it is *unique* in that respect. That from the beginning has been my aim. I have never in my life been so pleased by a piece of criticism." [44]

Whatever its conscious or unconscious motivation, Mrs. Craigie's conversion was surely rooted in deep personal unhappiness. Her new religious faith offered her spiritual consolation which the church of her family did not offer. But, more important, it had intellectual and aesthetic appeal. It was a retreat literally—she kept an apartment at the Convent of the Assumption in Kensington where she would go, from time to time, for several days of rest and contemplation—and spiritually. It helped her to reconcile at least temporarily those jarring qualities of her nature which her peculiar situation of socially prominent and respectable divorcée constantly aggravated. Most important, it gave a new direction to her thinking and her writing.

II

The School for Saints (1897) and its sequel, *Robert Orange* (1900), are the most ambitious novels of Mrs. Craigie's career.

Here, without abandoning the brittle social satire for which she was already celebrated, she tackled the more weighty subject of religion itself, creating in her hero Robert Orange a man of destiny, one whose stride covers the secular and spiritual worlds of his age (the late 1860's). Orange's destiny, his vocation, is the church. He ends as a Roman Catholic monsignor, but not until he has first been exposed to some enticing worldly temptations—success as a society novelist, power and prestige in politics, love offered generously by several exquisite women, including the young heroine Brigit whom he in turn loves ardently. The theme of these two novels is Robert's devious, painful, but inevitable journey to Rome—a journey made *through* the world, not out of it: the "School for Saints," Mrs. Craigie reminds her readers, "has often been called the way of the world."

There is no denying the brilliance and audacity of her choice of subject. Her purpose was no less than to create in Orange a mythic nineteenth-century hero who would mirror the entire spiritual and political history of the times. In his brief political career he is witness to and participant in the major developments of English parliamentary government (Reform and the emergence of a new ruling-class coalition) and of European government (movements of popular national revolution, encapsulated here in the Spanish Carlist rebellion). It is not by mere whim that she introduces Disraeli as an active character in both novels, refers specifically to his novel *Lothair,* and actually borrows details of her plot from it.[45] However, she also conceives Orange as the symbol of nineteenth-century man's struggle for religious faith. His worldly career is modeled on Disraeli's career, but in his spiritual life he is John Henry Newman—scholarly, ascetic, soul-searching, and ultimately dedicated to what even the staunchly Church of England Disraeli comes to recognize as "his true vocation." *Robert Orange* concludes with a letter Disraeli writes in 1879, some time after Orange's death, to an author working on a history of English Catholicism who has applied to him for information on Orange. Monsignor Orange, Disraeli reports, had difficulties when he entered the priesthood: "Rome did not smile at him at first." Eventually, however, he rose to high position in the church, but he remained always ascetic, withdrawn from the world: "He lived himself in great seclusion and simplicity, and died . . . of overwork last year."

This blend of Disraeli and Newman produces, not surprisingly, a hero who is a mixture of contradictions. Robert Orange is born English but of an aristocratic French family. His parents, who had married against their families' wishes are dead. Through his father he descends from a distinguished old line, the De Hausées. They are Bretons, of ancient Celtic race, carrying in their hearts a "spiritual rapture"—a dedicated, passionate idealism—"a mental thrill which wears away and kills the bodily life." But he also carries an English strain, "the Puritan instinct," which, in his youth and early manhood, prevents him from "going over" to Rome. Disraeli recognizes this conflict long before Robert sees it: "Don't protest; you will become a Roman Catholic because you will find nowhere out of Rome, poetry and the spirit of democracy and a reverence for authority all linked together in one irrefragable chain. But I must warn you that such a step would prejudice your whole political career." True to Disraeli's prediction, Robert becomes a Catholic, but his religion does not handicap his political career. He wins a seat in Parliament, plunges into political intrigue, fights in the Carlist rebellion in Spain, and kills a man in a duel of honor: "Robert was an ambitious man. This passion, like a sleeping dragon, lay side by side with the unselfish romance of his nature—a romance which had received a kiss of Gallic gaiety as well as the thorn of medieval asceticism."

Such ambivalence of character accounts for, if it does not excuse, the ambivalence of Mrs. Craigie's point of view. At one moment she is attempting to write fabulous romance, at the next a slick social comedy, at another topical political commentary, and at still another, profound metaphysical and spiritual analysis. *The School for Saints* begins like a fairy tale—Orange growing up in remote Brittany, pacing the medieval walls of St. Malo as he reads *Amadis of Gaul* and *Le Morte d'Arthur,* an orphan with a kindly but aloof godmother guardian. His entry into the world is made in a lushly idealized encounter with a beautiful woman who lives in a castle and "enchants" him. But Mrs. Craigie suddenly and clumsily shifts gears. The lady is an actress whom Robert follows to Paris and into a society of the *demi-monde*.[46] Before long, however, we are in another kind of fairy tale—this time the more modern one of the late nineteenth-century romantic novel with *Prisoner of Zenda*-type intrigue, international society with archdukes, morganatic marriages, crafty noblemen maneuvering for power, spies, and impossibly beautiful women.

Robert's career thus becomes a kind of upper-class, highbrow exercise in dream fulfillment, both for the reader and the author. This romantic-idealist hero schooling himself for sainthood in "the way of the world"—brilliant, ambitious, but doomed to frustration and sorrow—is a creation of Mrs. Craigie's imagination woven out of the very fabric of herself. His religious struggles, his yearning for faith and certainty, are literally hers. His adventures are hers imaginatively. And if Robert is to a degree Mrs. Craigie transvestitized, idealized, and sublimated, so too do the three women in the novel reflect her. They are all rich, beautiful, and formidably intelligent. One, the widow Pensée Fitz Rewes, loves Robert hopelessly but with unswerving loyalty. She wields considerable political influence and is helpful in his contest for a parliamentary seat. Another, Lady Sara De Treverell, who also loves him passionately, is bored with "the flippancy of the lives around her, the inanity of her relatives' pursuits, their heedlessness of those inner qualities which make the real." Like Mrs. Craigie, she has a strong-minded father, "who entertained clear views of 'the right thing' and 'the wrong thing' in social ethics." Also, like Mrs. Craigie, after disappointment in love she is drawn to the Church, but she goes all the way, becoming a Carmelite nun.

The principal heroine is Brigit—"a divinity," a character who would be implausible in a fairy tale and who, in the *mélange* that is Mrs. Craigie's story, is simply absurd. Robert lacks the substance but at least reflects a working idea in the book; Brigit is sheer fantasy. The daughter of the Archduke of Alberia and the actress with whom the adolescent Robert had been infatuated, convent-educated and devoutly religious, she appears in *The School for Saints* at sixteen, and by the conclusion of *Robert Orange*, one year later, she has been married twice (platonically,

Mrs. Craigie carefully emphasizes); she has taken an active role in the Carlist rebellion and risked a fiery death; she has been the pawn of a sinister and hopelessly confusing political plot involving her claim to the throne of Alberia; she has been the innocent cause of two duels and a scandal that has rocked international society; and when we last see her she has nobly renounced Robert and taken up a career on the stage.

Granted that Brigit is to be approached throughout the novel as pure fable, it is nevertheless impossible to accept her as the ethereal ideal to which Robert aspires. Mrs. Craigie's intention is clear enough. Brigit is to represent the ultimate sacrifice which Robert must make for God. As such she must offer both worldly temptation (her extraordinary beauty) and spiritual temptation (a soul as noble and devout as his own): "Suddenly, however, he had found presented to him, a mind and a nature in such complete harmony with his own that it seemed as though he were the words and she the music of one song." Sexually she is unawakened ("her womanhood still slept"), but "her lightest touch could sway his body and his spirit," and when he marries her, Robert, ordinarily the most self-possessed of men, becomes uneasy: "Was she perhaps some straying angel . . . a being of the elfin race?" The discovery that Brigit's first husband is still alive prevents the embarrassing confrontation of that question. Their marriage unconsummated, Brigit and Robert part. Although there are ample grounds for annulment of Brigit's first marriage, they both appear reluctant to follow so sensible a line of action. Instead they suffer, each convinced in his own way that his lot is a foreordained martyrdom: "His father sinned, and my father sinned," Brigit says. "We were born for unhappiness. Unhappiness and misgivings are in our very blood." Robert more philosophically reasons: "Submission to the severities of God, whatever they might be, obedience to authority, a companionless existence—these were the conditions, he knew, of the meagre joy permitted to those who, full of intellect, feeling, and kindness, undertook the rigorous discipline of a solitary journey."

Clearly, if such incredible characters are to be viewed with any degree of seriousness, they must be accepted in the spirit

in which they were intended. How seriously did Mrs. Craigie
take these novels? What did they mean to her? Over the years of
their composition her attitude toward her material changed.
Originally (about 1895) *The School for Saints* was conceived as
a play, a comedy about a middle-aged married couple, which she
planned to write for Henry Irving. She discussed the plot with
the actor and began to sketch her hero as a "Disraeli-type." Over
the next eighteen months the character grew and changed in her
imagination. "Orange is a highly idealized portrait of Disraeli,"
she wrote. In 1896 she drafted a play introducing the principal
characters of the novel but containing "only one situation which
was also used in the novel." The plan continued to grow larger
and more ambitious. She traveled to Brittany, Tours, Paris: "I
need 'models' as much as any painter. That is my method of
work as I study from the life—every line I write is based upon
my own observation." [47] With all the good intentions of a journalist filing a news report, Mrs. Craigie was nevertheless also a
fabulist. She modeled many of her characters on real-life per-
sonages (some like Disraeli and General Prim appear under their
own names; others were immediately recognized by her readers
as drawn from Sir Robert Peel and Lord Bentinck), incorporated
incidents from history, and provided footnotes for her more
recondite allusions. But she could not write a realistic novel.
The effort to write one was so strenuous here, so clumsy and
obvious, that it destroyed the book as romance as well.

Her failure was recognized by most of the first reviewers
of the books. "The hero and the heroine are elusive, they seem
more minds than persons," the *Athenaeum* observed (December
11, 1897). Some time later Vincent O'Sullivan, though generally
respectful toward the novels, called Orange "that cold, dull
phantasm, penny-in-the-slot machine for aphorisms." [48] But others
were impressed with Mrs. Craigie's wit and erudition. The London *Bookman* (August, 1900) said that *Robert Orange* "touches
a string not often sounded. The keen, bright manner, the sparkle
of epigram . . . are French. . . . Madame de Sévigné might have
written this account of the 'born priest' who moves steadily on
through fire and flames toward the fulfillment of his vocation."

Modern readers will probably find *The School for Saints* and *Robert Orange* unreadable. Mrs. Craigie's inability to construct a plot, create believable characters, or write dialogue that has even the faintest resemblance to human utterance is all the more obvious in a long and ambitious work like this. Her shorter novels bounce along airily on fizz and bubble, but her subject here demands solidity and craftsmanship. That the admiration of her contemporaries was exaggerated and ephemeral is proved by the swift oblivion into which these novels fell. By the time of her death in 1906 Mrs. Craigie was already regarded as passé. The coterie of her admirers grew smaller, until it all but vanished.[49]

Nevertheless, the momentary splash that these two books made was significant, as her whole career was significant, for what it reveals of a fine mind and a sensitive spirit seeking expression through the medium of the didactic-polemical novel. Essentially they must be read as fantasy. If they are approached with perhaps more than average willingness to suspend disbelief, they cease to appear as absurdities. Grudgingly at first, and then gradually more curious and admiring, one reads on. The mind that conceived this story was an excellent one. For every clumsy mannerism of narrative and style there is some bold stroke of wit or inventiveness. In her very "badness" one begins to suspect an intentional, not accidental, paradox—a contrariness that deliberately reflects the personality of her hero. Within half a dozen pages of *The School for Saints*, for example, she moves from unblushing sentimentality like this (describing a sensitive adolescent's first love):

> In his boy's nature, passion still lay profoundly dormant, but in its place he felt that infinite vague longing of the soul for an answering voice. What to him had been the nightingale's note or the coming of May or the blue pinions of a night in June? . . . His soul was swayed by the music of the spheres; and, swinging with the planets in their course, he saw the stars dance, he followed the eagle's flight.

to the detachment of this:

The poor boy suffered as all young, ardent, candid creatures must suffer when they make mistakes and are deceived, not by life, but by their own experience. Robert's intelligence was too pure in quality to confound even this first over-whelming and apparently inexplicable disappointment with any foolish theory adverse to the wisdom of Divine Provi-dence. A sigh certainly escaped his lips that the discipline of life should be so severe, but he never doubted that the trial was a discipline, and a necessary one.

On one level—that of personal, deeply felt religious expres-sion—she writes impressively at times.[50] On another level—that of the satirical "society" novel—she is unfailingly competent and sometimes witty. For example, she offers a dinner party conversation:

> One statement, made by Penborough, caused flutter.
> "If Catherine of Aragon had been immoral and Mary Stuart virtuous, the whole course of European History would have been different. The Reformation, for instance, would have found no favour in England."
> "That's *very* advanced," murmured Lady Larch.
> Sara, at dessert, tried to encourage a debate on the egoism of the Saints compared with the egoism of Mon-taigne.
> "They were selfishly bent on pain and renunciation, he was selfishly bent on pleasure and indulgence. Isn't that the one difference between them, Mr. Orange?"
> Orange refused to be drawn, but he promised to lend her the *Acta Sanctorum* of the Bollandists in sixty volumes in folio.
> "After you have read them," said he, "I will tell you my ideas about Montaigne."
> Many other remarks were probably more amusing: these, however, were the most characteristic.

The two novels swing wildly back and forth from one level to another. Not only do they fail as realism, but they also fail as fantasy. Mrs. Craigie's imagination was pulled down—or held back by her determination to tell a "real" story in a recognizable setting. She dared the impossible. Her goal was to write Newman's *Apologia* with the spirit of Disraeli's *Lothair,* in the modern, updated style of Oscar Wilde's drawing-room comedies. Her failure was inevitable.

III

Mrs. Craigie's last novels—*The Serious Wooing, Love and the Soul Hunters, The Vineyard,* and *The Dream and the Business*—show increasing technical mastery, owing in part at least to her experience in the theater.[51] There, while she was never able to repeat the success of her first play, *The Ambassador,* a drawing-room comedy sprinkled with Wilde-ian epigrams, she learned valuable practical lessons in construction, economy, and the writing of dialogue. She became all the more conscious of the seriousness and importance of her writing—not that she was ever prone to underestimate her talents. But commercial success, much as she pretended to scorn it, proved sweet to her taste. With a curious mixture of boldness and innocence, she never hesitated to appeal to the "masters" for help and advice. She invited the eminent Sir Arthur Wing Pinero to collaborate with her on a comedy, an invitation he gracefully declined. She sent the manuscript of her verse tragedy *Osbern and Ursyne* to W. P. Ker for his criticism of its medieval setting. She submitted several of her works, dramatic and nondramatic, to Edmund Gosse, who responded sympathetically and gave her quite detailed criticism.

A lesser master, though ultimately a more famous one, was George Moore. Their association began as a collaboration on plays. It developed into a personal, controversial, and, for Mrs. Craigie, a disastrous relationship. To this day she is remembered, when she is remembered at all, as the lady whose bottom George Moore kicked one day as they were walking in Hyde Park.[52] The most damaging scandals of her life—that she was in hot pursuit of Lord Curzon; and of her death—that she committed suicide when Curzon, then a recent widower, refused to marry her—may be traced to Moore. Since Moore, even by the testimony of his friends, was an incorrigible liar, it is impossible to rely upon his accounts of their relationship. And since Mrs. Craigie's letters to him are so butchered in her father's biography, it is equally impossible to balance and verify his testimony. All that is known with certainty is that Mrs. Craigie's efforts to promote her literary career by seeking George Moore's advice and cooperation had nonliterary and personally harmful consequences.

Moore left two or three slightly different versions of their first meeting. One is a polite letter to John Morgan Richards in 1909, printed in the second edition of the *Life of John Oliver Hobbes*. Recalling their first meeting, he says, that he had received a copy of the novel *Some Emotions and a Moral* with a tactful letter from the author inviting him to collaborate on a dramatization of the book:

> I wrote to John Oliver Hobbes telling him (for I had no suspicion that the author was a woman) how highly I thought of his story, but could not see my way to suggesting a dramatic version. Some months afterwards I heard that John Oliver Hobbes was a woman, and that her name was Mrs. Craigie, and feeling that the letter I had written was not exactly the letter I should have written if I had known the author to be a woman. I wrote another letter explaining my mistake, certain that the humour of the situation would appeal to the witty writer that concealed herself behind the well-chosen name of John Oliver Hobbes.

In the account Moore gave Barrett H. Clark, in 1922, he claimed that he thought it merely a "pretty" book and took no interest in the matter until Arthur Symons told him that John Oliver Hobbes was an attractive young woman: "That—was a different matter! I saw her some days afterward at the theatre and thought she was amazingly beautiful. Well, one thing led to another, and I fell in love with her." [53] In still another version, his autobiography *Memoirs of My Dead Life* (in the section called "Lui et Elles" of the 1921 edition), Moore describes in great detail his first meeting with her, using fictitious names (he says her real name was Mary but she wrote under the pseudonym

"Mark Anglewood," and his own name for her was "Agate").
Agate is wealthy but middle class, the daughter of "commonplace" parents. The sitting room in which he first visits her is
tastelessly furnished, "filled with engravings of Doré pictures
and marble statues"—a description that is confirmed by other
visitors to the Richards house in Lancaster Gate. Agate encour-
ages his attentions, although she rejects him as a lover:

> By some word or letter, sometimes even by acts she would
> dissipate suspicions. I might also say the belief, that my
> courtship would bring me to her bed. To be quite truth-
> ful, she hinted in the beginning that sex relations did not
> appeal to her, but such hints are so common among women
> that one attaches no real significance to the confession, or
> interprets it in the opposite sense, that sex relations are the
> one thing of interest to them. No one's talk turned oftener
> on the subject of sex than Agate; she admitted sex to be
> her subject; her brain was certainly possessed of it, and
> though sometimes it seemed about to descend from her
> brain when we returned from the theatre in the family
> brougham, I was not sure that our relations would become
> less and less restrained.

Agate teases and mocks him, introduces him to good music (Mrs.
Craigie urged Moore to attend concerts and to study the piano),
leads him on, but finally tells him, while they are strolling in
the park, that she does not wish to see him again:

> At last my stunned brain awoke, and I saw she was enjoying
> my grief as she might a little comedy of her own invention,
> conscious of her prettiness in black crepe de chine, with a
> hat to match. We were walking towards Kensington, I on
> her right side next the railings, and the ill-repressed smile
> that I caught sight of under her hat cast me out of myself;
> a great selfquake it was, and my left foot, flinging itself
> forward, hit her nearly in the center of her backside, a little
> to the right. She uttered a cry, and I met her look, which
> curiously enough was not a detestation, for lack of percep-

tion was not Agate's failing; and I think she took pride in the fact (I know she did later) that her power over me should have caused me to put off all conventions and to have become, as it were, another George Moore.

Susan L. Mitchell described Moore aptly as a lover who "didn't kiss but told." [54] However, there is enough detail in Moore's account to confirm an impression which Mrs. Craigie herself gives. The general outlines of his sketch of an intelligent, respectable woman who yearned secretly for sexual excitement and adventure are not inconsistent with the portrait that her own letters, bowdlerized as they are, reveal. For example, he quotes Agate: "I can't live without men's society; if I am deprived of it for about a week I begin to wilt." Yet he notes her sexual frigidity, her delight in playful teasing relationships that have, to today's reader, clear sexual implications. In 1902 she wrote to a friend, not identified in her father's edition of the letters, describing her visit to Ireland, in the course of which she quarreled with X (probably Moore, who had been in Ireland with her):

His latest runs as follows: "I never feel any anxiety about *your* relations with your men friends, because I am sure that you are *constitutionally* incapable of an indiscretion!" L. and A. regard this as an acute insult!!! Y., in rapture, rolls on the floor. M.P. tells me that A., B., and C. and D. discussed me once recently at the Club. They said my "charm" was that of an enchanting boy—that there was never the least *arrière-pensée* in my manner—(I make no *demands*, in fact!)—so different from that of most women. . . . They all agree that I am a little paragon!![55]

The Moore-Craigie collaboration produced little by way of stage drama, however much personal drama it engendered. They completed two acts of a comedy, "The Fool's Hour," then abandoned it. The first act was published in the first number of *The Yellow Book* in April, 1894, under their joint names—a slight, witty fragment that sounds more like the Wilde-ian idiom of

Mrs. Craigie than anything of Moore's. There was some collaboration, though to what degree remains a matter of dispute, on
the one-act play in which Ellen Terry appeared in 1894, *Journeys
End in Lovers Meeting.* In the letter that Moore wrote to Mr.
Richards in 1909, he claimed credit for only a rough draft of
this comedy, which was based, he said, on an old French story of
an erring wife, her lover, and her husband. He generously attributed "all the charm of the dialogue" to Mrs. Craigie. To
others, however, Moore complained bitterly that he had done all
the work, Mrs. Craigie only adding some epigrams—"her little
liver pills," he called them.[56] The program for the play listed
both as co-authors, but in 1902, when Mrs. Craigie included it
in her volume *Tales for Temperaments,* Moore's name did not
appear. By that time Moore and Mrs. Craigie were estranged.
The notorious rump-kicking episode, if it ever happened, had
presumably taken place in 1895, provoked not by disagreements
over playwriting but by more intimate conflicts.

Except, apparently, in Moore's overstimulated imagination,
their relationship was not sexual. They were seen together in
society. It was widely known that they were working together. It
was also widely known that Mrs. Craigie was separated from her
husband. Still, there might never have been any serious consequences had Moore not talked so publicly about his association
with her. At this stage in his life, though an established author,
he was busily working his way up the social ladder. The rich and
socially prominent Mrs. Craigie was a conquest of which he
could be proud. He gossiped about her in that witty but utterly
irresponsible fashion for which he was famous. When Vincent
O'Sullivan, for one, objected to his "uncontrollable babbling,"
Moore replied: "My dear fellow, you don't seem to realise that
I have collaborated with her. Now when a man has collaborated
with a woman it is the same as if he had slept with her. She has
no secrets left to reveal." [57]

In 1895 Mrs. Craigie was preparing to get her divorce. She
was also involved in a more subtle campaign of social climbing
than Moore's and was reaching rather dizzying heights. Gertrude
Atherton's cruel portrait of her in *Ancestors* emphasizes above
all her ambition to marry into Burke's *Peerage,* and gossip had

already linked her name with two highly eligible bachelors, Arthur James Balfour and George Nathaniel Curzon, both of whom were launched on brilliant political careers. Other reports had her engaged to the socially prominent artist Walter Spindler, who illustrated some of her books in *art nouveau* style and did her portrait.[58] Those who knew Mrs. Craigie knew that her religion would forbid her to remarry ("The step to the Roman Church," she wrote T. Fisher Unwin on May 13, 1897, "has cost me much also. It has made the idea of re-marriage absolutely out of the question"), but nothing could prevent her from mingling freely in the highest social circles—except the kind of scandal that Moore was circulating. In 1895, also, one of her closest women friends, the American heiress Mary Leiter, married Curzon. Since Mrs. Craigie's name had already been linked to to his by gossip, many people concluded that it was her association with Moore that had caused Curzon to look elsewhere for a wife. Such rumor, ironically, appears to have originated with Moore himself. No doubt it soothed his wounded ego to report that Mrs. Craigie had been rejected, as she had rejected him. The truth, however, is that Curzon and Miss Leiter had planned marriage since 1890 but waited prudently—in view of Miss Leiter's American and Jewish background—until they could secure the approval of Curzon's father.[59] Mrs. Craigie's "designs" on Curzon seem to have been purely social. He was the center of the most brilliant set in fashionable London society. After the Curzon marriage, Mrs. Craigie maintained a warm friendship with both of them. When Curzon was appointed Viceroy of India in 1902, she traveled to India as their guest at the inauguration ceremonies. Lady Curzon died in July, 1906, after a long illness. Less than a month later Mrs. Craigie died—with scarcely time in between for her to have proposed to the widower and been refused, as Moore implied. Two years after her death Lord Curzon was the principal speaker at the memorial ceremonies in her honor at University College, London.[60]

Moore could never forget or forgive Mrs. Craigie's dropping him in 1895. He took his revenge in several vicious literary portraits. The best of these, probably because it was modeled on her only superficially, is in *Evelyn Innes* and its sequel, *Sister*

Teresa. The worst, both ethically and artistically, are "Mildred Lawson," a short story first published in *Celibates* in 1895 and considerably amplified in later editions, and "Henrietta Marr," in *In Single Strictness* (1923, Carra edition). Mildred Lawson is a well-to-do bourgeois girl, intelligent but selfish and unfeeling, who enjoys leading men on ("She didn't want to marry, but she would like to have all the nicest men in love with her"). She breaks the heart of a sensitive artist, Ralph Hoskin, whose reddish hair and pale blue eyes remind us of Moore. Hoskin is her art teacher and her professional rival:

> She would do everything, yes, everything, except marry him. She couldn't settle down to watch him painting pictures. She wanted to paint pictures herself. . . . She must succeed. Success meant so much. If she succeeded, she would be spoken of in the newspapers, and, best of all, she would hear people say when she came into a room, "That is Mildred Lawson."

Mildred finally falls in love with a worldly Frenchman who is married. Under his influence she is converted to Catholicism. Her conversion is emotional, springing from her bitterness and depression; she describes her faith in words which Moore simply lifted from one of Mrs. Craigie's letters:

> Mildred: "I am a Catholic, but my Catholicism is my own. I am a Newmanite. If there be no future life and all is a mistake, then Catholicism is a sublime mistake."
> Mrs. Craigie: "Of course, in all Catholic matters I am so much a Newmanite, that, if Newman be unacceptable to the officials, I am not a Catholic." [61]

In "Henrietta Marr" Moore attempted an even more intimate and unsympathetic fictional portrait of Mrs. Craigie. The story is a fairly thorough reworking of "Mildred Lawson." Mrs. Craigie had been dead now for many years, and Moore had moved along to many presumably more rewarding relationships with women in high positions in society. Yet he did not forget, and with a tastelessness that was remarkable even for him, he soiled Mrs. Craigie's death as he had soiled her life. In this version the heroine is a more sophisticated woman than Mildred, but she wears "Watteau" dresses and is attracted to Catholicism. This time the married man she falls in love with is a powerful and wealthy French count who has been appointed Governor of Algeria. Henrietta accompanies the Count and his wife to the inaugural ceremonies in Algiers. As if the parallels were not sufficiently obvious, Moore even added the detail that the count suffers from a spinal disease which forces him to wear iron supports. His English readers all knew, of course, that Lord Curzon had suffered from a spinal injury since boyhood and that he wore a harness and had a stiff walk. The Countess dies, and when the Count refuses to marry her, Henrietta commits suicide. The public is informed that she has died of heart failure.

Some of these cruel portraits—*Evelyn Innes, Sister Teresa,* and the first version of "Mildred Lawson"—were published during Mrs. Craigie's lifetime. She read *Evelyn Innes* in galley proofs which T. Fisher Unwin sent her and reacted, understandably, with horror and disgust:

> I have not had the courage to mark the objectionable passages. The whole tone is false and an abomination. . . . The heroine isn't convincing—there never was such a girl. . . . Honestly, I have never read the like in any language. . . . I assure you the book is revolting & no amount of cheap Cathedral effects & religious humbug at the end can save it. It is corrupt in conception—it is false to nature & therefore false to morality.

Yet only a year later, in 1899, she met Moore by chance in Bayreuth and wrote to her father: "George Moore is here! So pleasant—these reunions." They did not apparently meet again until September, 1904, when she invited him to Steephill Castle, her father's home in the Isle of Wight. The purpose was to collaborate on another comedy—the bitterness of their earlier collaboration having apparently been forgotten. The play was "The

Peacock's Feathers," which Moore later claimed for himself and finished after her death.[62] He described the visit in a letter to Edward Dujardin written September 13, 1904:

> "The Lake" is nearly finished, and it would be finished if I had not come here to write my comedy along with the lady about whom I talked to you ten years ago. It will be signed by both of us, but almost all of it is mine. . . . The lady [identified in a footnote as John Oliver Hobbes]—I ought to tell you that she has a great deal of talent and is a well-known author—read the play yesterday and said she would not venture to touch it. . . . She says now there are repetitions, and this afternoon she has been doing a little clearing up. She is very strong on the business side, and has charge of all the arrangements; and in the morning she walks on the terrace and in the garden in the most delicious costumes *à la* Watteau, rose-coloured silks and flower-decked hats. Her great friend is a priest [probably Monsignor Brown, her confessor at that time].[63]

From Mrs. Craigie's point of view the visit was sheer disaster. Any hope that she might have had for a reconciliation with Moore was dashed by his behavior at Steephill. "He is not a gentleman & he is mad," she wrote to Unwin. In another letter she warned Unwin against publishing anything further of Moore's:

> Seriously, I believe his brain is touched. His conversation with men and women guests at Ventnor was found highly offensive. Tales reach me from Dublin. I am sorry for him, because it is now a case of mental disease . . . he is the "limit." I had to soothe some enraged *husbands* at Ventnor! My sister-in-law and my cousin (young married women) were terrified by his conversation. . . . The Vicar-General of Southwerk was also much disgusted.[64]

Moore himself never forgave Mrs. Craigie—whether for failing to acknowledge, to his satisfaction, his share in their collaboration on the plays, or for spurning him as a lover we shall probably never know. Long after her death he continued to talk of her with bitterness. As late as 1922 he told Barrett Clark that she had summoned him to Ventnor in 1905 to open her heart to him: "It seems that the Lord's wife was an invalid and P— wanted the lady to die, so that he might marry *her,* but she refused to die. That was why P— came back to me." [65]

IV

By 1922 it mattered little what the truth was. Perhaps even within her lifetime Moore's gossip did Mrs. Craigie no irreparable harm. Her position in society was secure. She was received everywhere. Along with Lady Randolph Churchill and the concert artist Nathalie Janotha, she played in a Beethoven trio at a reception for Queen Alexandra. In 1902 she was part of the glittering social company that formed Lord Curzon's entourage at the Great Durbar in Delhi, which she reported in a series of letters for the London *Daily Graphic and Collier's Weekly* (these were published the following year as a book, *Imperial India*). She traveled extensively in Europe, participated actively in literary societies, and lectured in both England and the United States. On her last American visit, in November, 1905, she was interviewed by the press when she landed, was received by President Theodore Roosevelt in the White House, toured as far west as Minnesota lecturing on "The Science of Life" (St. Ignatius, Wesley, and Tolstoy), "The Artist's Life" (Balzac, Turner, and Brahms), and "Dante and Boccaccio," and wrote articles on society news for the New York *American* and the New York *World*.

In contrast to all this brilliant activity and social success, however, is a note of despair in her letters in this last decade of her life which may, to a degree, reflect a deeply felt reaction to Moore's gossip. Some of her friends observed that after 1895 "she declined shockingly both in looks and spirit." A further source of her unhappiness was her mother's mental state, which made life at home unbearable at times and had a damaging effect on her own health. Explaining her renting of rooms at the Albany in 1904, she wrote to Unwin:

I shall continue to live at home, but it is impossible to *work* any longer in the home circle. . . . For obvious reasons it is often difficult for me to bring this fact home to my mother, who is extremely kind but very difficult to live with. My sister is only able to remain with her a certain length of time in the year, but I have endured the strain of this existence practically ever since I was born. I have reached the limit of my endurance . . . my mother is a very clever woman and very interesting in a number of ways. I can control her better than any other member of the family, not excepting my father, but my nervous system has suffered under the strain.[66]

On July 9, 1906, only a month before her death, she wrote again to Unwin of her mother: "She has driven me almost out of my mind—the incessant worry and strain effect my brain . . . her temper and excitability wear us all out. . . . Last month I was on the verge of an absolute breakdown."

Physically Mrs. Craigie may have been failing more rapidly than even her doctors recognized. The fatigue of which she had complained for years no doubt had its physical as well as its psychological origins. She was herself well aware of the interaction of body and state of mind. In February, 1905, she had written:

I don't believe I shall live much longer. There is nothing organically wrong with me, and doctors are always surprised at my actual health, which is most unusually good, but I flag—the pulse stops, and it is impossible for me to keep going. For some years I have been trying to cheat exhaustion; my mind is as active as ever but I can't struggle against this fatigue. My life has been sad and eventful. I have lived two lives in one: I take everything to heart and I have thought far too much. . . . My knowledge of the world has not embittered me, but it has *tired* me.

In this same letter she anticipated the very circumstances of her death eighteen months later: "[Doctors] told me some years ago that I should go out like a candle: my heart was broken with grief long ago, and although it is sound physically, and I *ought* to live by all the rules of the physical game,—the laws of the spiritual game are more determined—if more elusive." [67] She died, according to her own simile, like a candle going out. Presumably in good health, working on a new novel, to all appearances happy, she had returend to the Richards' London house on August 12, 1906, from a visit to her family on the Isle of Wight. She was found in her bedroom the next morning by a maid, having died in her sleep, her rosary in her hand. The coroner's inquest ascribed the death to cardiac failure from natural causes. A curious note in her will instructed that her body be cremated, but since she had also requested burial "according to the rites of the Roman Catholic Church," she was interred in St. Mary's Cemetery, Kensal Green, following a requiem mass, on August 17. She left the bulk of her estate of £24,502 to her son, but stipulated that royalties from her books up to the sum of £3,000 go to Monsignor Brown for his church in Vauxhall. [68]

The physical life that flickered out so suddenly was no more fragile than the work that Mrs. Craigie produced. In her last years there was a decided sobering of tone and strengthening of technique that—while it promises more than it delivers—does give her last novels some interest for the modern reader. The perverse, the odd, the arch and clever strain still dominate, but there is decidedly less self-consciousness. No longer the precocious young ingenue society-novelist, Mrs. Craigie viewed herself with solemnity. She had always taken her work seriously. Since writing her Robert Orange novels, however, she began to take her ideas seriously as well. Significantly, in 1901, a year which marks a subtle but unmistakable shift in her work, she had immersed herself in a study of George Eliot, preparing a sketch of her for the tenth edition of the *Encyclopedia Britannica*. Long an admirer of Eliot, and of some of that novelist's literary favorites like George Sand and Saint Teresa, Mrs. Craigie was drawn increasingly to her profound intellectuality, her capacity for the most strenuous mental discipline, her "speculative" as opposed to what she called her "emotional genius." Like many of her contemporaries at the turn of the century, Mrs. Craigie lamented the consequent loss of passion: "The highly trained brain suppressed the impulsive heart." She was nevertheless perceptive enough to conclude that even George Eliot's later novels, so often tagged as lumbering and pedantic, were in their own way masterpieces: "But one has only to compare 'Romola' and 'Daniel Deronda' with the compositions of any author except herself to realize the greatness of her designs and the astonishing gifts brought to the final accomplishment."

Her sketch of George Eliot is sensitive; at points, in fact, there is a positive empathy, leaving the reader suspicious that he has learned more about John Oliver Hobbes than about Eliot:

> No right estimate of George Eliot, whether as a woman or as an artist, or a philosopher, can be formed without a steady recollection of her infinite capacity for mental suffering and her need of human support. . . . She suffered from bodily injuries the greater part of her life, and but for an extraordinary mental health, inherited from the fine yeoman stock from which she sprang, it is improbable that she could have retained at all times so sane a view of human conduct or been the least sentimental among women writers of the first rank—the one wholly without morbidity in any disguise.

Characteristically, Mrs. Craigie identified herself with this wise, long-suffering, idealistic, and disillusioned but not embittered spirit. The morbidity which we detect in her work was no doubt unconscious. While she would probably have admitted to cynicism and bitterness—with a degree of pride at that—she felt that these qualities drew her all the more closely to the master who had succeeded in sublimating them. Her last two novels, *The Vineyard* (1904) and *The Dream and the Business* (1906), are the works of a thoughtful, mature writer attempting the intense moral analysis that George Eliot excelled in. Catholicism and fashionable society, the two topics that had most interested her up to this time, are subordinated here and become merely a background for the exploration of larger problems of human nature. In both novels she strives for, although she only rarely achieves, an atmosphere of recognizable English reality. *The Vineyard* shows unmistakable Eliot influence. Set in a provincial farm-market town, it has echoes of *Middlemarch,* with village gossip and homely humor—spinster sisters warn the day-dreaming heroine against the example of her late mother: "She followed her fancies wherever they took her. . . . When she was dying she put up her hand to gather those very roses [on the wallpaper] off the wall. She followed a fancy to the last." In contrast they recall approvingly their father's dying words: " 'If I fall asleep, take care of the candle' . . . that will show you, Jennie, that there is some sense all the same in our family" (Ch. VI).

The idealistic heroine Jennie Sussex, refined, intelligent, bookish, plunges into a heart-breaking romance with an attractive but morally weak hero. All similarities to George Eliot cease as soon as the machinery of the plot begins working, but there remains at least a hint of the theme of egoism in Mrs. Craigie's principal characters—Jennie, who learns painfully to subdue her ego in a good but unromantic marriage; the hero Gerald Federan, who indulges his ego and destroys his happiness by marrying a wealthy, neurotic girl. This character, Rachel Tredegar, is human egoism personified and magnified to grotesque proportions. She is half mad and sexually frustrated, bored and friendless until she sees Federan and resolves on possessing him: "She swayed in his direction as a vine seems to grow toward a tree, and as the morning mist will hang round a root, her will enveloped his. Was he not the one relief she had ever found for the starving egoism of her own nature?" Federan's egoism is less complicated. He loves Jennie but he covets wealth. His materialism unmans him and drains his moral strength: "Yet there was something in Rachel herself—a delicacy of body, a lassitude of soul—which seemed to fascinate and penetrate his own indolence. . . . Rachel called to some reluctant force of his being of which he seemed to have no experience, and over which he had, apparently, no control."

The Vineyard is a relatively uncluttered novel, for John Oliver Hobbes—one simple love triangle with a few trivial subplots involving disappointed lovers. In *The Dream and the Business* she reverts to the old pattern, weaving and interweaving human relationships with precise detail but lofty detachment. Here, however, she seems more emotionally engaged than in the earlier novels. Althoug much of the book is set in the rarefied atmosphere of London upper-class society, a substantial part of it deals with the family of a comfortable but not wealthy Dissenting clergyman. The complications of the plot involve the tangling of both religious and social problems, as well as the usual emotional ones. While the work was still in progress, Mrs. Craigie summarized her plot:

> The novel is a study of the Nonconformist life, political life, and social life in England. The main interest is a love interest. The chief man is the son of a rich Nonconformist merchant [in the final version a clergyman]. The chief woman is the daughter of a poor Roman Catholic old family. The second woman is the sister of the chief man. The second man is the son of a rich peer. . . . There are no religious controversial matters introduced, although the clash of the different religions comes into the story.[69]

As in most of her novels, the lovers here are all mismatched at the outset, and there is the usual shuffling about. The "second woman," Sophy Firmalden, loves a talented singer, Lessard, who cannot marry her because he is already married. Her brother, the Dissenting clergyman, falls in love with the "chief woman," Tessa Marlesford, a Catholic married to a man who became a Catholic himself to marry her. The main conflict concerns the rivalry between Sophy, who seeks to win Marlesford back to Protestantism, and Tessa, who seeks to convert the Dissenter to Catholicism. This battle is conducted in refined and flawless taste, with almost Jamesian delicacy. The outcome is ironic. Tessa dies and Sophy, having fallen in love with Marlesford, becomes a Catholic herself and marries him.

The Dream and the Business (the title is from Ecclesiastes: "For a dream cometh through a multitude of business") was an appropriate conclusion to John Oliver Hobbes' career. It is a novel, in fact, of conclusions—compromises, reconciliations, peace made not after glorious victory but in weary resignation. Mrs. Craigie put herself into this book more completely than she had in any other. The glamorous heroines of the Robert Orange novels represent facets of her personality idealized in dream fantasy. But the two heroines of this novel are projections of her real self, and, for want of more accurate records, we must look to them for whatever insights we may have into her strange and complex character. Sophy Firmalden, refined and earnestly Protestant, is an intellectual who writes book and art criticism for a weekly paper, studies Greek from six to eight each morning, reads French, German and Italian literature, plays the piano, and moves with poise through the highest London society. Superficially she resembles Mrs. Craigie in many ways. But Sophy is energetic, practical, and—in a not-unfriendly sense—self-serving. She therefore survives the ordeal of life.

Mrs. Craigie drew only the outline of herself in Sophy. Her real self, as she conceived it, was in the beautiful, sensitive Catholic Tessa, who dies young, a victim not of any specific ailment but crushed by the burden of life itself. She leaves behind a letter that might well have served as Mrs. Craigie's epitaph upon herself:

> Women of my type, who are not strong enough physically to bear the strain of moral suffering, very soon, and gladly, flicker out. We are designed to be *filles de joie* (not in the sinister sense), and although we may have the courage to face hard things, and the faith that can accept hard sayings, God mercifully allows us to die early in the fight. My religion helps me to die; it cannot make me live. All I have ever allowed myself in the way of indulgence is an occasional wonder (I will not call it a regret) at the destiny of creatures like myself, who can crowd so much despair into so short a time (Epilogue).

There is a *fin-de-siècle* weariness and self-pity in this fragile heroine, as there is in the author who created her—a late-romantic charm, an appealing air of hopelessness and helplessness.

Even Tessa's religion only half fulfills her need. Tessa, of course, was denied the outlet of self-expression and fulfillment in art or literature that Mrs. Craigie had. But where the medium of the novel so admirably served the needs of other sensitive, intelligent women, ultimately it too failed John Oliver Hobbes. Lacking the energy and drive of Eliza Lynn Linton, the passionate commitment to social ideals of Olive Schreiner, and the cool, firm intellectual control of Mrs. Humphry Ward, she never really focused her talents or directed her writing toward the public who would receive it. She approached her work with the same seriousness and zeal. She had a sense, both spiritual and intellectual, of mission, of a vocation to educate and reform. In choosing the novel of "high society," she was working after all with a setting she knew best, from first-hand experience. But in thus limiting the range of her vision, she removed and even alienated herself from the substantial bourgeois novel-reading public that so loyally supported her sister novelists. Late in her career this "misdirection" apparently began to dawn upon her. In a letter to the publisher William Heineman in 1904 she spoke with characteristic self-confidence about her success in literature but betrayed a frustrated yearning for a popular audience:

> I know that I have a large unexpected public—not the bookish public, but the working public—in addition to those who are by way of being educated, who are supposed to like epigrams and read "literature" only. During the last few years I have deliberately made for this human—as opposed to the merely fashionable—class, because they are the more constant and the more sound in their judgment of a book's truth. Style they do not understand, and the arts of combination and the like they cannot appreciate, but they respond to the meaning, anyhow, of one's little story.

But in her heart she remained aloof, remote from this "working public" that she sought. Unlike her sister novelists she persistently confused her talent with some lofty personal notion of "art." Perhaps she revealed herself most honestly in a letter to her publisher just a few months before her death: "I can't attempt to cope with the 'Jungle' public: sensationalism is not my line. I am an artist." [70] Too clever, too sophisticated, too proud to court not a "jungle" public but the solid middle-class and working class reading public, John Oliver Hobbes was the truly singular anomaly of that novel-writing age.

APPENDIX: MAX BEERBOHM'S PARODY OF JOHN OLIVER HOBBES*

ISAIAH, WATTEAU, AND STRAUSS

[A lecture delivered by Mrs. Craigie at the Royal Institute; at the Bar of the House of Commons; in the Albert Hall (hired by Mr. J. Morgan Richards for the occasion); at the Imperial Palace in Potsdam; and elsewhere.]

Perhaps in this distinguished audience there will be some who will wonder why I have grouped these three great men together. My excuse for doing this is that each of them had two legs, ten toes, eight fingers—or ten, if I may reckon the thumbs as such—and a pair of eyes, ears, and nostrils. That is my *excuse;* but my private motive (between you and me and Papa's Little Liver Pills) is that I have nothing whatever to say that has not already been said about Isaiah

---

* Beerbohm's copy of *The Artist's Life* is in the Berg Collection of the New York Public Library. It is printed here with permission of the Berg Collection, William Heinemann, Ltd., and the Estate of the late Max Beerbohm.

The following is written, in Beerbohm's hand, on the end pages of his copy of John Oliver Hobbes' *The Artist's Life* (London, T. Werner Laurie, 1904), a collection of lectures: "Balzac, Turner and Brahms"; "Dante and Goya"; "Dante and Botticelli." These lectures were delivered by Mrs. Craigie at the Philosophical Institution, Edinburgh; Literary Society, Glasgow; Ruskin Society, Birmingham; Dante Society, London, and various places in the United States, including Barnard College, New York.

In the same volume, also in Beerbohm's hand, are the following: on the engraving of Dante, wearing a laurel wreath, facing the title page—the signature of Pearl Mary Teresa Craigie, October 26, 1904, and J. Morgan Richards, with "Dante's Little Laurel Leaves. But see that they *are* Dante's." Beside the engraved Dante portrait he has written: "J. O. Hobbes, photo by Lafayette."

or Watteau or Strauss—nothing, that is, to say above the level of any high-school girl who has dipped into a popular encyclopedia—whereas by making a trio of them I can seem to be doing something very thoughtful and profound— or rather I can seem throughout my lecture as if I were *going* to be very illuminating about / the differences between these three great men, and about their points of resemblance; and when at length I suddenly resume my seat, I shall smile round on you so sweetly, with such modest brilliance, that you really won't be able to realise that I have merely succeeded in making fools of you, and a fool of myself. My hat, at which so many of you are looking, cost 17 guineas. And now to the subject of my lecture.

Isaiah was a Prophet, Watteau was a Painter, Strauss is a Musical Composer. Strauss was born in the 19th century, Watteau in the 18th, but Isaiah was born so long ago as the 7th century B.C. Thus between Isaiah and Watteau there is a far greater interval of time than between Watteau and Strauss. There have been very few feminine Prophets. In the nature of women there seems to be [I say it with a giggle] something / that prevents them from prophesying. But Isaiah was not a woman. Isaiah was a man. About his parentage and early education little is known. It is likely enough that, in his boyhood, people did not foresee his future eminence. There were people who did not foresee mine. And yet here I am. Watteau, when he grew up, was essentially a *Court* Painter. He delighted in all that is graceful and gay and distinguished in the outer aspects of life. In this he was very different from Rembrandt, who probed deep into character. That is what *I* do, but then I don't only do that, you bet your bottom dollar: I've got culture, but I'm a right smart Amurrican gurl, and don't you make no darned error about it. Watteau painted mainly in oils, which is more difficult to do than water-colour; but he also painted in water-colour. Strauss' earlier compositions show signs of immaturity—etc., etc., etc.

Notes

1. *The Life of John Oliver Hobbes* (hereafter *Life*), ed. John Morgan Richards (London, 1911), pp. 83–84. There is a large collection of unpublished materials relating to Mrs. Craigie—mainly her letters to friends, family, and publishers—in the Berg Collection, New York Public Library. I have drawn upon this material (as indicated in the notes below) wherever possible to supplement the rather sketchy material in the biography.

2. In commenting upon this novel in the mid-1960's, Lettice Cooper recalled that "trying to be clever" was "a frequent source of reproach in our youth" (*A Chaplet for Charlotte Yonge*, eds. Georgina Battiscombe and Margharita Laski [London, 1965], p. 33).

3. "The Fiction of John Oliver Hobbes," *North American Review*, CLXXXIII (October–December, 1906), 1251.

4. Commenting on a visit to Bayreuth in 1894, she wrote: "I think the thing is, on the whole, mere sensationalism of a rather vicious kind. In less than ten years Wagner will be 'off' " (*Life*, p. 169).

5. *Bookbuyer*, X (April, 1894), 127.

6. "Billy Booth and his Amelia," *Letters from a Silent Study* (London, 1904), p. 229.

7. Introduction to George Sand's *Mauprat*, tr. Stanley Young (London, 1902), p. xiv.

8. Mrs. August Belmont, *Fabric of Memory* (New York, 1957), p. 52. Mrs. Belmont, the former Eleanor Robson, was a very popular actress early in the century. Both Mrs. Humphry Ward and John Oliver Hobbes sought her for roles in their plays and the letters that she received from these writers are now in the Special Collections of Columbia University.

9. Lord David Cecil, *Max* (Boston, 1965), p. 367. Beerbohm's parody of a lecture by Mrs. Craigie, written in a copy of her *The Artist's Life* in the Berg Collection, is reproduced here; see appendix to this chapter, pp. 266–68.

10. *Life*, p. 19. Numerous unpublished letters to T. Fisher Unwin in the Berg Collection show her to be a practical woman concerned with royalties and promotion of her books.

11. *Life*, pp. 66, 67.

12. *Ibid.*, pp. 258–59.

13. Mrs. Craigie was a generous patron of the arts and contributed heavily to various societies for the benefit of authors: see her letter of February 13, 1896, to Mr. Woods of the Society of Women Journalists, with the postscript: "I am *delighted* to read the account of the Benevolent Fund. I will send a further donation but of course *anonymously*" (Fales Collection, New York University, her italics). After her conversion to Catholicism she concentrated most of her philanthropy upon the Church; see *Life*, pp. 346–48. When the artist William Rothenstein applied to her in 1904 for help to aid the then struggling writer Joseph

Conrad, she replied: "I am deeply concerned to hear of Mr. Conrad's troubles. I have the greatest admiration for his work. . . . My own liabilities with regard to the R. C. Church are extremely heavy—(a matter of thousands) & I simply *cannot* give any money till that obligation is cleared" (July 13, 1904, Houghton Library). Some of Mrs. Craigie's publicized philanthropy, however, may have been a cloak concealing personal debts. Among her unpublished letters there are numerous references to expenses involved in producing her plays, travel, and interest on loans—most of which she attempted to conceal from her father. See her letter of July 4, 1905, to her friend Tip (otherwise unidentified): "I fancy Papa thinks that a good deal goes to R. C. charities. This is not the case: I make my cheques payable in that form sometimes, but they go to Hebrews!" (Berg).

14. *Life,* p. 123.
15. *Ibid.,* p. 330.
16. *Ibid.,* pp. 80–81, 323.
17. *Ellen Terry's Memoirs,* eds. E. Craig and Christopher St. John (New York, 1932), p. 244.
18. Mrs. George Cornwallis-West, *The Reminiscences of Lady Randolph Churchill* (London, 1908), p. 285.
19. *Life,* p. 363.
20. *Adventures of a Novelist* (New York, 1932), pp. 248–49.
21. *Opinions* (London, 1959), pp. 93–94.
22. "A Literary Letter," *The Sphere,* August 24, 1918.
23. C. Lewis Hind, editor of *The Academy,* wrote in his autobiography *Naphtali* (London, 1926), p. 107, that Richards "idolized his daughter, and I soon learnt that if I pleased her I pleased him." Mrs. Craigie took an active but not dominating interest in the magazine; see *Life,* p. 124. According to Hind they occasionally disagreed on a book review: ". . . but a call upon her . . . made all smooth and smiling again" (p. 109). In 1903 she wrote a series of short essays for the magazine which were collected in the following year as a book, *Letters from a Silent Study.* Also, in 1903, Richards bought the periodical *Literature* from the *Times* (which was then starting its *Literary Supplement*) and incorporated it with *The Academy* (see his *With John Bull and Jonathan* [New York, 1906], p. 161, and *Life,* pp. 208–209).
Most of Mrs. Craigie's novels were favorably reviewed in *The Academy,* but the magazine could not be accused of puffing them. An editorial on her death, published August 18, 1906 (by which time Richards had sold his interests), was completely objective, observing that she never realized the promise of her "brilliant, if excessive" early novels, and concluding:

> The gravest charge that can be brought against her work, the fault which mars it all, is a coldness. an aloofness, a want of sympathy with human nature. It reveals, in fact, a scorn of humanity which is fatal to good work. It is not too much to say that most men and women, in the eyes of "John Oliver Hobbes," were beneath notice. How much of this sentiment was due to her birth and training, this is not the place to inquire. The result of it is that she remained in her unreal exquisite world, weaving fantasies that became more and

more remote from life, wrapping herself in a cold superiority that robbed her work of its life-blood. And so an exceptionally brilliant mind has left no worthy memorial behind it.

24. Hind, *Naphtali*, p. 108.
25. *Life,* p. 4.
26. "On Atmosphere and Character," *Letters from a Silent Study*, p. 217.
27. (London) *Times*, July 4, 1895, p. 12 (from account of Craigie divorce proceedings).
28. "John Oliver Hobbes," *Munsey's Magazine*, X (March, 1894), 640.
29. *Life,* p. 16.
30. *Munsey's*, p. 640.
31. (London) *Times*, July 4, 1895.
32. *Life,* p. 91.
33. Letter in Fales Collection, July 5, 1895.
34. *Life,* p. 167.
35. *Ibid.,* p. 42.
36. *The Letters of George Meredith,* ed. by his Sons, II (New York, 1912), 529, 550–51.
37. *The Feminine Note in Fiction* (London, 1904), p. 65.
38. Florence Hardy, *The Later Years of Thomas Hardy* (New York, 1930), pp. 26, 120. Mrs. Craigie denied the Hardy influence, but it is too apparent to be ignored. See her comment to Unwin in an unpublished letter of November 10, 1896, referring to a review of *The Herb Moon:* "My style bears no sort of resemblance to Hardy's & if I am like Meredith it is because we both belong to the same school. His English, however, is not my English. He is at his best when he writes under the influence of Victor Hugo, Charles Reade & Disraeli" (Berg).
39. *Life,* p. 94.
40. *Ibid.,* pp. 88–89.
41. *Ibid.,* pp. 341–42.
42. *Real Conversations,* recorded by William Archer (London, 1904), pp. 61, 63.
43. *Life,* p. 318; her italics. The religious experience of Althea Rees in Stuart's novel *Fenella* (see above, p. 225) is strikingly similar to Mrs. Craigie's, religion bringing her not happiness and tranquility so much as simply an outlet for intense, overwrought emotion:

> Even after her conversion she liked to play at heresy—to be the *enfant terrible*—to have grave monsignori wag their fingers half reprovingly at her. Her religion remained intensely personal, and she was never impressed, as some worthy converts have been, by the spectacle of the Church as a "great, going concern." Its dogma oppressed her; she was not strong enough, physically or nervously, to endure its elaborate ritual, and would often leave her seat in church, suffocating, in the very middle of high mass. What she liked best was to creep away at dusk, when the world is busiest with shopping and tea, and, before some dimly-lit altar in Farm Street or Brompton, to set herself adrift upon an ocean of sentiment that, with a little more conviction and a little less self-consciousness might almost have become ecstasy.

44. *Life,* pp. 295, 118; her italics.
45. *Lothair's* plot, inspired by the real-life conversion to Catholicism of the Marquis of Bute, carries its idealistic, fabulously wealthy young hero through a course of political intrigue, participation in the Italian nationalist wars of 1867–1868, and a perilously close flirtation with Catholicism. Disraeli introduces characters clearly identifiable with real figures—notably, the brilliant and persuasive Cardinal Grandison, who is Cardinal Manning. But, unlike Orange, Lothair remains in the Church of England and ends up happily adjusted to the secular society of his time and rank. In *The School for Saints* Robert Orange describes his first meeting with Disraeli:

> Disraeli's kindness passes all belief. . . . At the moment he, too, is writing a novel, some chapters of which he has shown me. They are the most brilliant things of their kind in any language. The book is to be called *Lothair.* Roman Catholicism plays a great part in the plot, and it is delightful to hear him utter his views on the subject. They have changed a little since he wrote *Sybil,* whereas he was, in his sympathies *Roman* Catholic then, he is *Pagan* Catholic now. He knows a lot; in fact, he possesses real learning. It is more than a great mind; he is a great spirit (Ch. VII).

46. Details of the life of this actress, Henriette Duboc, were certainly suggested to Mrs. Craigie by the life of Sarah Bernhardt—her Brittany retreat was modeled on the Grand Sarah's summer home Belle Isle, a rugged island off the Quiberon peninsula of Brittany.
47. *Life,* pp. 107, 110.
48. *Opinions,* p. 137.
49. Mrs. Craigie's good friend Owen Seaman, editor of *Punch,* wrote a delightful parody of these two novels, "Robert Porridge," published in his *Borrowed Plumes* (London, 1916), pp. 15–27. It reads in part:

> Robert was passing through that crisis which is inevitable with those in whom the ideals of childhood survive an ordered scheme of ambition. His head was his Party's; but his heart was in the "Kingdom under the sea," Lyonesse or another, not in the maps. He spent long hours of vigil over Jules Verne's *Twenty Thousand Leagues,* in the original. . . . Dépaysé by arbitrary choice, his adopted name of Porridge stood merely for the cooked article, the raw material being represented by his family name of Hautemille, a stock unrivalled in antiquity save by the Confucii and the Tubal Cains; and to the last even in the intervals of the most exalted abstraction, he was prey to poignant irritation when the comic journals (ever ready to play upon proper names) anglicized it phonetically as Hoatmeal. He repeated the *Chanson de Roland* verbatim every night in bed.

> The convent-bred heroine's name is Midget: "Consolatory platitudes exude from her brain with the facile fluency of her own saucy ringlets. Artlessness, in her case, has grown into an accomplishment so close to nature that it borders on sincerity."

50. Margaret Maison considers *Robert Orange* "the finest Catholic novel of the day" (*The Victorian Vision* [New York, 1961], p. 165).
51. See her comment to Ellen Terry: "I am changing all my views about so-called 'literary' dialogue. It means pedantry. The great thing is to be natural" (*Ellen Terry's Memoirs,* p. 245).

52. In a letter to the Editor of the *Spectator*, August 21, 1959, the novelist Graham Greene wrote that he reads and enjoys the novels of John Oliver Hobbes. "I even before the war contemplated a biography of this woman whose intimacy with Lord Curzon so angered George Moore that he kicked her bottom in Hyde Park."

53. *Intimate Portraits* (New York, 1951), p. 144.

54. Malcolm Brown, *George Moore: A Reconsideration* (Seattle, 1955), p. xvi.

55. *Life*, pp. 215–16; her italics.

56. Clark, *Intimate Portraits*, p. 144. As late as December 2, 1915, Moore wrote to John Richards complaining that, in the biography of his daughter, Richards had not corrected the "libel" that Moore had merely made suggestions to her concerning the play *Journeys End in Lovers Meeting*. By this time Moore had even forgotten the title: he refers to it twice as "Journey's End and Lovers Meeting." He concludes, however, on a friendly note: "The cloud is no bigger than a man's hand, it is true, and does not prevent my hoping that you will call and see me when you next come to London" (Berg).

57. *Opinions*, p. 31. Moore and Mrs. Craigie attended the inaugural dinner for *The Yellow Book* together: "Gossip was already linking his name with the handsome Mrs. Craigie's and his behavior did nothing to scotch the rumor" (Katherine Mix, *A Study in Yellow: The Yellow Book and its Contributors* [Lawrence, Kans., 1960], p. 82).

58. *Bookman*, March, 1897, reported the rumor of her engagement to Spindler but expressed surprise because, although Spindler was rich, "he can hardly minister to the new ambition that has sprung up in the mind of his fiancée—an ambition to shine in the world of *la haute politique*." The article adds that she travels in prominent Tory circles and has been seen "so much in the company of Mr. Arthur Balfour as to give rise to sporadic rumours of their engagement." Actually Mrs. Craigie did give serious consideration—in spite of her religious scruples—to marriage to Walter Spindler in 1902. In unpublished letters to her father of November 10, 24, and 25, she writes:

> Walter is in London, as you know. He is *very* determined in the marriage question. . . . I have not decided finally in the matter, but he will not stand much more temporising. The step would be a serious one. . . . Saw Walter yesterday. He wants announcement made at once. But of this more anon. Have not decided absolutely. . . . With regard to Walter, I must settle the question before I go [to India] as he is getting very irritable and "ill-used." We would not marry in any case before next spring (Berg).

59. Leonard Mosley, *The Glorious Fault: The Life of Lord Curzon* (New York, 1960), p. 54. Mrs. Craigie's unpublished letters give no hint of any "designs" on Lord Curzon. She speaks with genuine concern of the failing health of Lady Curzon and treats of Curzon himself with respect and no suggestion of intimacy. She was obviously impressed and flattered to be friendly with so prominent a figure.

60. In 1907 a memorial fund was established for a medallion-bust of Mrs. Craigie at University College, where she had been a student, and for scholarships in her memory. Among members of the committee formed

to raise subscriptions were Max Beerbohm, Winston Churchill, Edmund Gosse, Lady Margot Tennant, and Mrs. Humphry Ward. Nearly £1,000 was collected, £600 of which was reserved for scholarships. See *Life,* pp. 360 ff. and "The John Oliver Hobbes Memorial," a pamphlet (London, 1908; privately printed) in the Widener Library, Harvard University.

61. *Life,* pp. 323–24. See Helmut E. Gerber's comment: "It is possible that more than a little of Mrs. Craigie appears in the character of Mildred Lawson" (*George Moore in Transition: Letters to T. Fisher Unwin and Lena Milman, 1894–1910* [Detroit, 1968], p. 102). As Gerber observes (p. 110, n. 24), Moore's "heroines" were no doubt amalgamations of many women—at this point in his life Clara Lanza, Lena Milman, Maud Cunard. But the specific detail in "Mildred Lawson" is certainly drawn most heavily and intimately from his knowledge of Mrs. Craigie.

62. Unpublished letters to Unwin (March 16, 1898) and to her father (August 14, 1899) in the Berg Collection. The play on which they worked was produced under the title *Elizabeth Cooper* by the Stage Society in June, 1913, and published the same year. Moore rewrote it again as *The Coming of Gabrielle* in 1920; this version was produced for three matinees at the St. James' Theatre in July, 1923 (R. H. Davis, Preface to *George Moore: Letters to Lady Cunard* [London, 1957], p. 9, n. 1).

63. *Letters from George Moore to Edward Dujardin, 1886–1922,* tr. John Eglinton (New York, 1929), pp. 53–54.

64. February 1, 1905 (Berg).

65. *Intimate Portraits,* p. 146. According to Mosley (*The Glorious Fault,* pp. 164 ff.), some years after his first wife's death Curzon had a tempestuous affair with another literary lady, Elinor Glyn, to whom he sent a tiger skin after seeing her in a dramatized version of her novel *Three Weeks.* The affair lasted from 1908 to 1916, when Mrs. Glyn's husband died. Evidently she then expected him to marry her, but that same year he became engaged to a wealthy American widow, Mrs. Alfred Duggan, and resumed the political career from which he had been retired for several years.

66. July 19, 1904 (Berg).

67. *Life,* pp. 288–89. See also her letter to Mrs. Meynell, July 7, 1905:

> Do forgive the delay in replying to your kind letter. I became steadily more tired physically after the Dinner & I have to spend the last few days in bed getting my pulse back to its *normal* slowness! These collapses are the greatest bore—they don't effect my head but they make it impossible for me to keep engagements. I have to remain by wide-open windows (in *all* weather) & breathe "delicately"! (Fales).

68. (London) *Times,* August 16 and September 29, 1906.

69. *Life,* pp. 246–47.

70. March 16, 1904, and June 15, 1906 (to Mr. Naylor, of Fisher Unwin) (Berg).

*. . . it was the puritan in John Sargent who was perpetually dissatisfied
with that spontaneous imaginative vision of his, inclining him to the
recondite and far-fetched, and compelling him to an arduous search
after the unsuspected aspects and innermost qualities of whatever he
painted.*
                    —Vernon Lee, "J. S. S.: In Memoriam"[1]

*. . . although my salad days were passed, alas, in Victorian times . . .
yet I had put forth crops of (sere and yellow) leaves in this autumnal
twentieth century, nay in this discontented post-war weariness.*
                    —Vernon Lee, August 17, 1929[2]

*I have tried to bite into the apple of aesthetic knowledge on various
sides.*
                    —Vernon Lee, November 19, 1909[3]

5.

The Puritan Aesthete:
Vernon Lee

I

Vernon Lee does not properly belong in this study of women
novelists. Her only fiction of any enduring value is a small group
of short stories, mainly fantasies and ghost stories. Her four
novels are out of print and extremely difficult to find, even in
the best research libraries of Britain and America. During her
lifetime her fame—more accurately her reputation, because she
never achieved any really popular success—rested on travel
writing, essays, and studies of eighteenth-century Italian literature
and music. Yet in a sense almost everything that Vernon Lee
wrote bore the stamp of fiction. She did not write narrative often,

235

but she made history, biography, and aesthetics accessible to her readers by using the techniques of prose fiction. Her failure to reach as wide a public as, say, Mrs. Humphry Ward is easily explained. She was too far removed both physically (living most of her life in Italy) and intellectually from that public. She was unaware of the precise nature of their tastes and needs. But she worked tirelessly to educate and to enlighten. Her zeal, the sense of purpose in her writing, is as striking as it is in any of the ladies studied here. The great difference is that Vernon Lee was the only one of this group who approached the novel as an art form rather than as a medium for public expression and communication. Paradoxically, she was at once a puritan preaching a strict morality and an aesthete reveling in the absolute moral detachment of pure art. But that paradox is no more remarkable than was Vernon Lee herself, as some of her contemporaries remembered her—a homely, rugged-featured spinster in tailored dark clothes, bicycling furiously over the sun-drenched Italian campagna in search of some long-forgotten ancient ruin or a neglected mouldering medieval chapel in a remote farm village. Nor does it tease the imagination more than does the portrait of her by Sargent that hangs in the Tate Gallery—a plain, mannish-looking woman in black relieved only by a white collar, thin hair carelessly tossed back off the forehead, heavy jaw, irregular teeth, and only slightly smiling mouth—but behind the severe, silver-rimmed spectacles, eyes that twinkle with intelligence and humor and a zest for life. Vernon Lee was an oddity but not an eccentric, a mixture of contradictory qualities but not inconsistent. A Victorian who lived to 1935, an Englishwoman who had been born in France and made her home in Italy, a writer more intellectual than imaginative, of ebullient talent rather than of creative genius, she was in many ways a spiritual sister to the other women novelists we are studying here.

As a practicing novelist Vernon Lee contributed little to the progress of art. Her only "realistic" or contemporary novel, *Miss Brown* (1884), was both a personal and an artistic disaster. It was a bungled and amateurish book with characters drawn crudely from life and so thinly veiled that they outraged the few readers who had the patience to plough through it. Thereafter, except for one lapse in a short story in which Henry James figured, much to his pain and embarrassment, she prudently avoided the local and the topical. Her historical novels—*Ottilie* (1883), *Penelope Brandling* (1903), and *Louis Norbert* (1914)—are slight, delicate, but charming studies, with faithful and evocative period detail. Of more weight perhaps are her curious, exotic stories of the supernatural, also rich with historical detail and remarkably effective in re-creating the mood and scenes of the past. In many of her works of nonfiction, notably *The Countess of Albany* (1884), a biography of Princess Louise of Stolberg who married Bonnie Prince Charlie, and her vastly ambitious *Studies of the Eighteenth Century in Italy,* done largely as a series of sketches of personalities, she writes with the flair of the creative artist.

Vernon Lee indeed was more thoroughly committed to art than was any other woman of her generation. She practiced aesthetics consciously and professionally. Everything that she studied (and whatever she studied she tackled with seriousness and professional competence—art, music, literature, history, philosophy, and psychology) became the material of her aesthetics. Not surprisingly, therefore, she viewed the novel as an art form in an age in which formal criticism of it was only just beginning to emerge. Along with her friend and mentor Henry James, she was one of the first to write criticism (rather than reviews) of fiction, to analyze technique, to examine the psychology not only of the writer and his characters but of the reader who responds to the novel. Though her own novels are negligible, what she thought and wrote *about* the novel is today recognized as sound and significant. Desmond McCarthy's prophecy in 1941 that "Vernon Lee will be read by posterity, for her work is a rare combination of intellectual curiosity and imaginative sensibility," is being realized, but on a smaller scale perhaps than he had anticipated. One of her books at least enjoys a healthy survival, *The Handling of Words* (1923). It is not a novel but a book about the making of novels, a subject upon which she could speak with experience, her theory developing out of years of practice.[4]

Unlike many of her contemporaries, Vernon Lee did not have to purge herself of the puritan-philistine morality which regarded art suspiciously as, at best, a useful teacher of practical ethics. Her friend Bernard Berenson, for example, described the shock to "a boyish intellect as Puritanical in outlook as mine" when he discovered, on reading George Eliot's essay on the poet Young's *Night Thoughts,* "that art values deserved as much consideration as those of life or of morals for shaping and directing actuality." The course of his life was changed by this discovery: "It stuck fast . . . like a seed sending out numberless roots and the problem has never ceased to occupy me." [5] For Vernon Lee the discovery was neither sudden nor startling. Growing up in the art centers of western Europe, free from her childhood to taste and explore to her heart's content, to cultivate and indulge her sensibilities, she had from the outset a reverence for art that was nothing short of religious in its intensity. But simultaneously, and for reasons so deeply rooted in her character that it is difficult to do more than merely speculate about them, she also had a bristling distrust of "pure" aesthetics and a downright distaste for aestheticism and "art for art's sake." Operating always within her was a kind of puritanical vigilance far more subtle and refined, thanks to her European background, than that of the English philistine—but persistent and persuasive. Art is good, not because it is good in itself (though she believed this) but because its effects on us are good. It arouses our better instincts, exhilarates and stimulates us to loftier thought and nobler action. Vernon Lee pondered long and deeply on the subject. Over the years, although she altered many of her views, she never abandoned this fundamental position.

Her puritanism betrays itself the instant she raises the question of the purpose and value of art, and that question is the essence of everything that she writes about art. "The contemplation of beautiful shape is . . . favoured by its pleasurableness, and such contemplation . . . lifts our perceptive and empathic activities, that is to say a large part of our intellectual and moral life, on to a level which can only be spiritually, organically, and in so far, morally beneficial." Art is therefore socially useful, producing happiness, spiritual refreshment, and tending "to inhibit most of the instincts whose superabundance can jeopardise individual and social existence." [6] In her essay

"The Use of Beauty," she traces the relationship between the aesthetic and the altruistic instincts, the sense of "aesthetic harmony" and the sense of "the higher harmonies of universal life," the taste for aesthetic pleasure and "the nobler growth of the individual." Illustrating from her own experience, she describes how on a dreary day in London, looking out of her window over a scene of drab, grimy rooftops, she heard from a distance someone playing a strain of Handel's: "And then it seemed as if my soul, and according to the sensations, in a certain degree my body even, were caught up on those notes, and were striking out as if swimming in a great breezy sea; or as if it had put forth wings and risen into a great free space of air." [7]

In emphasizing, then, the constructive, affirmative purposes of art, Vernon Lee in no way dilutes its purer values. Commenting on the spiritual evolution of her friend Walter Pater, she noted precisely the course on which she too was embarked:

He began as an aesthete and ended as a moralist. By faithful and self-restraining cultivation of the sense of harmony, he appears to have risen from the perception of visible beauty to the knowledge of beauty of the spiritual kind, both being expressions of the same perfect fittingness to an ever more intense and various and congruous life.[8]

If, however, the evolution from aesthete to moralist produced a narrowing of sensibility or any restriction or limitation upon the province of art itself, Vernon Lee would have deplored it. But as she traced its course, and demonstrated it in her own development, this heightened moral sense actually extended one's appreciation. The Italian Renaissance, in which, like Pater, she was particularly knowledgeable, proved a good testing ground. The moralist in Vernon Lee was revolted by the corruption of that age: "the moral vitality of the Italians was rapidly decreasing; and a horrible moral gangrene was beginning to spread; liberty was extinguished; public good faith seemed to be dying out; even private morality flickered ominously." But the aesthete in her was drawn irresistibly toward the age's beauty and charm.

Happily, like Pater, Vernon Lee was able to adjust her sights. She had the sophistication and breadth of knowledge to see the age in its largest social and cultural context, in its multiplicity of colors rather than in strict black and white. She saw the totality, "the strange ebullition of the Renaissance, seething with good and evil . . . the picture of a people moving on towards civilisation and towards chaos." The visiting Englishmen of the sixteenth century brought back impressions, not without awed delight, of the horrors of Italy which Webster, Tourneur, Ford, and Marston immortalized in their blood-drenched tragedies— depravity, adultery, murder, incest. But there was also another Italy, perhaps less appealing to thrill-seeking tourists: "the bright and thoughtless rhyme of Lorenzo dei Medici . . . the sweet and tender poetry of Bembo and Vittoria Colonna and Tasso; the bluff sensuality of novelists like Bandello and Masuccio . . . the stately sweet matrons and noble senators of Titian, the virginal saints and madonnas of Raphael, the joyous angels of Corregio . . . this strong and serene Renaissance." [9]

There is no element of compromise in the thinking of Vernon Lee. She was often superbly wrong-headed and unyielding. But her puritan aesthetic was a logically based position, not the result of any timid yearning to make art useful and respectable. She clearly affirmed the independence of the "Beautiful" from mere codes of right and wrong, rejecting, for example, Tolstoy's condemnation in *What Is Art?* of all art that does not serve an immediate moral purpose, with the argument that art "like science itself, like philosophy, like every great healthy human activity, has a right to live and a duty to fulfill, quite apart from any help it may contribute to the enforcement of a moralist's teachings." [10] The question of moral good or bad is irrelevant. Beauty, she wrote, is "aesthetically good . . . pure, complete, egotistic; it has no other value than its being beautiful." [11]

So firm is Vernon Lee's faith in art that she holds it essentially incorruptible and, therefore, divine. "For even if beauty is united to perverse fashions, and art (as with Baudelaire and the decadents) employed to adorn sentiments of maniacs and gaol-birds, the beauty and the art remain sound." Her fundamental optimism is the fruit of faith: "Art is a much greater and more cosmic thing than the mere expression of man's thoughts or opinions on any one subject. . . . Art is the expression of man's life, of his mode of being, of his relations with the universe, since it is, in fact, man's inarticulate answer to the universe's unspoken message." [12] Early in her life Vernon Lee rejected orthodox Christianity because it seemed to her "man-made" and arbitrary. In its place she substituted her own form of humanism, grounded, not surprisingly, on man's supreme creation—art. She conceded that art lacks the center, the sense of community with others, and the reciprocity of love which the Church offers. In spite of these limitations, however, art remains for her the only answer to man's hungry need for religious faith:

> But in all this talk of man's emotional wants our ob-scurantists overlook that there exists a way of satisfying the soul's cravings other than that of belief: the way of Art. . . . they do not perceive that a good half of all mythology is not dogma, but poetry, a good half of ritual is Art . . . that the legitimate satisfaction of our wants, spiritual as well as temporal, is not through believing . . . but through *making*— that is, through the creation in the world outside or the world within, of those things, those shapes, those satisfactions whereof we stand in need.[13]

With art conceived in such lofty terms as these, inevitably Vernon Lee met practical difficulties when she confronted the problems of writing criticism of the novel. The art form that she conceives as almost a way of life and of faith is painting, followed closely by architecture, sculpture, and music—all in the grand classic sense, though not necessarily in the classic style. The chief problem was the always elusive aesthetic question of the nature of beauty. The aim of art, she insists, is to produce the beautiful. The more "abstract" arts of architecture and music (i.e., those not primarily concerned with imitating reality) are those which most directly produce the desired effects of beauty. Painting seems to be more restricted since, at least up to the period in which Vernon Lee was writing, it attempted to suggest some kind of reality and consequently often represented the less than ideal, even the ugly. But the painter controls his reality, arranging the elements to create the *effects* of beauty, if not actually representing beauty itself. He can show the ugly (the agony of the Crucifixion, for example) in such a way as to produce in the viewer the impressions of beauty in ugliness. By the skillful manipulation of details, light, shadow, etc., he can make a raging storm more beautiful than a conventionally beautiful day. But the writer is far more strictly confined to the materials of reality, truth-to-life—human emotions and actions, sense impressions, value judgments:

> The beautiful . . . can exist in literature only inasmuch as literature reproduces and reconstructs certain sensuous impressions which we name beautiful; or as it deals with such moral effects as give us an unmixed, direct, unutilitarian pleasure analogous to that produced by these sensuous impressions of beauty. Now, human character, emotion, and action [do] not merely present us with a host of impressions which, applying an aesthetical word to moral phenomena, are more or less ugly, but, by the very fatality of things, nearly always require for the production of what we call moral beauty a certain proportion of moral ugliness to make it visible. It is not so in art. . . . The beautiful, as such, has a far smaller share in the poem, novel, or the drama than in painting, sculpture or music; and, what is more, the ugly has an immeasurably larger one, both in the actual sense of physical ugliness and in the metaphorical sense of moral deformity.[14]

Literature lacks the purity, the precision, the definiteness, the "massive certainty" of the other arts. It is, she once declared, "a mode of merely imparting opinion or stirring up emotion, the instrument not merely of the artist but of the thinker, the historian, the preacher, and the pleader." [15]

Such dogmatic pronouncements are characteristic of Vernon Lee, but they represent only one side of the coin. Read in context they reflect no disparagement of literature, only a kind of dogged determination to define precisely the boundaries of the arts. In removing literature, specifically the novel, from the realm of the aesthetic, she was not excluding it from the realm of art but simply from the Beautiful, where indeed far too many of the more unsophisticated critics of her time had insisted that it must flourish. At one point, writing of literature as "infinitely less aesthetic" than the other arts, she conscientiously adds a footnote: "By *aesthetic* I do not mean *artistic*. I mean . . . that which relates to the contemplation of such aspects as we call 'beautiful,' whether in art or in nature." [16] The novel is only slightly less artistic than the other arts, and if a value must be placed upon it, one must also acknowledge its ethical function. There is more than a hint of puritan conscience in her remark: "The novel has less value in art, but more importance in life. . . . Hence, I say, that although the novel . . . is not as artistic, or valuable as painting, or sculpture, or music, it is practically more important and more noble." [17]

The novel, then, needs no excuse or apology. Vernon Lee shared the outrage of her contemporaries at the "excesses" of the French novel. In 1886 her spokesman Baldwin, in a dialogue "On Novels," condemns *Une Vie* and *Mlle de Maupin* as unfit for English readers and adds that he would like to cut ' whole passages, sometimes whole chapters," out of Balzac, Daudet, and Flaubert. He advocates "absolute liberty of selection and treatment of subjects"; but he hastily excludes from that noble principle "all abnormal suggestion . . . prurient description . . . [and] pessimistic misrepresentation." But once more the aesthete in Vernon Lee confronts the puritan. What she mainly objects to in Balzac, for example, is not questionable morality but a tendency she detects in many other French novelists as well to probe character too clinically and microscopically, to concentrate on merely one aspect of character or of society rather than on the flux and complexity of life. Thus Balzac isolates one peculiarity in Père Goriot, "the Bump of Philoprogenitiveness. The rest of the brain, one might say, has been cut away." In contrast, Thackeray portrays in Colonel Newcome a loving father and a whole human being, "connected with a half dozen cognate qualities," while Goriot's "paternal infatuation arises from nothing, and is connected with nothing; it is inorganic, at best utterly maniacal

—in truth it is a literary diagram." It is the novelists whom we grasp intuitively, for their compassion, their total identification with their characters—Tolstoy, Stendhal, Thackeray—that Vernon Lee most admires. "The novel of this school seems not written but lived." The analytic novel may be more precise and perfect in art because the novelist has almost scientific control over his subject. But the "synthetic" novel (in the sense of bringing together feeling *and* form) gives us the real sense of life.[18]

This is the subjective approach to the novel. Yet Vernon Lee's criticism is as minutely analytical as the type of Balzac-ian characterization which she disliked. But here she was dealing with technique rather than with character. Her essays on the writing of fiction, published over some forty years and collected in 1923 in *The Handling of Words,* are today read with appreciation by students of the novel because they are pioneer attempts in the close literary analysis of selected texts. A great deal of the book, to be sure, is dogmatic and wrong-headed. She writes as if the craft of fiction were a game, with rules and percentage points to be awarded for "good" or "bad" technique. Stories that use multiple narrators (like *Wuthering Heights*) or dramatic scenes, or are told in the form of autobiography, are "dodges"; "it represents a compromise with that difficult thing, straightforward narrative." Her suspicion of "analytic" characterization like Balzac's produces blind spots in her taste. For example, she shared the obtuseness of many of her late Victorian contemporaries with regard to George Eliot, faulting her for "sacrificing" warmth and humanity to "her passion for abstract scientific terms and scientifically logical exposition." Much as she respected George Eliot's intellect and admired, as an exception among her novels, *The Mill on the Floss,* she objected to her use of dramatic scenes, her precise, carefully calculated construction of character, and her

> little dry, neat, ironical essay-style . . . which creates an impression of the excessive trumperiness of human struggles and woes which, Heaven knows, she never felt to be trumpery; while at the same time she is making the limited feelings of obscure individuals into matters of state of the

Cosmos by the use of terminology usually devoted to the eternal phenomena of the universe.[19]

Although Vernon Lee objected to minute analysis as a technique of art, she favored it as a technique of criticism, a tool for the study of art itself. All her aesthetics is based on exhaustive study of the psychological reactions of the viewer to art, the listener to music, the reader to literature.

> I conceive the actual book or poem or essay to be but a portion of the complete work of literary art, whose completion depends upon the response of the Reader to the suggestions of the Writer. . . . I conceive Writing to be, spiritually: the art of high and delightful perception of life by the Writer; and technically: the craft of manipulating the contents of the Reader's mind.[20]

The Writer-Reader relationship is two-sided. The Reader is not passive but is in constant mental activity. In several places in her writings Vernon Lee quotes Coleridge's lines from "Dejection: An Ode": "O lady! we receive but what we give, / And in our life alone does Nature live," which, she says, sums up "the fundamental principles of modern psychological aesthetics." [21]

The essays in *The Handling of Words* examine the specific techniques by which the novelist manipulates the mind of his reader—techniques of construction (point of view, for example) and language (quite literally the choice of words, hence the title of the book). Because the writer, unlike the painter, sculptor, or musician, must work with only the fragments of consciousness—memory, association, moods—he must carefully select among those fragments so as best to play upon the mind of his reader. Point of view, the "angle of narration," is, she writes, the "supreme constructive question in the novel . . . exactly analogous to that question in painting." Whether the author is inside, outside, even nowhere precisely in relation to his presentation controls the whole nature of that presentation. Here, happily,

Vernon Lee does not fall into the games-and-points logic of other parts of her book. There is no "best" point of view. Favoring as she does, however, the "born," subjective, synthetic character as opposed to the rationally analyzed and constructed one (without recognizing, apparently, that equal or perhaps greater and more conscious effort might have gone into the creation of the intuitive, synthetic character), she emphasizes the advantage of flexibility of point of view:

> The synthetic novelist, the one who does not study his personages, but *lives* them, is able to shift the point of view with incredible frequency and rapidity, like Tolstoi, who in his two great novels really *is* each of the principal persons turn about; so much so, that at first one might almost think there was no point of view at all. The analytic novelist, on the contrary, the novelist who does not *live* his personages, but studies them, will be able to see his personages only from his own point of view, telling one what they are (or what he imagines they are), not what they feel inside themselves; and, at most, putting himself at the point of view of one personage or two, all the rest being given from the novelist's point of view; as in the case of George Eliot, Balzac, Flaubert, and Zola, whose characters are not so much living and suffering and changing creatures, as illustrations of theories of life in general, or of the life of certain classes or temperaments.[22]

The most interesting sections of *The Handling of Words* are those in which she demonstrates her critical principles by analyzing specific passages (of about 500 words each) chosen at random from a variety of types of narrative. Long before the formal study of semantics and the "communication arts" Vernon Lee was exploring questions of connotative meanings, patterns of association, the effects of sentence length and prose rhythms. Her studies reflect a certain amount of pedantry, mere adjective counting, but in the main they are surprisingly suggestive.[23] "Flaubert, by his enormous abundance of precise visual adjectives . . . turns passing effects into unchanging attributes." D'Annunzio's long, latinized sentences, where adjectives are rare and verbs vague, leave the impression of everything happening far slower than it possibly could in reality . . . an impression of something empty, featureless, gaping, but irresistibly emphatic, eerie and tragic, which allows one to read the most revolting or preposterous stories without, as one otherwise would, disbelieving in their possibility outside a madhouse.

Analyzing a passage from *The Ambassadors* she notes James's heavy use of personal pronouns, inferring that they suggest questions of *belief,* the characters moving by degrees toward insights and knowledge of each other:

What the people *do* has no importance save as indicating what motives and what spiritual manners they have, and how these affect the consciousness of their neighbours. And, in this quotation, a considerable amount of extremely vivid feeling of concrete things becomes merely so much metaphor, illustrating purely subjective relations.

Finally, and most important, she recognizes the importance of words in the total construction of a work of fiction. Her most telling criticism is of a descriptive passage from *Tess of the D'Urbervilles:* "This page is so constructed, or rather not constructed, that if you skip one sentence, you are pretty sure to receive the same information in the next; and if you skip both, you have a chance of hearing all you need later on. This makes it lazy reading; and it is lazy writing." [24]

Vernon Lee's critical judgments are never tainted with humility or false modesty. She found lazy writing in Hardy (though she concludes her analysis of this passage by conceding its appropriateness to the overall effect of dreamy, sensual life in nature that he was striving for), carelessness and fatuousness in Landor, deficient logic and haste in Kipling. She even dared to improve upon the writer whom she most admired and imitated, Walter Pater. Where he describes Marius slowly and laboriously climbing a mountain path, she ventures to suggest that his phrase "they passed along" would read better if amended to "they went up a

steep road," because Pater's phrase suggests a flatness of landscape that is inappropriate here.[25] But Vernon Lee's tendency to
carp, her abrasiveness of expression, her dogmatism, and an irritating habit of repetition weaken the really perceptive observations in *The Handling of Words*. One is tempted to see in her
strictures on other and far better writers all her own manifold
weaknesses. "Pater strikes me, so far, as a person who insists on
carrying too much mental luggage; and, not being at all acro-
batic, trailing some of it and getting it all mixed."

If ever a writer was weighed down with mental luggage it
was Vernon Lee herself. Her childhood, her early education, and
her background were unique. Even in the most ordinary person
they would have produced extraordinary qualities: in one as
extraordinary as Vernon Lee they were almost bound to produce
a prodigy. She was trained for art and literature as most girls of
her generation were trained for marriage and domesticity. She
was dedicated to her career and actually embarked upon it before she was in her middle teens. The only choices she had to
make were whether to become a French or an English writer and
how to be herself as a writer:

> Among my own contemporaries, especially in the one I know
> best, I can recognize long preliminary stages of being *not
> oneself;* of being; *being,* not merely *trying* to be, an adul-
> terated Ruskin, Pater, Michelet, Henry James, or a highly
> watered-down mixture of these and others, with only a late,
> rather sudden, curdling and emergence of something one
> recognizes . . . *as oneself.*[26]

II

In middle age, after suffering a series of nervous break-
downs, Vernon Lee came to the very sound conclusion that in
order to understand oneself, one must know "one's own history
and evolution, that is, one's parents and one's own childhood."
Writing to a friend who had had a similar illness she confided:

> I recognize now that my family is on one side acutely neuro-

pathic and hysterical; and that my earlier years were admirably calculated, by an alternation of indiscipline and terrorism, by excessive overwork and absolute solitude, to develop these characteristics. Had I known this at 22 or 23, instead of learning nearer forty, I should now be a good deal sounder and happier.[27]

The side of the family to which she refers is the maternal one; the small, domineering figure of her mother looms large over Vernon Lee's early life and quite thoroughly overshadows her father. Vernon Lee, born Violet Paget in a chateau near Boulogne, October 4, 1856, was her mother's second child. Some years earlier her mother, Matilda Adams, of an old Welsh family that had accumulated a considerable fortune from banking and trade in the West Indies, had married a Captain Lee-Hamilton, by whom, in 1845, she had had a son, Eugene. The captain died in 1849 and six years later his widow, having settled in France, married her son's tutor, Henry Ferguson Paget, son of a French *emigré* nobleman who had anglicized his name, De Fragnier, to Ferguson. Henry Ferguson Paget elected to take his mother's family name. He was a man of somewhat obscure background, educated in Warsaw where his father conducted a school for *emigré* children, and was involved briefly in Polish revolutionary activity. By 1855 he seems to have been satisfied to settle down in marriage to the mother of the boy he tutored, and for the remainder of his life he drifted aimlessly about in the wake of his fiery, restless wife. He was a man of no particular cultivation and spent most of his time hunting and fishing. Visitors to the Casa Paget in Florence recalled seeing him occasionally, but he never appeared at meals, where Mrs. Paget ruled over sessions one guest described as "feasts of reason and flows of soul." [28]

Mrs. Paget ruled everywhere. She was a frail-looking woman, with soft hair and pale eyes—but a sharp tongue and, apparently, an iron will. Though she had been born in 1815, her lonely childhood in remote Wales and the fact that she spent much of her adult life on the Continent, made her more an eighteenth-than a nineteenth-century woman. Her daughter remembered years later, in a tender but candid portrait of her, that she clung to certain eighteenth-century words and pronunciations, "and to heresies which I later identified as Voltairian, or derived from Rousseau and Tom Paine; and her politics were those of Charles James Fox." She was deeply, perhaps morbidly, attached to her son Eugene, a talented boy with a gift for languages and the writing of poetry. For her homely, precocious little daughter she may have had less affection but certainly no less interest. Violet's education was her mother's absorbing, if somewhat fitful, passion. Schooled herself in eighteenth-century rhetoric, she gave her daughter heavy doses of Blair's *Rhetoric* and Cobbett's *Grammar,* "supplementing them with elaborate and admirably written commentaries of her own, and with horribly painful object-lessons in *corpore vili* of my adolescent works." She also gave her scraps of Euclid "during our walks, by way of word of mouth, and without allowing me to glance at a diagram or even draw one furtively in the road's dust." It was an education that could have produced either an ignoramus or a great intellectual—and in either case was almost certain to produce a neurotic. "She was briefly," Vernon Lee wrote of her mother,

> a mass of contradictions; but these were all grown into each other, made organic and inevitable by her passionate and unmistakable individuality which recognized no law but its own. . . . She was tyrannical and self-immolating . . . overflowing with sympathy and ruthlessly unforgiving; dreadfully easily wounded and quite callous of wounding others; she was deliciously tender, exquisitely humorous, extraordinarily grim and at moments terrifying; always difficult to live with and always adorable.[29]

Mrs. Paget had evidently resolved that her clever little daughter was to become a writer, another Madame de Staël "at the very least." The wandering way of life of the Paget family ideally supplemented the child's informal but impressive education. They drifted about Europe: Germany, Italy, France—not as later English and American tourists did, hungrily absorbing "culture," but in an idle, aimless way. They were not "travelers"; they scorned tourism and sight-seeing:

We moved ourselves and our luggage regularly . . . and, obeying some mysterious financial or educational ebb and flow, backwards and forwards between the same two places, and every now and then between a new couple of places in a different part of the globe. But we were careful to see nothing on the way, save the inns where we slept, the refreshment-rooms where we ate, and the Custom-houses where we opened our boxes, whose contents must have been familiar to the officials.[30]

Actually, of course, the child was seeing everything. As her travel writings years later testify, Vernon Lee early developed an unusual sensibility. Scenes, people, smells, sounds—the spirit of places or what she later called the *genius loci*—made indelible impressions. It was a unique spirit that she absorbed: the rapidly vanishing old-world Europe, its eighteenth-century vestiges persisting into the second half of the nineteenth until the Franco-Prussian War of 1870 ruthlessly pushed Europe into the modern world. The Germany in which Vernon Lee spent so much of her childhood, for example, was the quaint storybook country of "pepperpot towers and covered bridges," of folk legend and songs, "when no one talked of Teuton superiority or of purity of Teuton idiom." Her German governesses were stolid and conscientious, cramming her full of music and poetry and sweets. She recalled one who played the Jupiter Symphony with her mother at the piano "instead of hearing me through my scales, and lent me volumes of Tonkunstler-Lexikons to soothe her conscience, and gave us honey in the comb out of her garden of verbena and stocks." [31]

But her real school was Italy, then only beginning to discover its national identity and still largely an eighteenth-century civilization. The Paget family spent the winter of 1868 to 1869 in Rome. There Violet had for playmates two American children whom she had met earlier in Nice—John and Emily Sargent. The painter-to-be was only a few months her senior and provided the brotherly companionship she was later to seek in her half-brother Eugene—at this stage a young man, too "old" for the little sister he called Baby. With Johnny Sargent she played

splendidly gruesome historical charades, the boy "either decapi-
tating Mary Queen of Scots with the fire shovel, or himself offering a bared neck on a footstool in the character of the Earl of
Essex, myself figuring as Queen Elizabeth." They read together
—*Notre Dame de Paris, The Marble Faun,* Fenimore Cooper;
they painted together; they discoursed "on elevated topics": "We
were much of the same juvenile priggishness; but John's was a
steady, boyish priggishness, and borrowed the Dionysiac element
from my already adolescent passion for all Rome meant." Mrs.
Paget had a lofty contempt for tourism, but Mrs. Sargent was a
sympathetic guide for the children's exploration of Rome. Fortified with Murray's *Guide* and Smith's *Smaller Dictionary of Antiquities,* they searched out hidden corners and absorbed
impressions thirstily: walks in the Borghese gardens where they
met cardinals and sometimes even Pio Nono himself, "a white
sash round his portly white middle, distributing benedictions
with two extended fingers"; visits to mass at St. Peter's and the
smaller "tinsel-hung churches, where tapers shone dim through
the stale incense, and the little organs scrunched out chords as
prelude to the *bravuras* of fluted sopranos and cooing throaty
falsettos." [32] She was already, in her own words, "a half-baked
polyglot scribbler," having discovered the magic of dingy old
bookstalls, "the rows of useless and dirty old books exhibited for
sale along the walls of palaces and churches," and the fascination
of old coins and other antiquities. By 1870 she was a published
author with a French *feuilleton,* "Les Aventures d'une Pièce de
Monnaie" (tracing the adventures of a Roman coin from ancient
times to the present) in *La Famille,* a Lausanne paper. But she
was also in pursuit of far more ambitious plans—a biography of
Metastasio, the eighteenth-century Italian playwright and lib-
rettist—and studies of eighteenth-century Italian music. Mrs.
Paget and brother Eugene had reason for pride in this amazingly
precocious girl, but the atmosphere of "prodigy-worship," as her
friend Ethel Smyth shrewdly observed some years later, gave her
"but slight chance of becoming a normal human being . . . her
life was cramped and her personal happiness rendered unattain-
able by the perpetual repression of human needs she had trained
herself to ignore." [33]

III

The largest part of Vernon Lee's writings, both fiction and nonfiction, deals with the past. She was not, however, an escapist, and was always deeply engaged in the present—actively concerned with issues such as socialism, pacifism, and world government. It is therefore curious that so little of her fiction should have a contemporary setting. The explanation is probably that her earliest efforts to write fiction in the contemporary scene proved painfully embarrassing, both for the friends and acquaintances she none too subtly portrayed and, consequently, for herself.[34] From such finger-burning, she should have promptly learned the lesson of fire-shunning, but caution and moderation were not in Vernon Lee's character. Having made one unfortunate blunder in her three-volume novel *Miss Brown,* which shocked polite society of the 1880's with its tasteless attack on aestheticism, she made the supreme gaffe of introducing her friend Henry James into a short story, "Lady Tal," that displayed him, unmistakably and unfairly, as a prig and a stuffed shirt. The irony was that in both cases Vernon Lee had only the best of intentions.

Miss Brown cannot be excused as merely the innocent clumsiness of a fledgling novelist. By 1884, the year it was published, Vernon Lee was a writer of considerable experience and reputation. At twenty-four she had published her *Studies of the Eighteenth Century in Italy,* a volume that was received everywhere with respect and, when the youth and sex of the author were discovered (early reviewers referred to "Mr. Vernon Lee"), with wonder and admiration. A year later she published *Belcaro,* subtitled "Essays on Sundry Aesthetical Questions," and early in 1884, some months before *Miss Brown* appeared, *Euphorion: Studies of the Antique and the Medieval in the Renaissance.* She had also experimented promisingly, if not brilliantly, in imaginative literature with a children's story, told in *commedia dell' arte* manner, *The Prince of the Hundred Soups,* and *Ottilie.* "An Eighteenth-Century Idyll," a short novel about life in Germany. And, finally, she had published a solid work of biography, *The*

Countess of Albany, in W. H. Allen's Eminent Women Series. Little wonder then that the *Atlantic Monthly* early in 1885 hailed her as a shining example of the "new" professional woman writer who "emancipated, encouraged and enlightened women of the now rising literary generation." [35]

In 1881 Vernon Lee made her first visit to England as an adult, having previously spent only the summer of 1862 on the Isle of Wight. She came prepared with letters of introduction to the most distinguished artistic and literary society, and she had many English friends whom she had known in Italy, among them the beautiful Mary Robinson, an aspiring young poet and novelist, with whom she stayed in London. She met scores of writers and artists—Edward Burne-Jones, Theodore Watts, William Rossetti, Lawrence Alma-Tadema, William Morris, Oscar Wilde, Edmund Gosse, Leslie Stephen, Andrew Lang, the Humphry Wards. Mrs. Humphry Ward took a friendly interest in her, arranging lodgings for her visit to Oxford and introducing her to Walter Pater, whom she had long venerated. She returned to England in 1882 and in 1883, widening her circle of friends and her knowledge of the literary and artistic scene, impressing everyone she met with her brilliance, though not with her charm, overwhelming and antagonizing many with her endless stream of talk and her argumentativeness. John Addington Symonds, who disliked her for several personal reasons—pique over her failure to use his work in her studies of the Italian Renaissance and jealousy over her close friendship with Mary Robinson—wrote to her candidly in April, 1884:

> I feel that you imagine yourself to be so clever that everything you think is either right or else valuable. And your way of expressing yourself is so uncompromising that your belief in yourself grates upon my sense of what is just and dignified. . . . It is possible to be frank without being flippant, rude, or patronising. You can be firm without posing as an oracle.[36]

It is the oracular pose that dominates the unfortunate *Miss Brown.* Having surveyed the arts in London for two or three

seasons, Vernon Lee felt entirely competent to judge them decadent and to warn of ominous things to come. The novel is a
remarkable demonstration of her ambivalence: the aesthete writing knowledgeably about pure art, the puritan sternly judging
the moral implications of certain types of art. In the conventional three-decker format in which the eminently respectable
Scottish firm of Blackwood published it, *Miss Brown* might be a
typical Victorian novel—a beautiful but poor heroine rescued
from the misery of servant-life by a well-to-do poet and artist who
educates and ultimately marries her. There is a sinister villainess
who lures the hero away temporarily and a stalwart rival suitor
for the heroine, but the intrigue, having padded out the requi-
site number of volumes, is evaporated by the inevitable happy
ending. This, however, is merely the barest outline of the plot.
The readers who picked up the somber-looking volumes were
soon plunged into a scene of absurdity and affectation, of postur-
ing poets and painters, and of more sinister things—a sensual
adultress, drug addiction, alcoholism, and various unnamed and
unnamable debaucheries. The fact that the scene was London,
the time immediately contemporary, and most of the characters
readily identifiable as members of the very circles in which
Vernon Lee was moving, added shock and sensation. It is not
surprising that the *Spectator* (December 13, 1884) found the
novel "too repulsive" to review at length and, while praising the
author's earlier achievements, chided her for not always knowing
"what it is good to say or leave unsaid." A few reviewers were impressed by the novel's "originality" and "purity of intention,"
but even the most sympathetic, like her friend Cosmo Monkhouse
in *The Academy* (January 3, 1885), deplored her personal satire:
"Vernon Lee has forgotten that to trick up an imaginary character in the clothes of a well-known person, though it will not
prejudice that person in the eyes of those who know him, may
well do so in the eyes of those who know only his clothes." And
privately he wrote her that he thought the book "very nasty.
Whatever made you write about such beastly people, do you
want to rival Ouida?" [37]

There seems little doubt of the high-mindedness of Vernon
Lee's intention. She did not mean to offend; she meant only to

castigate what she termed "the cheap-and-shop shoddy aestheticism" of pre-Raphaelitism, the phony "medieval sort of thing—no stays and no petticoats, and slashings, and tags and bootlaces in the sleeves, and a yard of bedraggled train," the houses cluttered with "weird furniture, partly Japanese, partly Queen Anne, partly medieval," the poets—harmless and ineffectual young men themselves who wrote descriptions "of the kisses of cruel, blossom-mouthed women, who sucked out their lovers' hearts, bit their lips, and strewed their apartments with coral-like drops of blood." Her criticism of the pre-Raphaelites, however, is based not on these merely superficial mannerisms, but on their fundamental philosophy of "art for art's sake," their "moral indifference" to society and its problems. Early in the novel the conflict is anticipated when the hero, Walter Hamlin, an Oxford educated aesthete-poet-painter, tells the heroine, Anne Brown: "The world is getting uglier and uglier outside us; we must, out of the material bequeathed to us by former generations, build for ourselves a little world within the world, a world of beauty, where we may live with our friends and keep alive whatever small sense of beauty and nobility still remains to us." Miss Brown, at first under his influence, gradually begins to think independently. She criticizes his poetry for its affectation: ". . . the poetry of pure beauty sickened her." When she calls his attention to the poverty and misery of the cottagers on his country estate and urges him to build a factory to give them work, he objects on aesthetic grounds and reaffirms his decadent philosophy of the ugliness and hopelessness of everyday life.[38]

Through this puritanical zeal of the plainly named Miss Brown and her radical M. P. cousin Richard Brown, Vernon Lee herself speaks, wagging her finger and banging her fist, preaching her own brand of idealistic socialism. If art were properly used, it would serve society, not scorn it. Even the aesthetic movement may redeem itself, for Miss Brown acknowledges to her cousin: "I don't think that aestheticism has had much generosity of aspiration in it so far, except in isolated men like Ruskin and Morris, but I am sure it will eventually improve such matters even for the lower classes." The resolution of the novel, however, offers no hope for the future. Full of guilt and remorse for now despis-

ing Hamlin, the man who had so generously educated her, Miss
Brown marries him in order to save him from the life of de-
bauchery into which his weak nature has led him. Even the
Victorian readers of the novel were more shocked by this morbid
act of self-immolation than by the villainy of "the other woman,"
the sinister and depraved Madame Elaguine. Within the novel
itself Miss Brown's cousin Richard warns her that for all her
purity, a loveless marriage motivated only by gratitude for
worldly favors is prostitution of the soul, "prostituting it as any
common woman would prostitute her body." And the *Spectator*
observed with horror that, "noble as Anne's figure is, her final
act is revolting and shows an utter perversity in the author's conception of nobility. It is intended, we suppose, to indicate the
last extremity of self-abnegation; but a Una who prostitutes herself is a monstrosity." [39]

The main target of Vernon Lee's heavy-handed satire in this
novel was aestheticism. In the course of firing at it, she peppered
many individuals with her gunshot. There was no actual malice.
She was careful, we have noted, to exclude Morris and Ruskin
from her indictment, recognizing in their enlightened social
philosophies views to which she was herself sympathetic. But with
the obtuseness that comes of limited imagination and unlimited
self-confidence, she never apparently dreamed that people would
be offended to find details of their private lives revealed, and indeed caricatured, in her novel. Perhaps she was misled by W. S.
Gilbert's satire in *Patience* (which she saw performed at Oxford
and "thoroughly enjoyed" [40]), into thinking that her poet, Pos-
thlewaite, with "a Japanese lily bobbing out of the button-hole
of his ancestral dress coat," was as witty and inoffensive as Bunt-
horne. Certainly she did not have Walter Pater consciously in
mind when she named her weak-willed Oxford aesthete Walter
Hamlin—she proudly sent him one of the first presentation
copies—but anyone except a sublime egoist would have sensed
the possible embarrassment. Similarly, it seemed never to have
occurred to her that William Morris, whose wife was as statuesquely beautiful as was Miss Brown, and who lived in Hammer-
smith, as does Hamlin, would be distressed; or that others—the
Rossettis in particular and Edmund Guerney, who had married

a gardener's daughter whom he educated himself, or the dowager Mrs. Charles Tennant, who held salons uncomfortably like those of the fat "lion-hunting" hostess in *Miss Brown*—would recognize themselves and be offended.

None of this seems to have occurred to Vernon Lee in the heat of composition, but in the chilly air with which the novel was received she soon became aware of her blunder. Many of her former friends avoided her. Wilde, the Rossettis, the Morrises, and Theodore Watts were unforgiving; and it was not until 1894 that Wilde spoke to her, and then only to inquire about her half-brother Eugene. The Humphry Wards, after a brief coolness, resumed social relations, but the damage had been done. She read her reviews with shock and dismay: "Here I am accused of having in simplicity of heart, written, with a view to moralise the world, an immoral book . . . of doing, in a minor degree, the very things for which I execrate Zola or Maupassant." Vernon Lee was not without courage, however. With characteristic tough-mindedness she contemplated the possibility that she had been terribly mistaken, that

> at the bottom of this seemingly scientific, philanthropic, idealising, decidedly noble-looking nature of mine [may] lie something base, dangerous, disgraceful. . . . May I be indulging a more depraved appetite for the loathsome, while I *fancy* that I am studying disease and probing wounds for the sake of diminishing both?

These speculations Vernon Lee confided to her journal.[41] On the surface she moved boldly, even brazenly, in society, but the doubts troubled her for years to come. "Everyone," she remarked to Maurice Baring long afterwards, "ought to write one novel, if only to lose the desire of ever writing another." [42]

Unfortunately, the lesson learned in 1885 was forgotten in 1892 when Vernon Lee published the short story "Lady Tal" that caused acute pain for a man she admired and respected, Henry James. James also had been embarrassed, but less painfully, in the *Miss Brown* affair, since it was to him that she had dedicated the novel, although happily he did not figure in it. James and Vernon Lee had been acquainted since the 1870's when he visited the Paget family in Florence. Their friendship was resumed during her London visits in the 1880's, at first largely through the good offices of Mrs. Humphry Ward. James was much impressed with the young woman's intelligence and erudition: in 1884 he wrote to T. S. Perry: "I don't think I think Violet Paget *great,* but I think her a most astounding young female, & *Euphorion* most fascinating and suggestive, as well as monstrous clever. She has a prodigious cerebration." Undoubtedly flattered by his praise, she dedicated *Miss Brown* to him: "To Henry James I dedicate, for good luck, my first attempt at a novel." [43]

Not having yet even read *Miss Brown,* James felt himself already compromised. With characteristic gallantry he wrote off a note of thanks, but he delayed in sending her his considered judgment of the novel.[44] The reasons for the delay are obvious. Ever the gentleman, he could not bear to deliver his opinion bluntly. Ever the artist, he was of course appalled by the novel itself. He wrote in confidence to Perry in December, 1884, that

> as it is her first attempt at a novel, so it is to be hoped it may be her last. It is very bad, *strangely* inferior to her other writing & (to me at least) painfully disagreeable in tone. . . . It is violently satirical, but the satire is strangely without form as art. It is in short a rather deplorable mistake—to be repented of. But I am afraid she won't repent—it's not her line. . . . I am sadly put to it to what to write to her. I think I shall be brave & tell her what I think—or at least a little of it. The whole would never do.[45]

After months of pregnant silence, James at last summoned up courage to write to her in May, 1885. The letter is a jewel of delicacy and periphrasis ("I am on my knees prostrate, humble, abject, in the dust . . . I hereby declare to you that the rest of my days shall be devoted to removing from your mind the vile impression my ignoble silence must have produced upon it"). But when he got down to the business of criticism, James was sufficiently forthright. He found the novel, he says, "an imperfect but a very interesting book." He admired the nobility of Miss Brown's character. He was impressed with the *donnée* of the book ("a real subject in the full sense of the word"). He was generous in praise of her concern for moral, psychological, and intellectual life, as opposed to "the everlasting vulgar chapters of accidents, the dead rattle and rumble, which rise from the mere surface of things." Like most other readers, however, he strongly objected to the heroine's self-sacrificing marriage. His chief criticism was aimed unerringly at her intense moralizing, her "ferocity" which sacrificed art (her style at times becoming "a kind of intellectualized rowdyism") to indignation:

> . . . you take the aesthetic business too seriously, too tragically, and above all with too great an implication of sexual motives. There is a certain want of perspective and proportion. You are really too savage with your painters and poets and dillettanti; *life* is less criminal, less obnoxious, less objectionable, less crude, more *bon enfant,* more mixed and casual, and even in its most offensive manifestations, more *pardonable,* than the unholy circle with which you have surrounded your heroine. And then you have impregnated all those people too much with the sexual, the basely erotic preoccupation: your hand was over violent, the touch of life is lighter . . . you have been too much in a moral passion! That has put certain exaggerations, overstatements, grossissements, insistencies wanting in tact, into your head. Cool first—write afterwards. Morality is hot—but art is icy! [46]

By June, 1885, Vernon Lee had heard and read enough criticism of *Miss Brown* to accept James's remarks with good grace. They remained on the friendliest of terms. When she returned to Italy in the autumn he gave her letters of introduction to two American friends of his in Venice, Mrs. Daniel Curtis and Mrs. Arthur Bronson, both ladies celebrated for their artistic *salons* in their palazzi on the Grand Canal. On her visit to London in 1886 Vernon Lee was entertained by James at lunch and later that year, when he came to Florence, she returned his hospitality, receiving him at the Paget home (where he heard from Eugene Lee-Hamilton the story about Captain Silsbee that inspired *The Aspern Papers*). The friendship continued through the early 1890's. James had high praise for her Italian stories in her volume *Hauntings* (1890), and she responded enthusiastically with praise for his dramatization of *The American*. But in 1892 her volume *Vanitas,* containing the story "Lady Tal," was published. James had not read it when, late in that year, he suggested that his brother William, then traveling in Italy, visit the Pagets in Florence. In January, 1892, however, Henry James suddenly sent his brother "a word of warning about Vernon Lee." He had still not read the offending story (indeed he may never have read it), but he had been told that he was the victim of her satire—"a particularly impudent and blackguardly sort of thing to do to a friend and one who has treated her with such particular consideration as I have," he wrote indignantly: "draw it mild with her on the question of friendship. She's a tiger-cat!"

With less delicacy than his brother, William wrote a highly indignant note to Miss Paget:

> The portrait of my brother . . . is clever enough, and I cannot call it exactly malicious. But the using of a friend as so much raw material for "copy" implies on your part such a strangely *objective* way of taking human beings, and such a detachment from the sympathetic considerations which usually govern human intercourse, that you will not be surprised to learn that seeing the book has quite drenched my desire to pay you another visit.

Like so many brilliant and self-absorbed people, Vernon Lee was a total innocent in matters of human sensibility. She read William James's letter in amazement and horror: certainly proof that her portrait of his brother had no malicious intention. Contrite, she wrote to William begging his forgiveness and confessing that his accusation had made her burst into tears. Somewhat discomfited himself now, he replied briefly:

My dear Miss Paget,

A woman in tears is something that I can never stand out against! Your note wipes away the affront as far as I am concerned, only you must never, *never,* NEVER, do such a thing again in any future book! It is too serious a matter.

We are pulling ourselves together to go north in a couple of weeks unless something unforeseen prevents. My wife and I are to make some one or two day excursions first. When the time serves, I will (if you are willing?) come again and bid you goodbye.

> Sincerely yours
> Wm. James

By this time Henry James's feelings had been soothed, though the wound still smarted: "I don't find her note at all convincing," he wrote William; "she is doubtless sorry to be disapproved in high quarters; but her *procède* was absolutely deliberate, and her humility, which is easy and inexpensive, after the fact, doesn't alter her absolutely impertinent nature. Basta! Basta!" He was sufficiently magnanimous some years later to reply with kindness to a very humble request from her that they meet again:

I may well have regretted to have failed, of late years, of sight and profit of one [of] the most intelligent persons it had ever been my fortune to know—and as to whom you are right in supposing that my interest hadn't dropped. I hope that we *shall* meet again—let us by all means positively do so; at some time of full convenience. That occasion will turn up—in Italy if not here—and will give full pleasure to—yours, dear Violet Paget, always—Henry James.

The occasion did not "turn up" until 1912 when they met once, briefly, at the home of a friend.[47] The loser, of course, was Vernon Lee, and she was keenly sensitive of her loss. A particularly unfortunate consequence of the whole brouhaha is that, tasteless and unsubtle as is her portrait of Henry James in "Lady Tal," she was misjudged by William James and has since been misjudged by most readers of the story. Actually, as a careful reading of the story will indicate, she was not ridiculing Henry James but portraying him as the innocent victim of a domineering woman. The story admittedly invites misinterpretation by its many ambiguities and lapses in narrative technique. But it is not true that James is portrayed as "a selfish, heartless cad" (as Carl J. Weber stated), nor (in the interpretation of Burdett Gardner) as an unscrupulous artist preying on the heroine "with the quite cold and deliberate intention of putting her into a big and important novel of his own." [48]

The one certainty is that the central character *is* James. Jervase Marion is a successful "cosmopolitan," "psychological" American novelist, "an inmate of the world of Henry James and a kind of Henry James, of a lesser magnitude." He looks like James (portly, somewhat awkward), talks like him and has his mannerisms ("his well-adjusted speech, his precise mind, the something conventional about him"), lives like him (a bachelor, "a very methodical man, valuing above everything—even his consciousness of being a man of the world—his steady health, steady, slightly depressed spirits, and steady, monotonous, but not unmanly nor unenjoyable routine of existence"), writes like him ("his books turned mainly upon the little intrigues and struggles of the highly civilized society"), and shares his artistic credo:

> Indeed, if Jervase Marion, ever since his earliest manhood, had given way to a tendency to withdraw from all personal concerns, from all emotion or action, it was mainly because he conceived that this shrinkingness of nature (which foolish persons called egoism) was the necessary complement to his power of intellectual analysis; and that any departure from the position of dispassioned spectator of the world's follies and miseries would mean also a departure from his real duty as a novelist.

In a sense Vernon Lee produced a reasonably good imitation of a typical James character and theme, and "Lady Tal" is not unworthy of comparison with James's own work. There is something of the same irony—the speculation, in comic overtones but with deeper implications, about the price one pays for total dedication to the life of art. Jervase Marion is neither a fool nor a hypocrite. He is the victim of an artistic credo so demanding and rigid that it leaves him unprepared for the battles of real life. Having been the detached observer of others for so long, he has lost touch with humanity: "To be brought into contact with people more closely than was necessary or advantageous for their intellectual comprehension; to think about them, feel about them, mistress, wife, son, or daughter, the bare thought of such a thing jarred upon Marion's nerves." The ultimate sacrifice he has made for his art is a great one: ". . . for Marion, although the most benevolent and serviceable of mortals, did not give his heart, perhaps because he had none to give to anybody." When he meets an aggressive female who is all life-force, he is completely vulnerable. His plan to "use" her in a novel is foiled because, ironically, she "uses" him in infinitely more practical ways.

Marion has come to Venice for a holiday after finishing a three-volume novel for Blackwood. He is determined to rest but reluctantly finds himself eavesdropping on conversations, observing people, and mulling over "vague notions of new stories." When he meets Lady Tal (Atalanta Walkenshaw), a wealthy and statuesquely beautiful young widow, he becomes fascinated quite against his will. He learns that her jealous elderly husband had left her a fortune which she must renounce if she remarries. She has also recently lost a crippled half-brother whom she had nursed devotedly. Now alone in the world, though with many suitors, she decides to write a novel and enlists Marion to help her. Although he has resolved never to look at the manuscript of an amateur novelist, he soon finds himself reading, editing, and all but rewriting Lady Tal's clumsy efforts. He does not particularly like her; he finds her book appalling (he recommends that she study punctuation and Blair's *Rhetoric*); but he is powerless to resist her:

> It was this want of soul which constituted the strength of Lady Tal. This negative quality had much more than the value of a positive one. And it was Lady Tal's want of soul

which had, somehow, got the better of him, pushed him, bullied him, without any external manifestation, and by a mere hidden force, into accepting or offering to read that manuscript.

It is not Lady Tal's "hidden force" that finally conquers Marion so much as his own Achilles heel—his art. He cannot live without his work, without turning the raw material of every experience into art. Thus he promptly breaks another of his resolutions: ". . . not to drift into studying any character while on a holiday"—and begins to make mental notes on Lady Tal for his next book. Although he has "a twinge of conscience" for what he recognizes as "that hateful habit of studying people, of turning them round, prodding and cutting them to see what was inside," he cannot conquer it. The "demon of psychological study" overpowers him and meets its match in "an equally stubborn though less insidious demon apparently residing in Lady Atalanta, the demon of amateur authorship." Reading the first paragraph of her manuscript, "he registered the remark, to be used upon the earliest occasion in one of his own novels, that highly-connected and well-dressed young women of the present generation, appear to leave commas and semi-colons, all in fact except full stops and dashes, to their social inferiors." The more he studies her, both as she is revealed in her novel and in their many meetings, the more he discovers: first, that she has a soul, though it is well concealed; second, that he has misjudged some of her seemingly callous behavior; third, that she is "an intelligent woman of the world, with aspirations ending in frivolity, and a heart entirely rusted over by insolence."

Lady Tal is certainly intelligent, however lacking in delicacy. She understands herself intuitively and more accurately than Marion does, with all his subtle psychological analysis. And she understands him perhaps better than he knows himself. She recognizes shrewdly that he has been rewriting her novel for her: "It isn't fair to put it into an unfortunate creature's head," she accuses him, "that she is an incipient George Eliot, when you know that if she were to slave till doomsday, she couldn't produce a novel fit for the *Family Herald*." He acknowledges the justice of her charge, realizes to his pain that he has compromised himself, and berates himself "at feeling anything at all, and still more, in consequence, at feeling all this much." But the significant fact is that he has begun to feel. He confesses to Lady Tal that his next novel will be about a middle-aged artist "who was silly enough to imagine it was all love of art which made him take a great deal of interest in a certain young lady and her paintings." When Lady Tal asks what happens then, he replies, "What happened? Why—that he made an awful old fool of himself. That's all."

She will accept no such inconclusive ending. "Why shouldn't we write that novel together?" she asks, adding the suggestion that the artist and the young lady should marry: "Consider that both he and the lady are rather lonely, bored, and getting into the sere and yellow—We ought to write that novel together, because I've given you the ending—and also because I really can't manage another all by myself, now that I've got accustomed to having my semicolons put in for me—." The story ends there. We are not told that Marion and Lady Tal marry, but the conclusion is inevitable. It is in the spirit of high comedy not unworthy of the lesson of the master himself. Yet one can be thankful that James probably never read the story. What might have pained him far more than the merely tactless references to his personality and working habits is the implied identification of Lady Tal and Vernon Lee. It is absurd to suggest that Vernon Lee was here confessing a romantic passion for the master and equally absurd that she was the model for the beautiful Lady Tal. But with the total absence of creative imagination that so often marks the second-rate novelist, she drew upon herself for numerous details. Lady Tal's beauty is hard and masculine; she is blunt and forthright; her voice is loud; her laugh harsh ("Her power over man, if she had any, or chose to exert it, must be of the sledge-hammer sort,")—a "big woman in her stiff clothes." She had nursed a crippled half-brother through almost twenty years of a disabling illness. She plans to dedicate her first novel to Marion as Vernon Lee dedicated *Miss Brown* to James. Writing only a few years after the stinging reception of that novel, Vernon Lee has Lady Tal say, "Only, catch me ever writing another novel again!" Marion's criticism of Lady Tal's book has echoes of James's judgments on her own work:

> You are perpetually taking all sort of knowledge for granted in your reader. Your characters don't sufficiently explain themselves; you write as if your reader had witnessed the whole thing and merely required reminding. I almost doubt whether you have fully realized for yourself a great part of the situation; one would think you are repeating things from hearsay, without quite understanding them.

"Lady Tal" fails for a variety of reasons. One of these is purely technical. Not having herself mastered point of view, of which she speaks knowledgeably in *The Handling of Words*, Vernon Lee shifts so often from omniscient author to the consciousness of her characters that she produces serious ambiguities. It is extremely difficult to distinguish, for example, between Marion berating himself and the author condemning him. Little wonder then that the story was taken as a cruel portrait of James —when Marion is said to have no heart, to be incapable of human emotion, to be a veritable *voyeur* and exploiter of the feelings of others. But most of these accusations are his own, filtered through his consciousness. Vernon Lee attempted to draw a subtle, highly complex character in Marion, but lacked the skill (that she so much admired in James's work) of making the character reveal himself. Where it is clear that she is speaking from Marion's point of view, there are no ambiguities: "Jervase Marion, the next morning, woke up with the consciousness of having been very unfair to Lady Tal . . . he had not only behaved more or less like a cad, but he had done that odious thing of pretending to feel differently from how he really did." Neither is there any confusion as to her sympathies when she speaks directly as author:

> That gift, a rare one, of seeing the simple, wholesome, and even comparatively noble side of things; of being, although a pessimist, no misanthrope, was the most remarkable char-

acteristic of Jervase Marion; it was the one which made him, for all his old bachelor ways and his shrinking from close personal contact, a man and a manly man, giving this analytical and nervous person a certain calmness and gentleness and strength.

Unfortunately then what might have been a sparkling *jeu d'esprit* turned into a clumsy *roman à clef*. We can better appreciate the potentialities of "Lady Tal" when we look at a companion story in *Vanitas*, "A Worldly Woman." This too is a Jamesian story, even to the extent of introducing a direct reference to *The Princess Casamassima*. Its hero is a sensitive, self-examining, impoverished young man with a keen social conscience. An idealist dedicated to art, he fails to accept the challenge of reality and loses the young woman who might have made him happy:

> Greenleaf had a great disbelief in his own intuitions; perhaps because he vibrated unusually to the touch of other folks' nature, and that the number and variety of his impressions sometimes made it difficult to come to a cut-and-dry conclusion. There was in him also a sensitiveness on the subject of his own beliefs and ideals which made him instinctively avoid contact with other folk, and avoid even knowing much about them.

He becomes attracted to a well-born girl who shares his interest in ancient pottery. On reading *The Princess Casamassima* ("Do authors ever reflect how much influence they must occasionally have, coming by accident, to arouse some latent feeling, or to reinforce some dominant habit of mind?" Vernon Lee asks), he identifies himself with the poor young craftsman Hyacinth Robinson and the young lady with the glamorous but treacherous Princess. As a result, he fails to declare himself. Ten years later he meets her again. She is now the wife of a rich but repulsive man, having, as she tells him frankly, sold herself to the highest bidder. They are both aware of their mistakes now, but they can only part—he to his empty life of art, she to her shallow and frivolous one as a society matron. In this thin but touching story Vernon Lee achieves at least a degree of artistic detachment and objectivity. But she was not able to repeat her modest success; perhaps she did not care to try. The fact remains that after the publication of *Vanitas,* with the unfortunate "Lady Tal," Vernon Lee wrote no more fiction with a contemporary setting. She retreated to the past, where she was comfortable and secure. In re-creating the past, she found an outlet for her creative energies, her vast erudition, and her zeal to educate her readers. And, happily, in the dead past there were no living feelings to wound.

IV

Most children—at least I wish to believe it—are consumed by violent passions less material than those which are satisfied at the pastry cook's or the fruitstall. . . . To me, who had remained, like the Prince Parzival of Wolfram and of Wagner, a child and an idiot long after the legitimate period, there came, after the usual passions for Joan of Arc and Marie Antoinette, after the more fervid passion for the Natchez, the Sioux, and especially the inconvenient and entrancing Mohicans—a passion, be it said, which made me walk along the beach looking pathetically in the direction where America probably lies or swims—after all these childish passions, there came then to me an unaccountable passion for the people and the things of the eighteenth century in Italy. How it arose would be difficult to explain; perhaps mainly from the delight which I received from the melodies of Mozart and Gluck, picked out with three fingers on the piano. I followed those sounds; I pursued them, and I found myself in the midst of the Italian eighteenth century.[49]

Vernon Lee's passion for this age was both emotional and intellectual. The past was a reality for her, heightened and colored by an intense creative imagination which she seemed to lack in the writing of fiction set in the contemporary scene. But the past was historical reality, controlled and disciplined by her scholarship, exhaustive research, and careful documentation. She was not, however, in the strictest sense, a scholar or an historian. She generalized, exaggerated, and dogmatized. For a detailed, objective picture of Renaissance and eighteenth-century Italy one must go to other sources. But for a colorful and sensitive impression of scene and the spirit of an age, her writings cannot be surpassed. She assumed a disarmingly frivolous pose as a cultural historian, announcing in her preface to the second edition (1907) of her *Studies of the Eighteenth Century in Italy* that the book had been the work of her youth ("I really did know a great deal about Italian life and literature in the eighteenth century . . . and was well equipped as any other person of twenty for holding forth about them") and that it had so many "sins of omission and commission" that she could not bear to reread it herself. This was merely a pose. Actually, the high praise the earlier edition had received and the altogether imposing nature of the book gave her complete confidence in her scholarship.

Since the age of fourteen she had been poking about book stalls and museums priming herself on her subject. She had studied old prints and engravings and old musical scores. She interviewed old people who had dim memories of the eighteenth century: "What a moment when my dear old singing master suddenly remembered that he had heard Cimarosa sing some of his own comic songs." She ambitiously planned a biography of Metastasio and "a grand historico-musico novel, on the model of *Consuelo*" with an Italian tenor hero—"a perfect eighteenth-century ideal of the Télémaque, Sir Charles Grandison, and Re Pastore sort." [50] Because Vernon Lee found such deep emotional and imaginative appeal in the past, it is not surprising that her nonfiction has so many of the attractions of fiction: "I never distinguished between the novelist's plausibility and historic probability." [51] The statement sounds arrogant, but it is only candid. And because she had such sound knowledge of her subject, she knew that she was not sacrificing history to the novel, nor common sense to personal enthusiasm.

The color and vitality of her historical writing derives from her use, wherever possible, of first-hand sources, archives, documents, journals, autobiographies, and from her sensitive re-creation of place and milieu. Her work is reliable because she observed at first hand with extraordinary perception and sensibility. Henry James commented of her Italian stories in *Hauntings*: "I always taste, deeply, in all your work, the redolence of the unspeakable Italy, to whose infinite atmosphere you perform the valuable function of conductor or condenser." [52] Her younger friend Maurice Baring, himself an international traveler, considered her the supreme observer who could seize unfailingly on the *genius loci*:

> Sight-seeing with Vernon Lee was sight-seeing indeed. It was the opposite of scampering through a gallery with a Baedecker and ticking off what had been "done." For Vernon Lee and with Vernon Lee nothing was ever "done." It was there forever in the haunted, many-corridored and echoing palace of her imagination, and after you had seen such things with her, in yours as well. [53]

Her travel writings, like her histories, read like novels, but with no sacrifice of factual accuracy and precise detail. Her essay on Ravenna, indeed, is so evocative that it has been reprinted in an edition of her stories of the supernatural although only one segment of it contains a ghost story. Her description in this essay of the mosaics in the Church of Saint' Apollinare Nuovo in Classe, seen during a chilly winter sunset, is a striking example of her talent for combining subjective impressionism with objective observation:

> [the low sun shone] across the oozy brown nave and struck a round spot of glittering green on the mosaic of the apse. There, in the half dome, stood rows and rows of lambs, each with its little tree and lillies, shining out white from the brilliant green grass of Paradise, great streams of gold and blue circling around them, and widening overhead into lakes of peacock splendour.

Her prose becomes more impressionistic, her imagination flowers, but her eye remains steadily on the object: "For it is, after all, a

nest of ghosts. They hang about all those silent, damp churches
. . . They are legion, but I do not know who they are. I only
know they are white, luminous, with gold embroideries to their
robes, and wide, painted eyes, and they are silent." [54]

Studies of the Eighteenth Century in Italy has the same remarkable fusion of sensibility and observation; it is also an impressive work of scholarship. Concentrating primarily on
eighteenth-century Italian music, a field almost completely neglected by nineteenth-century musicologists before Vernon Lee,
she gives secondary (but considerable) attention to literature,
mainly in the form of opera *libretti, commedia dell' arte,* and the
works of the comic playwrights Goldoni and Gozzi. Painting
figures in the book only as illustration—portraits of the people
she discusses. In the passage from *Juvenilia* quoted above, she
conjectures that her passion for the eighteenth century began
with music—Mozart and Gluck. Certainly it developed with an
increasing absorption in music. Though not a gifted musician
herself, she studied piano and voice purely to make this "un-
heard" music of the past accessible to herself. She bought old
collections of songs and musical scores and copied "as much
music as fills a couple of much cherished volumes" in the libraries of the music schools of Bologna and Florence. In what
sounds like an echo of the career of Browning's Grammarian, she
dedicated her youth to her scholarship:

At eighteen I had written an essay demonstrating why Cimarosa's recitative was less good than, say, Leo's, and wherein
consisted the subtle superiority of Pergolesi's setting of *Se
cerca, se dice,* over Galuppi's. There were six weeks of
struggles to settle Mozart's position toward Sarti and Paisi-
ello, which made me appreciate the wrestlings of divines
with Predestination and the Procession of the Holy Ghost.
. . . My many love passages with various composers, my in-
fidelities and remorseless returns to this piece or that,
brought about a habit of comparison and classification not
unlike that recorded in Leporello's catalogue.[55]

In view of this all-consuming passion for music, it is the

more remarkable that the book is not a narrowly specialized study but a rich, many-faceted cultural history. Her chief virtue as a scholar was her ability to see her subjects in broad context. She describes her point of view as "neither exclusively literary nor exclusively musical, but generally aesthetic" and reminds her readers that the figures about whom she writes "cannot be well understood unless we previously reconstruct the society in which they lived." In re-creating a whole milieu, to be sure, she makes sweeping and sometimes questionable generalizations:

> Italy in the last century got her philosophy and philosophic poetry, like her dress and her furniture, from Paris and London; but Italy in the last century got her drama and her comedy neither from Paris nor from London, but from her own intellectual soil, where they had been germinating for centuries; and Italy, in the eighteenth century, gave her own spontaneous national music to the whole of Europe . . .

> The plastic arts were dead everywhere and had not yet been galvanized by criticism into a spectral semblance of life. Poetry in France and England, under Pope and Voltaire, was mere philosophy decked out in Dresden china pastoral furbelows; in Germany it was, when it re-appeared late in the eighteenth century, only partly spontaneous, and, in the main, philosophy again of a different sort, and either draped in classic garments, manufactured on Winkelmann's patterns, or trapped out with pseudo-medieval jingles.[56]

In her writing, as in her conversation, Vernon Lee allowed no interruption. She plunged ahead, so absorbed in her interests that she failed to see flaws and was, accordingly, often careless of style and detail, repetitious, and even illogical. But for all her excesses, *Studies of the Eighteenth Century in Italy* demonstrates that Vernon Lee was a brilliant and stimulating writer. Her enthusiasm is communicated to the reader not merely as emotion but fortified with scholarship and, in spite of her lapses, generally sound critical judgment.

She is at her best in evoking scenes of the past and in her

character portraits. People and places come alive. Indeed, she writes history in terms of the people who lived it: eighteenth-century Italy as seen through the eyes of Dr. Charles Burney touring Italy in 1770 to collect material for his history of music; eighteenth-century opera developing in the career of Metastasio; Italian comedy evolving from a decaying tradition of masks and pantomime into new life through the genius of Goldoni and Gozzi. She studies the portraits of her subjects and then brings them vividly to life. Gozzi, for example, is the "tall, gaunt man, stalking about in his old-fashioned clothes . . . silent, self-absorbed, his eyes fixed on the unseen world, his lips smiling at unspoken jests . . . he believed in the superior wisdom of child-ishness, in the philosophy of old nurses' tales, in the venerable-ness of clowns." The middle-aged Metastasio is "short, fat, rather languid and bent. . . . There is no strong life in the man, though there is a flickering semblance of life: he is amiable, bright, whimsical, humorous, can tell anecdotes well . . . when in com-pany; but he becomes dreary and apathetic when alone . . . complains of a mysterious nervous disease. . . . In reality what ails him is mental and moral *ennui*." Even more vivid is her re-creation of the eighteenth-century Italian scene:

> As soon as the sun had fairly set and the cool breeze risen, the townsfolk would waken, and having opened shutters, pulled up blinds, and breathed the fresher evening air, they would begin to think of hearing a little music, nothing grand or tragic, oh, no! no great singers who required tre-mendous applause; something simple, easy, and refreshing. So the men have exchanged dressing gowns for snuff- or puce-coloured light coat, and coloured handkerchief for well-combed little wig, and their wives and daughters have slipped on a tidy gown and a coquettish black veil, the population would slowly wend their way towards the comic theatres, pausing just a little to talk to acquaintances and breathe the fresh air in the white, pearly twilight.[57]

Vernon Lee employs the same technique of re-creating the past through personality and place in her biography of Princess

Louise of Stolberg, *The Countess of Albany*. She moves even closer to fiction here by introducing a more overt authorial *persona*, judging and moralizing about her historical characters' actions. Evidently she felt obliged to do this, in a volume commissioned for Allen's Eminent Women Series, because of the fairly delicate nature of her material—at least as it must have appeared to a reading public in 1884. The Countess led a life which many readers might have considered corrupt. (Vernon Lee's cousin, Mrs. Adah Hughes, was, in fact, so offended by *Miss Brown* and *The Countess of Albany* that she refused to meet their author again.[58]) She had left her husband, the dissolute Bonnie Prince Charlie, no doubt with good cause, but her subsequent life as the mistress of the poet Alfieri demanded explanation, if not apology. Vernon Lee was forced accordingly into the ambiguous position of apologist-critic. Devoting far too much space to explaining and judging the behavior of the Countess and her stormy lover, she ended by presenting a colorful but inconsistent portrait. On the one hand she condemns them for their weaknesses, their self-indulgence, their acceptance of their "illegitimate passion." On the other, she defends them:

> in the attempt to work out their happiness in despite of the evil world in which they lived, the Countess and Alfieri, infinitely intellectually and morally superior to many of us whom circumstances permit to live blameless and comfortable, were splashed with the mud of unrighteousness, which was foreign to their nature, and remained spotted in the eyes of posterity.

She justified the Countess' attraction to Alfieri by emphasizing that she saw in him not the debauched youth that he had been, but the reformed poet "who had broken through the base habits of his youth" and was ardently dedicated to the loftiest patriotic. and artistic ideals. She insisted that as long as the Countess lived with her husband her relations with Alfieri had been platonic and pure. And when the historical record forced her to admit that they finally became lovers (after "seven long years of platonic passion"), she hastened to point out that the Countess now had a legal separation from the Prince, which to her "was equivalent to a divorce."

Whenever the present impinges on the past, Vernon Lee's imagination seems to desert her. The more she writes with 1884 in mind, the less successful is her treatment of the past. There is a note of insecurity, at moments even absurdity, as when she describes the innocence of the poet's mother, the Countess Alfieri, "one of those persons into whose mind, high removed above all worldly concerns, no experience of vice, of weakness, nay, of mere equivocal situations, can enter." But when Vernon Lee regains her historical perspective, she writes with conviction and good sense. Her account of the growing boredom between the lovers, although at times it descends to the "she-must-have-thought" school of biography, is sophisticated and convincing. The Countess of Albany, now fat, dowdy, easy-going, indifferent, but still sensitive and intelligent, devotes herself to reading. Alfieri, more melancholy and introspective than ever, sensitive to his failure to achieve his lofty ideals, consorts with "low women": "he did not, perhaps, receive much pleasure from this stout, plain, prosaic lady (like one of Rubens's women grown old, as Lamartine later described her) whom he left to her letter-writing, her reading of Kant, La Harpe, and of Shakespeare, of Lessing; to her painting lessons and long discussions of art with Monsieur Fabre." When he dies, the Countess reveres his memory but also experiences a sense of relief: "she had acquired a possibility of being herself with all her tastes, the very existence of which she had forgotten while living under the shadow of that strange and disagreeable man."

Although based on sound historical research, *The Countess of Albany* is only a small step from historical fiction.[59] Eighteenth-century Italy is recreated with vivid and often poetic detail. The journey of the young bride through the bleak Apennine valleys to meet the bridegroom she has married by proxy but never seen is full of ominous, dark imagery, foreshadowing the disastrous marriage: "the scraggy outlines of the poplars, which rise in spectral regiments . . . these valleys . . . bare as a bone or thinly clothed with ilex or juniper scrub . . . rocks in a sort of catacomb open to the sky. . . ." Rome, the setting for the first unhappy years of that marriage, is described in rich Browningesque detail —the streets noisy with life and exploding violence:

> the blood trickling from the disembowelled sheep hanging, ghastly in their fleeces, from the hooks outside the butchers' and cheesemongers' shops; or returning home at night from the opera, amid the flare of the footmen's torches . . . the distant cries of some imprudent person struggling in the hands of marauders; or, again, on Sundays and holidays . . . the crowd gathered around the pillory where some too easy-going husband sat crowned with a paper cap in a hailstorm of mud and egg-shells and fruit peelings, round the scaffold where some petty offender was being flogged by the hang-man, until the fortunate appearance of a clement cardinal or the rage of the sympathizing mob put a stop to the proceedings.

An interesting example of the bridge that Vernon Lee attempted to build between history and the novel is *Ottilie,* which she carefully did not label a novel but "An Eighteenth Century Idyll" (she referred to *Miss Brown,* published a year later, as her first novel). In her preface she calls herself an essayist and speaks of the difficulties imposed by the essay form when the writer seeks to combine historical matter with imaginative interpretation:

> For an Essayist possesses, inasmuch as he is an Essayist, some of the instincts of the superior creature called a novelist: a certain half imaginative perception of the past, a certain love of character and incident and description, a certain tendency to weave fancies about realities; but as the centaur has hoofs, so the Essayist has peculiarities which exclude him from the pleasant places of fiction, which render it proper that he should run along on the beaten roads of history, and be tied up in the narrow little stable of fact.

Ottilie, however, reflects no serious conflict between fact and imagination. As fiction it is very slight: a brief recounting, through flashback, of the lives of a sister and half-brother in a small sleepy German town at the end of the eighteenth century. The sister's devotion to her indulged and self-indulgent younger brother is so great that she gives up an opportunity to marry and, after the failure of her brother's marriage, dedicates her life to his service. This theme of morbid and unnatural self-sacrifice might have been a sinister one. The implications of incest are unmistakable. The psychological interest of the story is heightened too when we note that there are direct parallels to Vernon Lee's relationship to her half-brother Eugene, who for almost twenty years was a helpless cripple, victim of a neurasthenic paralysis. But Eugene's attachment appears to have been to his mother rather than his sister. As a young man he seemed unable to break away from home. Like Ottilie's brother he was a poet; also like him he abandoned his university studies (at Oxford) without taking a degree, although he was a good student. He joined the diplomatic service but was unhappy in his work and, falling ill, returned home where his mother and sister nursed him. In 1893 his health began to improve slightly. In 1896, immediately after his mother's death, he made a complete recovery, left home, traveled abroad, and two years later married an American writer, Annie Holdsworth; they had one daughter who died in childhood.[60]

Thanks to Vernon Lee's talent for imaginatively reconstructing the past, *Ottilie,* instead of being a study in psychopathology, is truly the idyll she called it, a sensitive, charmingly sentimental evocation of the long-vanished romantic Germany of her childhood: gable roofs, window boxes filled with geraniums, a gentle green countryside. The brother's selfish attachment to his sister is seen as a form of moody *Sturm-und-Drang.* "Wild and stormy that generation truly was," he reflects years later; ". . . a boiling and seething of all things good and bad, which filled our literature with paradoxes of all kinds, the strangest being the co-existence of absurd whimpering sentimentalism by the side of a disgusting love of horrors." He pays a high price for his romantic whims, failing in a career and in marriage, but Ottilie remains loyal to him. They live on together, he a minor poet, she his guiding genius ("People at W— maintained that in all these productions the sister had done at least half the work, and indeed the general opinion seems to have been that she was the mastermind of the two"). The brief story itself is presented as the brother's autobiography, found after his death, titled, "My Confession—1809."

Ottilie is a personal history framed in the cultural history of eighteenth-century German Romanticism. The real challenge to Vernon Lee was the historical novel, which demanded wider exercise of the creative imagination. She made two attempts in this genre, neither particularly successful though both are interesting. In one, *Penelope Brandling* (1903), she experimented with the more conventional matter of popular historical romance: a love story, villainy, intrigue, suspense, and a literally smashing climax in which the hero blows up his family's castle because it has become a haven for a band of wreckers.[61] It is one of Vernon Lee's few works with an English setting—the wild coast of Wales that she knew from tales of her mother's childhood. Like *Ottilie* it is told in retrospect, the narrator, Penelope Brandling, recording for her grandchildren the story of the first years of her marriage when she and her husband were the prisoners of his wicked relatives. There is some suspense involving their gradual suspicions and discovery of their danger and their desperate efforts to escape, but the narrative portions of the story are poor —much of the mystery simply solved by a servant's confession. Its main interest is that of time and place. Vernon Lee cannot evoke this scene with the vividness of her eighteenth-century Italy and Germany. This is a purely literary reconstruction in which the narrator-heroine quotes Ossian, compares Brandling castle to Otranto, recalls meeting "the accomplished Mr. Walpole" in Paris, and describes landscape in terms of grand style and classic painting.

Louis Norbert (published in 1914 but probably written earlier) is a more ambitious and ingenious novel. Subtitled *A Two-Fold Romance*, it begins in the present and develops as a kind of scholarly detective story, reconstructing a mystery from the seventeenth-century past. Louis Norbert is the subject of an old portrait that hangs in the home of the well-to-do middle-aged Englishwoman, Lady Venetia.[62] Since childhood she has been fascinated by the portrait, knowing only the name of the young man and that he died in 1684, at the age of twenty-four. On a visit to the Campo Santo in Pisa, she comes upon his grave. Thanks to the interest and help of a young Italian archaeologist, she begins to reconstruct his mysterious life story and a tale of sinister intrigue is uncovered. The charm of the novel is that it makes scholarship itself exciting. Unfortunately, it is weak in construction. The mystery of Louis' birth (he proves to be the son of Louis XIV and Maria Mancini, niece of Cardinal Mazarin) and death (he is murdered at the instigation of a treacherous Italian monk) is solved not by the gradual unfolding of scholarly evidence but in a single letter that turns up accidentally. Too many of the discoveries along the way are made intuitively by Lady Venetia, although they are confirmed by the research of the archaeologist in old letters, documents, and archives. But Vernon Lee is at her best in suggesting the enthusiasm of a scholarly quest. Her Lady Venetia is a delightful woman, sensitive, whimsical, erudite, but charmingly scatter-brained. In one paragraph of a letter to the archaeologist she leaps from Cunninghame Grahame to Renan's *Peuple d'Israel* to Sir Willoughby Patterne to Racine. The young scholar, by contrast, is serious and methodical. His main interest is seventeenth-century music, and his research on Norbert is motivated by his interest in a musically gifted abbess of the period who, it develops, had been been in love with him. The past increasingly possesses these two modern figures until their lives become enmeshed with those of Norbert and the Abbess. With the common sense of her sex, however, Lady Venetia decides at last to marry her cousin, a man her own age: "For how can I expect, at my age, to find another Louis Norbert to fall in love with?" She counsels the young scholar to find a "living countrywoman" of his Abbess, "learned and lovely as she, with whom you can, in years long hence, when the cicada is sawing in the noontide, or the olive faggot crackling in the winter, discuss the strange story of what happened in Pisa in 1684. Or was it rather (the thought suddenly strikes me) in 1908?"

In *Louis Norbert* Vernon Lee speculates about the mysteries of time. Her characters yearn to penetrate its barriers and move back into the past but achieve no more than a fragmentary reconstruction of it with their scholarship. In her stories of the supernatural, however, the barriers of death and time are surmounted. These are by far her best works of fiction, where scholarship and imagination both flourish. They utilize her talent for colorful description and evocative period detail and make fewer demands upon those skills in which she was weakest—plotting, realistic characterization, and dialogue. As short stories they imposed upon her the quality so lacking in her other writing and in her conversation—economy. Her most purely imaginative work, they are also intensely personal. The past, she tells us repeatedly, was her passion. It came to life for her everywhere, but most especially in musty old Italian buildings, crumbling manuscripts and musical scores, in old engravings and paintings. The quest for the past in *Louis Norbert* begins with a painting. Her own quests often began in the same way and ended in a story.

In her essay on Dr. Burney, "The Musical Life," in *Studies of the Eighteenth Century in Italy,* she discusses the once famous tenor Farinelli, whose portrait she had first seen as a young girl in 1872 when she and John Sargent visited the old music school in Bologna. Subsequently she saw many other portraits of him: ". . . seated among clouds in the midst of allegorical figures with preposterous draperies and preposterous inscriptions: a long, slim, sober youth, looking on with the most absolute indifference at the puffy-cheeked Fame blowing her trumpet and the creasy little Cupids pelting him with roses"; or in performance, "colossal, dark, uncanny, mysterious, standing out sharply and strangely . . . from a vapoury, lurid background, filled with vague forms of elves and genii," or in rehearsal, "exquisitely well-dressed, well-bred, and on the whole rather virtuously insipid." [63] What mattered to her was the voice of the long-dead singer, a voice forever lost yet alive to her imagination.

Two years after she saw the first portrait she wrote a story, "Winthrop's Adventure" (published in *Fraser's Magazine,* January, 1881) in which a young artist hears an old song at a party and recognizes it, although he is sure that he has never heard it before. Then he recalls that a year earlier in a cluttered old

palazzo, a veritable museum of old music manuscripts and instru-
ments, he had been fascinated by the portrait of a singer, one
Rinaldi, who held in his hand a manuscript of this same song.
After learning that Rinaldi had been murdered ninety years before, he spends a night in the deserted house where the crime is
alleged to have taken place and during the night hears strange
music. Following the sounds to a lofty room, he sees a figure
dressed in eighteenth-century clothing playing and singing at a
harpsichord. It is Rinaldi as he appeared in the portrait. The
young artist falls unconscious. When he hears the song again at
the party he realizes that he has not been a victim merely of a
nightmare delusion but has seen a ghost. Some fifteen years later,
still haunted by this theme, Vernon Lee rewrote "Winthrop's
Adventure" under the title "A Wicked Voice." This is a much
more elaborate story, in which the singer, now named Zaffirino,
becomes a more overtly evil force, a man who uses his beautiful
voice to seduce and ultimately cause the death of a married
woman. His mocking voice haunts the narrator, a young Danish
composer who has bought an old portrait of him (posed like
Farinelli, "seated under a triumphal arch somewhere among the
clouds, surrounded by puffy cupids and crowned with laurels by
a bouncing goddess of fame"). The scene of this story is Venice,
and Vernon Lee evokes an atmosphere of decadence and corruption not unlike that of Mann's *Death in Venice:* "Venice seemed
to swelter in the midst of the waters, exhaling, like some great
lily, mysterious influences, which make the brain swim and the
heart faint—a moral malaria, distilled, as I thought, from those
languishing melodies, those cooing vocalizations which I found
in the musty music books of a century ago." Her young composer, haunted by the wicked voice, sees the singer's ghost and
relives a moment in the past. In the end, however, he pays an
even greater price than frustration and mystification. A Wag-
nerian himself, in the throes of composing an opera on the
legendary *Ogier the Dane* (also, incidentally, the victim of
enchantment), he had despised the human voice, concentrating
on massive orchestral effects. Now the voice haunts him and,
against his will and aesthetic principles, he must write music for

the voice, in the style of Handel, Gluck, and Mozart, loathing the music he is forced to compose.

The theme of most of Vernon Lee's stories of the supernatural is similar to this one: the impingement of the past upon the present.[64] Because these are ghost stories, the influence is usually sinister, but there is no suggestion that either the past or its pursuit in the form of scholarship is intrinsically evil— simply that these are isolated incidents produced by the obsessions of individuals, neurotics and madmen sometimes, but more often dedicated scholars exhausted and overwrought by their labors. In "Amour Dure" (the title is a word-play on "enduring" love and "hard" or cruel love), for example, a Polish scholar doing research in the archives of a small Italian town, learns of a wicked woman, appropriately named Medea da Carpi, who, two centuries earlier, had ruined the lives of her many lovers, driving them to crime and madness. She had finally been brought to justice by the reigning duke. Now, in 1885, the scholar pursuing her sordid life story sees her portrait and falls in love with her. He finally meets her ghost, who persuades him to destroy the statue of her enemy the duke. In the end, the scholar's body is found beside the mutilated statue. He has been stabbed to death "by an unknown hand." Evil and violence strike from the past again in "Dionea," in which a beautiful girl, mysteriously cast up from the sea and raised on a remote Italian island by a group of nuns, captivates a visiting German artist and drives him to the murder of his wife and suicide. She then disappears, but the superstitious villagers believe that she is the legendary pagan mother of Venus and swear that they last saw her sailing away on a mysterious Greek boat, leaning against the mast and "singing words in an unknown tongue, the white pigeons circling around her."

Only one of these stories, "Oke of Okehurst" (first published by Blackwood separately in 1886 as "The Phantom Lover"), has a contemporary English setting. Here again the past intrudes violently and tragically upon the present. The mistress of Okehurst, a fine old country house, becomes possessed by the spirit of an ancestor who, in the seventeenth century, had had a love affair with a poet and, for reasons never made clear, joined with her husband to murder him. As the wife relives the past she gradually goads her husband into a frenzy of jealousy until, thinking he has seen the poet's ghost, he kills his wife and himself. Somehow Vernon Lee was not at home in the English past. The story is colorless, the country house atmosphere more chilly than chilling, and the total effect far less exciting than her Italian-based tales.

Two of her most interesting stories of the supernatural, however, are not set in Italy, nor do they deal with the overlapping boundaries of time. One is the florid, exotic "Virgin of the Seven Daggers," so richly colored that it reads almost like a parody of her style. The scene is Spain of the baroque age, a period for which, strangely, Vernon Lee had little aesthetic appreciation. Her years in Italy had made her intensely sympathetic to Latin culture, but it was the joyous, wholesome open spirit of Italian life to which her puritan soul responded. Describing herself as "an old agnostic adorer of true Catholicism," she scorned what she considered the dark Calvinism of the Counter-Reformation, "with its sour aping of Geneva," and the grim morbid spirit of Spanish art with its cult of

> death, damnation, tears and wounds. . . . Asiatic *fleurs du Mal* sprung out of the blood of Adonis, and taking root in the Spanish mud half and half of *auto da fés* and bullfights . . . the melancholy lymphatic Hapsburgs of Velasquez, the lousy, greedy beggars of Murillo, the black and white penitents of Ribera and Zurbaran, above all the elongated ecstatics and fervent dullards of Greco.[65]

"The Virgin of the Seven Daggers" was conceived during a visit to Granada when she was recovering from a nervous breakdown. Its overwrought, sensuous imagery reveals a mind still shaken with illness and a fevered imagination, but it remains a characteristic Vernon Lee story—first because of its blending of pure aestheticism with stern moral condemnation, second because it draws on her impressive learning in literature and art.

The conception is witty but also bitterly ironic. Her "hero" Don Juan, not in his Mozartian or Byronic gaiety but a ruthless, arrogant seducer and murderer, is saved from the damnation he thoroughly deserves by one act of faith in a career of faithlessness —loyalty to the gaudy, sanguinary image of the Spanish Madonna of the Seven Daggers. Through necromancy he summons up the spirit of a long dead Infanta, said to be buried beneath the Alhambra. In a scene of dazzling sensuous imagery (eunuchs and dancing girls, riotous colors, the beautiful princess in veils and cloth "stiff with gold and gems . . . a wondrous opalescent radiance . . . her face was oval, with the silver pallor of the young moon; her mouth subtly carmined, looked like a pomegranate flower among tuberoses . . . and the orbits of her great long-fringed eyes were stained violet"), he is offered the love of the Infanta, provided he swear that she is more beautiful than the Virgin of the Seven Daggers. Unable to do so, he is beheaded, but his soul rises to heaven. The story concludes on an ironic note with a comment by Calderon to the Archpriest Morales that he wishes he might make this story the subject of a play, for it is "well calculated to spread the glory of our holy church."

The other story is set vaguely in the late seventeenth century but is really out of time and place, an almost pure fairy tale, beautifully realized as fantasy and also full of tenderness and pathos. This is "Prince Alberic and the Snake Lady" (first published in *The Yellow Book,* July, 1896). Alberic is a lonely orphan growing up in the court of his vain and selfish grandfather, the reigning Duke of Luna. The boy becomes fascinated by a tapestry which depicts a family legend of a lamia whose enchantment can be broken only by a man's faithful love. One day in the garden he finds a harmless grass snake and makes it a pet. Shortly after, a mysterious lady who calls herself his godmother appears, offering him companionship and affection. As he grows to manhood the prince keeps aloof from his grandfather's corrupt, pleasure-seeking court and lives in a private world, communing with the spirit of the enchanted Snake Lady. When he refuses a state marriage his grandfather's retainers kill his pet snake and the prince dies. Rumor has it that in the place of the dead snake the body of a beautiful woman was found.

The story is artfully simple and straightforward—a work of love and imagination, but also a subtle allegory of the struggle of pure beauty and art against worldliness and carnality. The young prince, remote and isolated, finds solace in the old Gothic tapestry depicting the legend of the Snake Lady. To foil him his grandfather destroys the tapestry: "Duke Balthasar Maria was a prince of enlightened mind and delicate taste; the literature as well as the art of the dark ages found no grace in his sight." But the boy persists in his hatred for the overdecorated treasures of his grandfather's palace; he is terrified by the sight of his grandfather's elaborate daily toilette. He watches in horror as the old duke, listening to fiddlers and "a lady dressed as a nymph" singing a serenade, is dressed by his valet:

In his green and gold wrappers and orange headdress, with the strange patches of vermilion and white on his cheeks, Duke Balthasar looked to the diseased fancy of his grandson as if he had been made of precious metals. . . . But just as Alberic was mustering up courage and approaching his magnificent grandparent, his eye fell upon a sight so mysterious and terrible that he fled wildly out of the ducal presence. For through an open door he could see in an adjacent closet a man dressed in white, combing the long flowing locks of what he recognised as his grandfather's head, stuck on a short pole in the light of the window.

The prince withdraws into a world of pure fantasy. With only the companionship of his pet snake and his godmother, he comes to manhood—handsome, sensitive, intelligent—completely repudiating the life led by his grandfather and his sinister retainers. But he is doomed. The corruptions of the world invade his isolation, destroying the things he loves, and ultimately they destroy him as well.

It is tempting but dangerous to read into symbolic stories like these all manner of personal reflections on the character of the author. Vernon Lee was a complex and highly emotional woman. From time to time she suffered severe mental disturbances and we have it on her own testimony that her family background was "acutely neuropathic and hysterical." [66] These highly wrought stories abound in passages that invite the speculations of amateur Freudians:

> Don Juan advanced. At the further end of the tank a peacock was standing by the myrtle hedge, unmovable as if made of precious enamels; but as Don Juan went by the short blue-green feathers of his neck began to ruffle; he moved his tail, and, swelling himself out, he slowly unfolded it in a dazzling wheel. As he did so, some blackbirds and thrushes in gilt cages hanging within an archway began to twitter and to sing.

> . . . there rose from the carved trough, from among the weeds and roses, and glided on to the brick of the well, a long, green, glittering thing. Alberic recognized it to be a snake; only, he had no idea it had such a flat, strange little head, and such a long forked tongue, for the lady on the tapestry was a woman from the waist upwards. . . . But the creature glided past and came around and rubbed itself against Alberic's hand. The boy was not afraid for he knew nothing about snakes; but he started, for, on this hot day, the creature was icy cold. But then he felt sorry. "It must be dreadful to be always so cold," he said; "come, try and get warm in my pocket."

Speculations, however, are profitless. The records of many who knew Vernon Lee indicate beyond speculation that she had pronounced lesbian tendencies.[67] Her choice of a masculine pseudonym was not apparently the merely conventional procedure that it was with so many other women writers. Her closest personal attachments were to women like Mary Robinson and Kit Anstruther-Thomson, who tended to be sensitive and artistic, like herself, but less gifted and therefore more inclined to defer to her dominant, assertive personality. Although she had many friendships with men, her best relationships were either with older men, who assumed a father-mentor attitude toward her (James, Pater), or with younger ones like Carlo Placci and Maurice Baring, who were not likely to make sexual demands upon her. But personality, not sex, dictated all her relationships. Strong personalities, whether male or female, that competed with hers were inevitably shunned or alienated. She tolerated no competition. She retained the friendship of a brilliant, strong-willed woman like Edith Wharton only because their meetings were infrequent. Percy Lubbock recalls Vernon Lee once dominating a conversation with Mrs. Wharton ("Vernon Lee's, most of it, but kept together and enlivened by Edith's quick repartees and ringing laughter" [68]). Bertrand Russell was less complaisant. Lady Ottoline Morrell described one occasion in 1909 when Vernon held forth:

> She did not attend or listen; her voice went persistently on, with its rather charming intonation . . . whenever she saw one of us attempting to answer she would hurry on, fearing an interruption. Bertie Russell grew very restive, and had visibly to control his longing to burst out and say something harsh. We all sat round watching.[69]

When she grew deaf in later years, she used a large horn as a hearing aid—and also as a social weapon, developing the habit, as Nicky Mariano noted, "of using it while she was herself talking and of dropping it at the moment she was expected to listen." [70]

Bernard Berenson, who admitted that he was "born to talk" and demanded that his audience accept him as "a talker worth their while," clashed with her almost from their first meeting: "I never heard such *spropositi* as she aired for an hour. I was scarcely polite in my stern dissent—when I got a chance to cry out a word." [71] And her long-time friend, the musician Dame Ethel Smyth, a talented, witty and mercurial woman who was herself never willing to share the center of the stage, found her socially intolerable. She admitted that Vernon Lee's talk was "brilliant fireworks, but to my mind the pyrotechnical charm was ruined by the Mount Sinai touch . . . she could not stand opposition, and if someone's views were diametrically opposed to hers, she was unwilling even to make an effort to understand them." Nevertheless, Dame Ethel, among all those who were less than enchanted with Vernon Lee, had a rare understanding of her peculiar nature. She recognized that her extraordinary childhood was hardly preparation for a "normal" social or personal life, and she observed shrewdly but sympathetically:

> Myself, I believe the tragedy of her life was that without knowing it she loved the *cultes* humanly and with passion; but being the stateliest and chastest of beings she refused to face the fact, or indulge in the most innocent demonstration of affection, preferring to create in a fiction that to her those friends were merely *intellectual* necessities. One of them once said—but this was after the friendship had come to grief: "Her kisses—very rare—were of the sacramental kind; you felt you had been to your first communion." . . . The thought, say, of a good bear-hug would have been, I fancy, as alien and seemed as vulgar to her as the use of such mild slang as we all indulge in now and then. One day, in an extra-expansive mood, I gave her a parting hug myself, and though she bore it with kindness and courtesy, I felt I had committed a solecism.[72]

Certainly Vernon Lee's close attachments to women betray a fundamental loneliness and insecurity which no amount of mere social activity could satisfy. The fact that she chose women whom she could dominate, who would defer to her, also reveals a frustrated desire for recognition and appreciation that we can better understand when we recall her mother's erratic nature. Coldly indifferent to her husband, protective of her only son and clearly favoring him over her plain but precocious daughter, Mrs. Paget had rigorously trained the girl for the highly specialized and demanding life of literature but had given her little maternal affection. Vernon Lee was always close to her family, breaking away only for annual visits to England during which she wrote long letters to her mother faithfully recording her activities. The home ties were severed only by her mother's death and her brother's amazing recovery of his health, but Vernon herself remained in the family house just outside Florence until her death. From her girlhood she turned to other women for the warmth and approval which her mother denied her—Mrs. Sargent, who introduced her to the joys of simple tourism, and Mrs. Jenkin and Mrs. Cornelia Turner, both literary ladies themselves, who encouraged her earliest writing efforts. As she grew to womanhood she found friends closer to her own age. One of these was Mary Robinson, a pretty young woman who wrote poetry and looked up to her as a paragon of intellect. When Mary became engaged to James Darmsteter in 1887, Vernon suffered her first nervous breakdown. Happily, by this time she had already met the large, handsome Clementina (Kit) Anstruther-Thomson, whose interests until then had been pretty evenly divided between horses and art. Sargent painted Kit's portrait—a striking woman with classic but definitely mannish features. To Vernon "her finely chiselled, rather statuesque features, and a certain—I can only call it—virginal expression made one think rather of a very beautiful and modest boy, like some of the listeners of Plato." [73]

The role of Plato was one that Vernon Lee delighted to play. Kit came to stay with the Paget family in Florence in 1888, first nursing Vernon, then her invalid brother, and finally Mrs. Paget, who died in her arms. But her first duty in the household was disciple and pupil. Ethel Smyth observed wryly that "if Vernon was seized with one of her *cultes* for anyone, that person was firmly manipulated into an expert on art, and incidentally into Vernon's slave and familiar friend. When no symposium was on, Kit spent her time stroking Vernon's hand; and, symposium or no symposium, in stroking her vanity." [74] Dame Ethel took a dim view of aesthetics and especially ridiculed the rituals of art appreciation in which Vernon and Kit indulged. They were collaborating at this time on studies later published under their joint names as *Beauty and Ugliness: and Other Studies in Psychological Aesthetics* (1912), a formidable, pretentious, but not insignificant book that attempted to relate the bodily responses of the viewer to the work of art in terms of empathy (*Einfühlung*), a concept that Vernon Lee had discovered in the writings of the German aesthetician Theodor Lipps. Kit served willingly as the aesthetic guinea pig, recording in elaborate detail her reactions (respiration, blood circulation, muscular tension, etc.) to art objects. But even the dedicated art scholar Bernard Berenson, who should have been more responsive to their efforts, was put off by their arrogant, humorless, dogmatic attitude toward their investigations. While he grudgingly respected Vernon Lee, Berenson considered Kit "profoundly stupid." His own prickly nature was offended by their sublime self-confidence, and he suspected that they were picking his brains: "There is a man she [Vernon] thinks who has done all the dirty work, all the unskilled labour. Let me use my *real* intelligence in exploiting him. You may imagine I don't too much like being exploited. . . . Fearfully ill-behaved. They have a way of turning to each other, and excluding you from the conversation." [75]

Berenson soon found what he considered real proof of their exploitation of him. In August, 1897, Vernon Lee sent him proof sheets of an article, "Beauty and Ugliness," that she and Kit were to publish in the *Contemporary Review*. He acknowledged these with a stingingly sarcastic letter, the essence of which was a charge that they had plagiarized his conversations.

> Do you remember my sustaining [i.e., maintaining] that Miss Anstruther-Thomson was quite without a memory, while you opposed that she had a memory superhuman, incapable of forgetting? I see from yr. paper that you were right. Her memory is indeed startling. I confess it inspires me with a certain awe; it is too much like conversing with a recording angel, I must add, a benevolent angel, one who stores up nothing against one, but takes the whole burden upon his shoulders.

Vernon Lee understandably reacted with indignation. Kit had just suffered a nervous breakdown, partly induced, they believed, by overwork on the article. Vernon defended her loyally. "For the plain English of your elaborate ambiguities," she wrote, proceeding to copy out his charges,

. . . the plain English of all this equivocating sarcasm is that Miss Anstruther-Thomson & I have stolen the larger part of our essay from our conversations. I set it down in all its crudeness, because I believe that whatever mean & absurd things your tendency to exaggeration and your pleasure in complicated utterances may have hurried you into writing, you will recoil from acknowledging that a thought so ludicrous and so detestable ever seriously formulated itself in your mind.[76]

The unfortunate explosion of tempers was ultimately regretted by both. Mrs. Berenson attempted to make peace, but not until 1922 were friendly relations restored between them. Vernon Lee had calmed down much earlier. In 1913 she wrote to their mutual friend Carlo Placci:

I have myself long since felt persuaded that just because Berenson was (passez-moi le mot) an ill-tempered and egotistic *ass* to mistake us for plagiarists, we, on the other hand, were not very intelligent in mistaking him for a slanderer and a villain. The whole incident was merely a comedy in which the usual (indeed perhaps more than usual!) human incapacity for understanding other people's ideas and the naive human demand that other people should *exactly* understand *one's own,* played the chief and not at all amusing parts.[77]

Ten years later when, after Kit's death, Vernon Lee was preparing her friend's papers for the volume *Art and Man,* she discovered that Kit actually had made notes on Berenson's conversations and that his charges, though crudely stated, were not entirely unfounded.

Kit Anstruther-Thomson continued to live at least part of every year with Vernon Lee in Florence until 1899. By that time Mrs. Paget was dead and Eugene had gone off on his travels. When, therefore, Kit decided to return to England to nurse a sick friend, Vernon felt herself completely abandoned. She traveled, she had many friends, both men and women, but no permanent ties to friend, family, or country, feeling herself an alien in England, knowing herself to be always a foreigner in Italy. More discouraging even than her isolation was her sense of failure as a writer. Never a popular writer—never indeed seeking popularity—she still suffered from the knowledge that except among a coterie her work was not appreciated or even generally known. Her career had begun brilliantly. She had never had the admiration of the mass public, but her early writing efforts had been praised by those whose approval she most sought—Henry James, Walter Pater, and Robert Browning, who paid an especially graceful tribute to her in his last volume, *Asolando* (1889), where in the poem "Inapprehensiveness" a speaker notes the odd way the weeds grow on a wall in Asolo and wonders if Ruskin had ever noted it:

"No, the book
Which noticed how the wall-growths wave," said she
"Was not by Ruskin."
I said, "Vernon Lee."

It was, nevertheless, disturbing to realize, as she did as early as 1893, that "at thirty-seven I have no public." But she was still hopeful and confident. "I am singularly far from being played out," and she consoled herself that she had never been forced to seek public favor, write for money to live on, or do anything "which did not happen to interest me at the moment." [78] But by 1906 her self-examination was becoming more candid. Someone had told her that she lacked one of the essentials for a writer—a sense of the reader at the other end.

"It is certain," she wrote to Maurice Baring, "that I can never imagine what I write being read, still less read by anyone in particular. (I know all my writings tend more and more to the soliloquy.) It gives, perhaps, a certain freedom and decency; but sometimes, not often, it makes one feel a bit lonely, as if one were the vox clamans—not in the desert, but inside a cupboard."

Two years later she reflected ruefully to him:

> It's odd, when people speak or write about my writings I
> always have the embarrassed feeling one has when others
> are making a gaffe, as if they were attributing someone else's
> work to me (as old Mrs. Tennant introduced me once as
> "Austin Lee")—work which I would sooner have died than
> written, flat, stale, unprofitable, certainly not *mine*.[79]

Vernon Lee was forty-four years old when the twentieth
century began. She was a Victorian not only by the accident of
time, but by choice, sharing with so many of her contemporaries
a melioristic faith and a reforming zeal. Like the Arnolds she
worshiped in the purely secular religion of culture. She saw
man's highest aspirations achieved in art, as did Ruskin, Pater,
and Matthew Arnold, because art was ennobling and uplifting;
art existed not in a vacuum of aestheticism but reached out to all
men in society. It was perhaps her misfortune to outlive the
Victorian age and to survive through the holocaust of World
War I, into the early years of Fascism and Nazism. Her social
consciousness was as sensitive as her aesthetic consciousness. As
early as 1887 Walter Pater had recognized this quality in her,
writing in a review of her *Juvenilia:*

> For in truth, together with all those fine qualities, there has
> always been traceable in Vernon Lee's work an unaffected
> sense of great problems, of the real probation of men and
> women in life, of a great pity, of the "sad story of hu-
> manity," bringing now and again into her exposition of
> what is sometimes perhaps decadent art a touch of something
> like Puritanism.[80]

It was therefore in many ways painful for Vernon Lee to
witness the emergence of the twentieth century. Art, she believed, was rapidly losing all touch with the masses of humanity.
In earlier societies art had had practical utility and relevance to
daily life. Working men had been artisans, craftsmen, and their

religion was interpreted to them by art—temples, cathedrals, and religious painting and sculpture. But in modern times art has become the province exclusively of the rich and leisured classes, "produced for the benefit of the classes who virtually do not work, and by artists born or bred to belong to these idle classes themselves." [81] Even more alarming to her, however, was the rise of political nationalism in Europe. Long before the outbreak of the First World War, she saw the ominous signs of crisis. She held and expressed her opinions on world politics with the same conviction and fervor as her opinions on art. She was positive, dogmatic, intolerant of other opinions. As a result she made many enemies, isolating herself even more in the lonely last years of her life, and her outspoken pacifism during the war cost her many friends in France and England.[82]

Her most ardent polemical work was a book called *Satan the Waster* (1920). It incorporated her allegory *The Ballet of Nations*, which she had published in 1915 with a dedication to Romain Rolland—"in terra pax hominibus bonae voluntas." This "present-day morality," as she designated it, described a dance of death performed by the human passions, the nations, and the institutions of western society. But the bulk of the volume consisted of lengthy notes and commentaries intended mainly to warn against the follies of the Armistice and the peace settlements, which she felt were only preparing the stage for an even more destructive dance of death. In the euphoria of the early postwar years the book was condemned or ignored by reviewers and the public. Only one reviewer spoke loudly in its praise. This was Bernard Shaw, writing in *The Nation*, September 18, 1920, who pronounced it a masterpiece. Characteristically, Shaw was more interested in seeing his own opinions confirmed here than in discussing the book itself and used the review as a bludgeon to beat Lloyd George ("Vernon Lee is a political psychologist: Mr. Lloyd George is a claptrap expert").[83] She had some satisfaction, however, ten years later when her publishers reissued *Satan the Waster*. In a new preface she observes that the rise of pacifism in the past decade made her book more timely: "In 1920, my own friends turned away from it in silence; and I myself felt rather ashamed of having written it."

In 1930, "people have listened without being scandalized, except with the war itself and its former promoters."

Vernon Lee spent her last years in Italy with brief but frequent visits to England in spite of her ill health and loss of hearing. For the most part she withdrew from old friends and associations. "Having what I want of you safe in the Past," she wrote to Carlo Placci in 1920, "I am reluctant to run risks with the present. We are neither of us the same and these war years have completed our transformation." [84] But she remained active up until almost the end of her life, publishing travel writings, collecting older essays for new editions, and assembling a vast amount of research on the aesthetics of music for *Music and Its Lovers,* published in 1932. There were rewards of a sort in the continued appreciation of a few readers—the praise of Aldous Huxley, Desmond MacCarthy, and Roger Fry, and the award of an honorary Doctor of Letters by the University of Durham in 1924.

Probably the most personally gratifying tribute came in April, 1934, less than a year before her death, with a performance in an Italian translation of a play she had written in 1899, *Ariadne in Mantua*. It was elaborately staged with lavish costumes and props at the Accademia dei Fidei in Florence by her friend Signora Flavia Cini, and several of her Italian friends were in the cast. *Ariadne* is a slight, rather precious romance. It was performed professionally only once, in London, in 1916. But as a poetic-symbolic work it has rather special significance in Vernon Lee's career. Like so many of her writings, the play was inspired by the past—by the composer Caccini's seventeenth-century air which Vernon Lee had discovered in an anthology of old music. Beside it was Monteverdi's *Lamento d'Arianna,* composed for his patron the Duke of Mantua. From such fragments of the past her imagination fabricated a tale which blended the themes of Viola, the lovesick girl disguised as a boy in *Twelfth Night,* and of the abandoned Ariadne of ancient legend. She placed the scene in Renaissance Italy. Her Theseus-Orsino is a Duke of Mantua; his Viola-Ariadne is a harlot, Magdalen, whom he once loved and who follows him now to his court disguised as a boy. The play is a work of love, a tribute to the old music that

had always haunted and delighted her. As she wrote it, she says
in her preface, the characters assumed real life for her. No longer
"puppets" of her fancy, they became symbols of the struggle between "mere impulse, unreasoning and violent," and "the mod-
erating, the weighting and restraining influences of civilization,
with their idealism, their vacillation, but their final triumph
over the mere forces of nature." At the end, the faithful Ariadne-
Magdalen sacrifices herself in suicide. The Duke, although he
loves her, must marry a woman of his own class and accept his
duties—"Tradition, Discipline, Civilization." This beautiful production was a rare and fitting tribute to its author. Unhappily,
she was by this time so deaf that she could not hear her beloved
music—Frescobaldi, Palestrina, Caccini, and Monteverdi—that
accompanied it. Less than a year later, on February 13, 1935, she
died. She was cremated, and her ashes were buried in the Allori
cemetery in Florence.

V

Ariadne in Mantua may well epitomize Vernon Lee's
achievement: a life dedicated to art, rigorously disciplined and
guided not by the "mere impulse, unreasoning and violent," of
pleasure and the "forces of nature," but directed conscientiously
toward the "restraining influences of civilization." In a larger
sense her play also epitomizes the achievements of the other novelists discussed in this book: those singular anomalies who, in an
era and a society which denied them other outlets of expression,
found in the novel (which is after all an art, however they may
have abused the form) a medium for disseminating their ideas
and their ideals. Vernon Lee is fittingly the last of these—not
only because she lived the latest, but because her aesthetics of
the novel anticipates the end of the Victorian polemical novel. In
her theory, though not in her practice, she recognized that the
novel was an art form. Not herself capable of writing the kind of
novel she could so perceptively analyze and criticize, she nevertheless had the advantage over her sister-novelists of understanding and appreciating it. The crudities of Eliza Lynn Linton's
fictional soapbox oratory, the shrill hysteria of Olive Schreiner's

poetic outbursts against injustice, the pedantry of Mrs. Ward's sugar-coated academic lectures, and the self-conscious preciosity of John Oliver Hobbes' drawing-room philosophy—all betray a blindness, or at least a confusion, regarding the nature of the novel. They *thought* that they were writing like George Eliot.

Interestingly enough, that confusion does not seem to have spread to their critics or to their public. Widely read and honored in their time, they never—for more than a fleeting moment—deluded the public into believing that they were great novelists. That public was discriminating enough, however, to recognize that these were better, more serious novelists than the host of others—the Ouidas, Marie Corellis, M. E. Braddons, and Hall Caines—who were mere entertainers. The late Victorian reader was more sophisticated in his taste for novels than some of us today credit him. He had grown up on Jane Austen, Scott, Dickens, Thackeray, George Eliot, Trollope, Mrs. Gaskell, George Meredith, as well as on the mediocre and blander fare of the "average" popular novel. The reader's approval and support of the works of the Lintons, Schreiners, Wards, Hobbes's, and Lees, was based less on lack of taste than on sound recognition that these novels also had their value. They educated the reader; they gave him insights into problems and issues of his day; they showed him honestly how other peoples and other classes of society lived and thought; they even suggested (without overtly preaching) new moral values, new ethical standards, new faiths with which to meet the chaos and confusion of "modern" life. And they entertained. Their novels are today of little importance, but they tell us much that is important about the Victorians themselves.

Notes

1. Published in Evan Charteris, *John Sargent* (London, 1927), pp. 235–55.
2. "Explanatory Note," Introduction to *A Vernon Lee Anthology*, ed. I. Cooper-Willis (London, 1929).
3. A. L. S. to Mrs. Shields, Berg Collection, New York Public Library.
4. See MacCarthy's essay "Out of the Limelight," in *Humanities*, ed. Lord David Cecil (London, 1953), pp. 189–93. For recent appreciations of her

criticism of the novel, see Kenneth Graham, *English Criticism of the Novel, 1865–1900* (Oxford, 1965) and David Lodge, *The Language of Fiction* (London, 1966). Graham considers her essay "On Literary Construction" in *The Handling of Words* "one of the most remarkable of all late-Victorian pronouncements on the craft of fiction" (p. 135). Lodge calls the book "a remarkable achievement, full of useful insights and suggestions" (p. xi). In 1968 Bison Books (University of Nebraska, Lincoln) published a paperback edition of *The Handling of Words*, edited and with an introduction by Royal A. Gettmann.

5. *Sketch for a Self-Portrait* (London, 1949), pp. 116–17.
6. *The Beautiful: An Introduction to Psychological Aesthetics* (Cambridge, 1913), pp. 151, 155.
7. *Laurus Nobilis: Chapters on Art and Life* (London, 1909), p. 14.
8. *Renaissance Fancies and Studies* (London, 1895), pp. 255–56.
9. *Euphorion* (second ed., London, 1885), pp. 28–29, 80.
10. *Gospels of Anarchy* (London, 1908), p. 141.
11. "Ruskinism: The Would-Be Study of Conscience," *Belcaro* (second ed., London, 1883), p. 210.
12. *Renaissance Fancies*, pp. 251–53.
13. *Vital Lies*, I (London, 1912), 242–43. For her religious views, see two essays, "The Responsibilities of Unbelief" and "The Consolations of Belief," in *Baldwin* (London, 1886).
14. *Baldwin*, pp. 202–204.
15. *Gospels of Anarchy*, p. 141.
16. *The Handling of Words* (London, 1923), p. 79.
17. *Baldwin*, pp. 207–209.
18. See her essay "Rosny and the French Analytical Novel," in *Gospels of Anarchy*.
19. "On Style," *The Handling of Words*, p. 161.
20. *Ibid.*, p. 35.
21. See her Preface to C. Anstruther-Thompson's *Art and Man* (London, 1924), p. 72. See also her comments on the viewer's reaction to painting:

> Also, like other painters of those ingenuous, unpsychological days, John Sargent did not know that *seeing* is a business of the mind, the memory and the heart, quite as much as of the eye; and that the *valeurs* which the most stiff-necked impressionist could strive after were also *values* of association and preference ("J. S. S.: In Memoriam," p. 251; her italics).

22. "On Literary Construction," *The Handling of Words*, p. 29.
23. See her comments in an unpublished letter to Mrs. Shields, who worked as her assistant and typist, November 19, 1909 (Berg Collection; her underlining):

> But there remains another side, and this is the one at which I myself am always working more or less and in which I want help. I want a pupil and successor! This is the purely *literary* side of aesthetic, i.e. the enquiry into what qualities are discoverable in the mere handling—the syntax and composition, *not* the rhythm of fine literary work *apart from the subject, the metaphors, etc. and all that*

belongs to the subject. It is, in fact, an attempt to discover in writing something analoguous to those various *modes of movement* which, according to us (and Lipps) are at the bottom of the aesthetic phenomenon in the visual arts. It is a question of counting and classifying words, and much more, of analyzing the prepositions between various kinds of words, for instance the richness and variety and complexity in tenses of verbs, in prepositions and conjunctions.

24. Ironically, this passage found an echo in Virginia Woolf's criticism of Vernon Lee's style: "But looseness quickly becomes slovenly. A little effort is needed to face a character or an incident which needs to be recorded. Nor can one let the pen write without guidance; for fear of becoming slack and untidy like Vernon Lee. Her ligaments are too loose for my taste" (*A Writer's Diary* [London, 1953], p. 14).
25. This analysis of Pater appears not in *The Handling of Words* but as a separate article, intended as a kind of postscript to the book—"The Handling of Words. A Page of Walter Pater," *Life and Letters*, IX (March, 1933–February, 1934), 287–310.
26. "Can Writing Be Taught?" *The Handling of Words*, p. 296; her italics.
27. Letter to Carlo Placci, August 9 [1894], quoted in "Carlo Placci and Vernon Lee," by S. Pantazzi, *English Miscellany*, XII (1961), 117–18.
28. Most of the biographical information on Vernon Lee is in Peter Gunn's *Vernon Lee* (London and New York, 1964). Gunn has had access to the large collection of Vernon Lee letters and papers acquired from her executrice Irene Cooper-Willis by Colby College, Waterville, Maine (see *Colby Library Quarterly*, III [November, 1952], 117–19). See also "In Casa Paget," by Madame Duclaux (Mary Robinson), *Country Life* (December 18, 1907), pp. 935–37.
29. "Can Writing Be Taught?" *The Handling of Words*, pp. 297 ff.
30. *The Sentimental Traveller* (London, 1908), p. 7.
32. *Hortus Vitae* (London, 1904), pp. 19–22.
32. "J. S. S.: In Memoriam," pp. 242–43.
33. *What Happened Next* (London, 1940), p. 51.
34. See Henry James' comment in a letter to his brother William, January 20 [1893]: ". . . her books of fiction are a tissue of personalities of this hideous roman-à-clef kind" (Carl J. Weber, "Henry James and his Tiger Cat," *PMLA*, LXVIII [September, 1953], 683).
35. Harriet Waters Preston, "Vernon Lee," *Atantic Monthly*, LV (February, 1885), 219–27. *Miss Brown* was published in England late in 1884 and was not included for discussion in this article.
36. Gunn, p. 97, and Phyllis Grosskurth, *John Addington Symonds: A Biography* (London, 1964), pp. 222–24.
37. Gunn, p. 102. Vernon Lee certainly had no desire to emulate the sensational Ouida, but she had personal respect for her (they knew each other in Florence) and healthy respect for her work. In an article in the *Westminster Gazette* (July 27, 1907), Vernon Lee wrote of her:

> I do not imply that her novels will be published in ornamental editions all through the ages. Still less that their every particular . . . woud meet the taste of my juniors. I do not hold that the chief function of literature is to suit the future. . . . the real business

of a book is to serve asd satisfy its own day. . . . this power of seeing and feeling and creating in a particular way—is what Ouida has given us . . . and this being so, what does it matter if the shapes, the symbols, the tricks of invention and expression . . . are not of the sort which we today happen to consider immortal?

38. See her criticism of art for art's sake in "A Dialogue on Poetic Morality," in *Belcaro* (London, 1883), where her spokesman Baldwin objects to it as:

> the sterile pleasure of perceiving mere ingenuity and dexterity of handling; they [aesthetes] hanker vaguely after imaginary sensuous stimulation, spiced with all manner of mystical rubbish, after some ineffable, half-nauseous pleasure in strange mixtures of beauty in nastiness. . . . In short, these creatures want art not for its own sake, but for the sake of excitement which the responsibilities of society do not permit their obtaining except in imaginative form (pp. 246–47).

39. See also Julia Wedgwood's review, *Contemporary Review*, XLVII (May, 1885), 748–50: "Vernon Lee thinks evidently that in painting a marriage impressing the reader as a kind of prostitution, she is describing the loftiest self-sacrifice."

40. Gunn, p. 79.

41. *Ibid.*, p. 105.

42. Baring, *Lost Lectures* (London, 1932), p. 88.

43. See Burdett Gardner, "An Apology for Henry James' 'Tiger-Cat,' " *PMLA*, LXVIII (September, 1953), 688–95. Gardner interviewed Percy Lubbock, who recalled "Jame's humorously exaggerated accounts of the eccentric behavior of Mrs. Paget on the occasions of his visits in the 1870's" (p. 695, n. 5). Gardner's theory that young Violet was the model for Christina Light in *Roderick Hudson* was refuted by Leon Edel, "Henry James and Vernon Lee," *PMLA*, LXIX (June, 1954), 677–78. See also Edel's *Henry James: The Middle Years* (Philadelphia and New York, 1962), pp. 332–35.

44. Be assured, dear Miss Paget, that this proposal touches the most sensitive parts of my being and produces there the most delightful agitation. It will be a great honour for me, as well as a great pleasure, to see my name on the threshold of your beautiful structure; it will never be written in a more distinguished place (quoted by Weber. *PMLA*, LXVIII, 674).

45. Quoted by Edel, *Ibid.*, LXIX, 677.

46. For the full text of the letter see *Selected Letters of Henry James*, ed. Leon Edel (New York, 1955), pp. 204–207.

47. Edel, *Henry James*, p. 334.

48. *PMLA*, LXVIII, 681, 693.

49. *Juvenilia*, I (London, 1887), 135–36.

50. *Ibid.*, I, 141–43.

51. Preface to *Studies of the Eighteenth Century in Italy* (second ed., London, 1907), p. xix. All quotations, unless otherwise noted, are from this edition.

52. Letter, April 27, 1890, quoted by Weber, *PMLA*, LXVIII, 678–79.
53. *Lost Lectures,* pp. 86–87. Royal A. Gettmann considers her travel writing worthy of comparison with that of Goethe, Henry James, and Norman Douglas:

> She also had a gift for translating colors, lusters, textures, shapes, and sounds into vivid words and ardent epithets. Some pages of her travel essays are indeed flecked with purple, but her characteristic practice was to place the acute observation and the deep-dyed sensuous particular in the context of her own memories and the historical experience of European man. The present moment is interpenetrated by knowledge, retrospection, and concern for the future. ("Vernon Lee: Exponent of Aestheticism," *Prairie Schooner,* XLII [Spring, 1968], 47–55) .

54. "Ravenna and Her Ghosts," in *Limbo* (London, 1908), pp. 160, 176. The essay was reprinted in *Pope Jacynth and Other Stories,* ed. Peter Owen (London, 1956). This collection in turn was reissued in paperback by Corgi Books (London, 1962) with the title *Ravenna and Her Ghosts* and a lurid cover illustration of the ghost story, showing a nude girl pursued by a demon hunter.
55. Preface, pp. xxiii–xxiv.
56. Introduction to first edition (1880) and p. 7 of 1907 edition.
57. Pp. 415–16, 330–31, 132–33.
58. Gunn, p. 109.
59. In the preface she cites, in addition to the standard biographies and Baron von Reumont's *Die Gräfin von Albany,* Taillandier's *La Comtesse d'Albany,* Alfieri's autobiography and letters, and numerous manuscript letters of the Countess, which she consulted in Milan and Siena. She expresses a special indebtedness to her friend the Italian novelist Mario Pratesi.
60. Gunn, pp. 22, 162–63. For other accounts of Eugene Lee-Hamilton, see *Country Life* (December 28, 1907), pp. 935–37, and *Colby Library Quarterly,* III (February, 1954), 217–18.
61. See her description of the story as "a virtuous and exciting tale, rather Stevensonian" (A. L. S. to T. Fisher Unwin, January 5, 1902, Berg Collection) . Gunn (p. 187) notes a similarity between her plot and Henry Brewster's libretto for Ethel Smyth's opera *The Wreckers.* Actually there is little resemblance. Brewster's story is set in eighteenth-century Cornwall and tells of lovers who defy their fellow villagers by lighting a beacon to warn off a ship from the rocky coast. The lovers are then put to death by the wreckers.
62. An interesting personal note is that Lady Venetia has been caring for her invalid brother. He has now, however, recovered and plans to marry, thus leaving her at loose ends: ". . . my poor silly old brother thinks fit to solemnise his comparative recovery by marrying a woman . . . who has been entangling him for the last two months, so that, having fought my fight against her, I shall have to depart from Arthington and become once more a wanderer on the earth's surface."

63. Introduction to *For Maurice: Five Unlikely Stories* (London, 1927), p. xxxiii.
64. One might note as exceptions a group of imitation saints' lives and religious tales written in a pseudoarchaic language, like "Pope Jacynth" and "St. Eudaemon and his Orange Tree." There is also the very moving "Legend of Madame Krasinska" (originally published in *Vanitas*), set in contemporary Florence and dealing with the punishment of a beautiful, frivolous young woman who mocks a wretched, mad beggar-woman and is gradually possessed by her spirit. Driven to the verge of suicide, she is saved by an apparition of the woman and repents by becoming a nun.
65. Introduction to *For Maurice*, p. xviii.
66. See above, p. 18.
67. Havelock Ellis suggested to J. A. Symonds that Vernon Lee and Mary Robinson might be a good case history for his section on lesbianism in his *Sexual Inversion* (Grosskurth, *John Addington Symonds*, p. 223 n.). Bernard Berenson, writing to Mary Costello (later Mrs. Berenson) in 1896, quoted the rather malicious observation of Maud Crutwell: "Miss C. thinks V. by nature very passionate and that her, V.'s, sourness is due to her never having had a man's love. As a little girl V. used to stay away when company came for fear people should ask, 'Who is this frightful child?' " (*Selected Letters of Bernard Berenson* [London, 1965], p. 37). The Berenson household appears to have been fully aware of her lesbian tendencies. In a letter to Mary Berenson in 1921, Nicky Mariano reported that their friends the Kingsley Porters liked Vernon Lee and saw her often, "in spite of Mrs. [Janet] Ross's [a friend, noted for her gruffness of manner] lugubre warnings. She has told Lucy that friendship with Miss Paget implicated the most horrible danger to Mrs. Porter's young niece, to her reputation, and actually to her virtue" (Nicky Mariano, *Forty Years with Berenson* [London, 1966], p. 102).
68. *Portrait of Edith Wharton* (London, 1947), p. 110.
69. *Ottoline: The Early Memoirs of Lady Ottoline Morell* (London, 1963), p. 183. Lytton Strachey, who met Vernon Lee at Ottoline Morrell's in 1916, found her "slightly boring," and wrote a verse: "Tastes differ: some like coffee, some like tea; / And some are never bored by Vernon Lee" (Michael Holroyd, *Lytton Strachey, A Critical Biography*, II [New York, 1968], 206).
70. Mariano, *Forty Years with Berenson*, p. 102.
71. *Sketch for a Self-Portrait*, p. 13; *Selected Letters*, pp. 11–12.
72. *What Happened Next*, pp. 28–29.
73. See Vernon Lee's long preface to *Art and Man*, a collection of writings by C. Anstruther-Thomson, p. 8.
74. *What Happened Next*, p. 26.
75. *Selected Letters of Bernard Berenson*, pp. 14–15.
76. *Ibid.*, pp. 55–60.
77. *English Miscellany*, XII, 120.
78. Letter to Eugene Lee-Hamilton, quoted in Gunn, p. 161.
79. Ethel Smyth, *Maurice Baring* (London, 1938), pp. 206–207, 211. See

Mario Praz' comment that by thirty-seven "her miraculous period was over; she was far from played out and crystallised, but her hold on a wide public was lost" (review of Gunn's *Vernon Lee* in *English Studies*, XLVII [August, 1966], 313).

8c. *Pall Mall Gazette*, August 5, 1887, p. 5.

8ɪ. *Laurus Noilis*, p. 231.

8ᴇ. See Gunn's summary of her quarrel with H. G. Wells, a former friend, over American trade with Germany in 1914 (pp. 204–205). This also made an enemy of one of her closest women friends, Madame Bulteau, a Frenchwoman, who accused her of being pro-German. Her position, however, won sympathy from another woman pacifist, Olive Schreiner, who wrote her in praise of her antiwar articles in the *Nation* (London) in 1915: "Can I tell you how splendid I think your articles on the war. You 'take away the shame of women from among us' " (Gunn, p. 207; see also *Letters of Olive Schreiner*, pp. 122, 338, 362).

83. Shaw acknowledged the lack of balance in the review by apologizing near the end for neglecting the book: "But this is by way of being a review of Vernon Lee's book and not a phrenologist's chart of Mr. Lloyd George's bumps. The book, of first-rate workmanship from beginning to end, is far too thorough to leave the reviewer anything to say about it that is not better said in the book itself." He thereupon quotes at length from it (pp. 758–60).

84. *English Miscellany*, XII, 122.

Index